Cape Ann and Vicinity

A GUIDE FOR RESIDENTS AND VISITORS

KARIN M. GERTSCH

ACORN PRESS
Essex, Massachusetts
1997

CAPE ANN AND VICINITY . . . A Guide for Residents and Visitors

© 1997 Karin M. Gertsch

Library of Congress Cataloging-in-Publication Data
Gertsch, Karin M. (1946–   )
    CAPE ANN AND VICINITY . . . A Guide for Residents and Visitors
    Includes bibliographical references and index.
    First edition / first printing   p.   cm.
    ISBN 0-9657413-0-3
    1. Massachusetts—Guidebooks.
    2. Atlantic Coast (MA)—Guidebooks.
    Library of Congress Catalog Card Number: 97-71571

Cover photograph: Motif #1, Rockport, by Nancy Dudley
Cover design: Alison Anholt-White
Copy Editor: Patti Picardi
Typography and Graphics: Compset, Inc.

At the time of publication all prices were confirmed; we recommend that users call ahead to obtain current information and rates. Every effort has been made to contact copyright holders for permission to reprint borrowed material where necessary. We regret any oversights that may have occurred and would be happy to rectify them in future printings of this work.

Your comments and suggestions are welcome. Please write to the author c/o the publisher: ACORN PRESS, P.O. Box 403, Manchester-by-the-Sea, MA 01944-0403.

Acknowledgments

This first edition of *Cape Ann and Vicinity . . . A Guide for Residents and Visitors*, has been a community effort. Without the help of many, it would not have been possible. During the researching and writing stages, I met many new people. In each community, people were willing to give unselfishly of their time, information, and expertise to assure that what I printed was accurate. My profuse thanks to all!

Thanks also to the enthusiastic, dedicated Gordon College interns who helped with research and writing: Jeff Spencer, Renae Terry, Peggy Miles, and Nathan Grace; Joy Levitan joined us from North Shore Community College.

In the early stages, friends Ralph and Priscilla Walter proofread. To all the librarians: Karen Rogati, Beth Cairns, David McArdle, Eleanor McKechnie, Eleanor Gaunt, Michael Segur, Steve Rask, and Gunilla Caulfield, I extend my appreciation.

To the historical society curators, archivists, and/or members: Judith McCulloch, Martha Oaks, Mary Conley, Jim Kyprianos, Tom McPherson, Cynthia Peckham, Marian Carter and Judy Gilliss, Tom O'Keefe, Barbara Ninness, and Gertrude Griffin, "Slim" Proctor, Eleanor Thompson, Kristen Porter, Courtney Ellis, and Ellen Nelson, my thanks for helping to make the digging easier.

When I had questions about community events or needed to know who to contact, cheerful assistance came from Fran Richards, Jane Bokron, Sally Soucy, Gretchen Wood, and Sheila Irvin. The following people provided information or verified text for content and accuracy: Andrea Cooper and Dennis Ducsik, Kathy Leahy and Robert Buchsbaum, Jim MacDougall, Janet Csencsits, and Teresa Ciavola. Mason Weinrich and Interns Katherine Sardi and Laurence Grisanti. Special thanks to Marcia Norton.

The architecture section proved a challenge and Prudence Fish provided much welcomed expertise. For help with the art, music, dance, and theater sections: Ellie Norris, Susan Burton, Ruth Brown, Ann Lainhart, Carol Linsky, Richard Emery, Anne White, and Frances Lowe gave expert guidance. Thanks for the interviews: Michael March, Richard Saltzberg, Ruth Toivainen, Bob Coviello, Dana Guarnera, Matt Jackson, Elaine Perkins, and Nan Webber.

The following gave helpful advice: Bob Hiltz, Janis Bell, Sean Nickerson, Michael Costello, and Eleanor Hoy. Barbara Parsons helped me with advertising. Thanks to Mary Hayes. My friend Ginny Hughes helped with publicity. The gorgeous cover photo was taken by Nancy Dudley, and the cover design, layout, and graphics were by Alison Anholt-White. Original pen-and-ink sketches were by artist Nancy Marculewicz and Wheaton College intern Liz Mackie. Jean O'Hara graciously allowed me to use her husband Tom's sketches from *Cape Ann: Cape America*. Thanks to my cheerleader Linda Mueffelmann, the Wizards in Newburyport, and Curtis Vouwie. Many of the local business people provided information and photographs. I appreciate the efforts of the hardworking staff at Compset for giving the book its personality. Thanks to Peter and Elizabeth and the faith and support of my confidant, roommate of twenty-seven years, proofreader, and not-so-silent partner, Emil, without whose help this book would have remained just a dream.

Dedicated to teachers past, present, and future,
and to my first teacher and grandmother,
Helene K. Kolbe, with love and affection.

*"The disadvantage of men not knowing the past
is that they do not know the present.
History is a hill or high point of vantage,
from which . . . men see the town in which they live
or the age in which they are living."*

G. K. Chesterton (1874–1936)

Introduction

What's the best time to be in the Cape Ann area? If you ask me in June, I'll tell you this is best. For in June, Cape Ann's rose gardens are in bloom; the air is pleasantly warm; seasonal shops, motels, and restaurants have reopened; and their window boxes have been filled with new flowering plants that have been set out against the freshly painted white clapboards. Ask me in July or August, I'll say this is the best time for enjoying the clean, fine sandy beaches; lovely perennial seaside gardens; all kinds of boating; eating seafood in the rough on outdoor picnic tables or served by candlelight on white linen-clad tables with an ocean view.

Ask me in the autumn months, I'll say this is a great time to come to Cape Ann. The days are cooler; the shops and beaches are far less crowded. The foliage colors are spectacular because the air is clearer and the sky is bluer at this time of the year. The marsh grasses display their colors more subtly as they begin to turn from shades of green to yellows and browns with hints of red and orange. Yes, autumn is best!

Ask me in winter, when the leaves have fallen from the deciduous trees and their skeletons are clearly visible. The landscape is laid bare and reveals its many nuances: millions of rocks in the thousands of rock walls or the squirrel and bird nests high in the forks of naked trees. The sunlight becomes more precious as the days shorten and, with the fall of winter's first snow, sounds become muffled and a pensive time of year arrives. Longer evenings encourage reading before the fireplace, flannel sheets replace cotton on the bed, and clam chowder tastes better than ever!

Ask me in spring, when the sunbeams lengthen and the tiny green shoots of bulbs magically pop out of the thawing earth. Cooped-up smiling residents and their dogs begin the spring pilgrimage to their favorite local beaches. Here they gulp the sea air to nourish their winter-weary lungs. The surf sounds stronger, the gulls look whiter, the sand has been washed clean by winter snows. Spring is definitely the best!

If I limit my answer to one time of year, there is so much I'll have to leave out. You and your family must experience this marvelous piece of earth for yourselves. Cape Ann and the surrounding area covered by this guide will not disappoint you. At any time of year, there are always places open where you can stay, eat, visit, shop, and rest. Come often, and enjoy the many pleasures of Cape Ann and its vicinity.

KARIN GERTSCH
Cape Ann resident since 1959

Contents

Acknowledgments **iii**

Dedication **v**

Introduction **vii**

Map of Cape Ann and Vicinity **xii**

CAPE ANN AND VICINITY

Facts About the Area **1**

Profile of the Area **2**

Calendar of Traditional Events **5**

What's Where? **12**

The Sea, the Land, and the People **16**

The Clam Industry **28**

Salt Marshes and their Industry **32**

Architectural Styles of the Area **35**

ESSEX

Map **46**

History of Essex **47**

Places of Interest **59**

Places of Worship **65**

Antiques **65**

Art **70**

Music **72**

Recreation **75**

Lodging **79**

Restaurants **80**

GLOUCESTER

Map **82**

History of Gloucester **83**

Places of Interest **89**

Places of Worship **111**

Antiques **113**

Art **114**

Music, Theater, and Dance **118**

Recreation **122**

Lodging **129**

Restaurants **132**

IPSWICH

Map **138**

History of Ipswich **139**

Places of Interest **144**

Places of Worship **152**

Antiques **153**

Art **154**

Music, Theater, and Dance **159**

Recreation **160**

Lodging **165**

Restaurants **165**

MANCHESTER-BY-THE-SEA

Map **168**

History of Manchester-by-the-Sea **169**

Places of Interest   **172**

Places of Worship   **180**

Antiques   **180**

Art   **181**

Music, Theater, and Dance   **182**

Recreation   **185**

Lodging   **186**

Restaurants   **187**

ROCKPORT

Map   **188**

History of Rockport   **189**

Places of Interest   **196**

Places of Worship   **203**

Antiques   **203**

Art   **204**

Music, Theater, and Dance   **208**

Recreation   **211**

Lodging   **214**

Restaurants   **216**

BIBLIOGRAPHY   219

INDEX   223

ORDER FORM   229

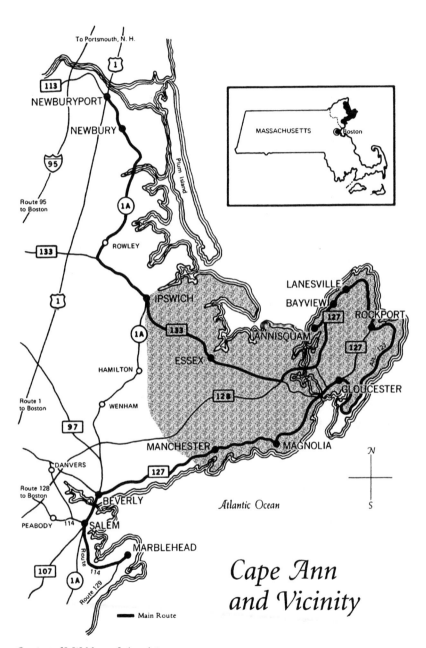

To Portsmouth, N. H.

1

113
NEWBURYPORT

NEWBURY

95

Route 95
to Boston

1A

133

ROWLEY

Plum Island

MASSACHUSETTS •Boston

1

IPSWICH

1A **133**

ESSEX

HAMILTON

97

WENHAM

Route 1
to Boston

LANESVILLE
BAYVIEW
127 ROCKPORT

ANNISQUAM

127 Alt. 127

128

GLOUCESTER

DANVERS

Route 128
to Boston

127

MANCHESTER

MAGNOLIA

Atlantic Ocean

N

S

PEABODY 114
BEVERLY

SALEM

107 **1A**

MARBLEHEAD

Route 114

Route 129

━━ Main Route

*Cape Ann
and Vicinity*

Courtesy of J. W. Murray & Associates

Cape Ann

FACTS ABOUT THE AREA

Location   32 miles north of Boston (the capital of the Commonwealth of Massachusetts) and only one hour's drive from the border of either New Hampshire or Maine (see map opposite page).

Arrival by Air   Boston's Logan International Airport.

By Rented Car   Automobile rental agencies are conveniently located at Logan International Airport. It's best to arrange a rental car through your travel agent before coming to Boston. Shuttle buses run every 15 minutes from airport terminals to car rental agencies.

By Private Car (from points south)   Take I-95 North to Route 128 North. Exits for Essex, Manchester-by-the-Sea, Gloucester, and Rockport are clearly marked. Ipswich can be reached by taking the Route 1A North exit from Route 128.

(from points north)   Take I-95 south to Route 133 East (Exit 54).

By Train   From Boston's North Station take a commuter train (call 1–800–392–6100 or 617–222–3200 for information) on the Rockport Line for Manchester-by-the-Sea, Gloucester, and Rockport. For Ipswich, take a commuter train on the Ipswich Line. Essex has no direct train service, but can be reached from either of these lines by taking a taxi from either Gloucester or

1

Ipswich (see transportation listing in the **What's Where** section).

Local Transportation Cape Ann Transportation Authority (CATA) call 283–7916 for the schedule serving Gloucester, Rockport, and Essex. Inquire about beach buses that meet trains.

Massachusetts Area Codes Please note the area code here is *508*. As long as you dial from place to place within the same community or telephone to a community directly bordering on the one from which you are calling, you do not need to dial the area code. For all other calls placed within this part of Massachusetts you must dial *1* then *508* and then the telephone number. Massachusetts has three area codes: 413 (Western MA), 508 (most sections of MA outside greater Boston), and 617 (greater Boston area). If uncertain when dialing, consult the telephone directory.

Zip Codes Essex (01929), Gloucester (01930), Ipswich (01938), Manchester-by-the-Sea (01944), and Rockport (01966).

PROFILE OF THE AREA

(Information current as of 1/97)

ESSEX

Population:	3,260
Area:	14.4 square miles
Incorporated:	1819
Emergency Phone Numbers:	
Police, Fire, and Ambulance:	911 or 768-6200
Hospital and Health Services:	
Addison Gilbert Hospital, Gloucester:	283-4000
Beverly Hospital, Beverly	922-3000
Visiting Nurse Assoc., Gloucester	283-2020
Cable Emergency Center, Ipswich	356-4366
Government:	3-member board of selectmen, town meeting
Town Clerk, Town Hall,	
30 Martin Street:	768-7111

Tax rate: $13.74 per $1,000
Avg. value of single family house: $185,000

GLOUCESTER

Population: 28,716
Area: 26 square miles
Incorporated: Town: 1642, City: 1873
Emergency Phone Numbers:
  Police: 911 or 281-9751
  Fire: 911 or 281-9760
  Ambulance: 911
Hospital and Health Services:
  Addison Gilbert Hospital
    298 Washington Street 283-4000
  Visiting Nurse Assoc., 8 Angle Street 283-2020
Government: 9-member city council
  Mayor 281-9700
  City Clerk, City Hall, 9 Dale Avenue 281-9720
Tax rate: $16.90 per $1,000
Avg. value of single family house: $135,000

IPSWICH

Population: 13,025
Area: 33 square miles
Incorporated: 1634
Emergency Phone Numbers:
  Police: 911 or 356-4343
  Fire: 911 or 356-4321
  Ambulance: 911 or 356-9800
Hospital and Health Services:
  Beverly Hospital, Beverly 922-3000
  Bay Area Visiting Nurse Assoc., Beverly 356-5055
  Cable Emergency Center, County Road 356-4366
Government: 5-member board of selectmen, town meeting
  Town Clerk, Town Hall,
    30 S.Main Street 356-6600
Tax rate: $14.15 per $1,000
Avg. value of single family house: $187,000

MANCHESTER-BY-THE-SEA

Population:	5,680
Area:	7.7 square miles
Incorporated:	1645

Emergency Phone Numbers:

Police:	911 or 526-1212
Fire:	911 or 526-4040
Ambulance:	911

Hospital and Health Services:

Addison Gilbert Hospital, Gloucester	283-4000
Beverly Hospital, Beverly	922-3000
Bay Area Visiting Nurse Assoc., Beverly	356-5055
Visiting Nurse Assoc., Gloucester	283-2020
Government:	5-member board of selectmen, town meeting
Town Clerk, Town Hall, 10 Central Street	526-2040
Tax rate:	$11.93 per $1,000
Avg. value of single family house:	$350,000

ROCKPORT

Population:	7,656
Area:	7 square miles
Incorporated:	1840

Emergency Phone Numbers:

Police:	911 or 546-3444
Fire:	911 or 546-6750
Ambulance:	911

Hospital and Health Services:

Addison Gilbert Hospital, Gloucester	283-4000
Visiting Nurse Assoc., Gloucester	283-2020
Government:	5-member board of selectmen, town meeting
Town Clerk, Town Hall, 34 Broadway	546-6894
Tax rate:	$14.36 per $1,000
Avg. value of single family house:	$185,000

CALENDAR OF TRADITIONAL EVENTS

Note Due to space limitations only a partial listing is given; see individual community sections for details or call the telephone number if provided.

MARCH

Essex:	One World Coffee House, First Universalist Church. Call 768-3690.
Gloucester:	Cape Ann Symphony Concert at Fuller School Auditorium. Call 281-0543.
	Hammond Castle Easter Concert. Call 283-2080.
Ipswich:	Along the Way Coffee House, United Methodist Church. Call 356-1636.
Manchester:	Community Center Party. Call 526-7626.
	Manchester Harbor Boat Club's winter lecture series. Call 526-4290.
Rockport:	Chorus North Shore, cathedral series. Call 546-1740.

APRIL

Ipswich:	"Panic Day," a town-wide giant yard sale in honor of a day in the Revolutionary War when people gathered belongings in a panic and fled; held at the Winthrop School. Call Ipswich Rotary Club 356-7571.
Manchester:	Big Yard Sale at the Community Center. Call 526-7626.
	Women's Chorus spring concert at the First Parish Church. Call 283-9021.

MAY

All:	"Earth Day," call Massachusetts Audubon, Essex County Greenbelt, or Trustees of Reservations for details.
	Memorial Day parades and observances usually begin at 9 a.m.

Essex:	Essex Shipyard Festival. Call 768-7541.
	Taste of Essex. Food and wine reception. Call 283-1601.
Gloucester:	Prince of Whales Ball. Call 283-1601.
	Mother's Day Concert at Hammond Castle. Call 283-2080.
	Rocky Neck Art Colony, at Eastern Point. Open for the season.
Ipswich:	International ALPCA (Automobile License Plate Collectors Association) Annual Meeting VFW Hall. Public welcome. Call 468-1234.
Rockport:	5-Mile Road Race. Call 546-6575.
	Motif #1 Day celebrates famous landmark. Call 546-5997.
	Rockport Art Association annual art auction. Call 546-6604.
	Chorus North Shore concert. Call 546-1740.

JUNE

Essex:	"Art in the Barn" at Essex County Greenbelt. Call 768-7241.
Gloucester:	Gloucester Stage Company live performances. Call 281-4099.
	Gallery Walk on Rocky Neck third Saturday of the month. Call 283-7978.
	Pipe Organ Concert at Hammond Castle. Call 283-7673.
	Music at Eden's Edge at Hammond Castle. Call 283-7673.
	New Fish Festival. Call 283-1601.
	North Shore Arts Association opens with a major exhibit. Call 283-1857.
	Saint Peter's Fiesta. Call 283-1601.
	Seaside Afternoon Teas at Beauport. Call 283-0800.
Ipswich:	Ipswich River Festival, all-day in and outdoor events for the whole family, boat cruises, antique cars, music, nature walks. Call 356-3116.

Pick-your-own strawberries, at Marini's Farm or Goodale Orchards. Strawberry festival held third Saturday of the month. Call 356-4083.

Manchester: Tennis Tournament at the Community Center. Call 526-7626.

Red, white and blue pancake breakfast with jazz at Tuck's Point. Call 283-1601.

Rockport: Chamber Music Festival, casual Sunday series. Call 546-7391.

Granite quarry tours every Saturday. Call 546-2997.

Swedish festival. Call 546-6575.

JULY

Essex: One World Coffee House at the First Universalist Church at 8 p.m.

Gloucester: Annisquam Sea Fair. Call 283-2908.

Blackburn challenge rowing race, a 21-mile rowing race around Cape Ann. Call 546-9022.

Cape Ann Symphony pops concert. Call 281-0543.

Fourth of July holiday parade. Call 283-1601.

Renaissance Faire at Hammond Castle. Call 283-7673.

Music at Eden's Edge at Hammond Castle. Call 283-2080.

Musical cruise aboard schooner *Ernestina*. Call 282-1399.

Clam Bake at Lanesville Community Center. Call 283-3471 or 281-4818.

Art Festival at Magnolia Library Center. Call 525-3343.

North Shore Art Association auction. Call 283-1857.

Rocky Neck Art Colony exhibits. Call 283-4554.

Church fair at St. John's Episcopal. Call 283-1708.

Local history lectures at Sawyer Free Library. Call 283-9763.

White elephant and rummage sale at
W. Gloucester Trinitarian Congregational
Church. Call 283-2817.

Ipswich: Art Show at the Winthrop School. Call 356-3602.
Clambake and Greek festival on second
weekend of the month. Call 356-4247.
Fourth of July children's parade at 10 a.m. on
the South Village Green, field events, games,
refreshments, sponsored by the VFW.
Greek food and dance, fourth weekend of the
month. Call 356-4247.
Independence Day celebration at Castle Hill.
Call 356-4351.
Jazz and blues concert at Castle Hill. Call
356-4351.
Olde Ipswich Days arts and crafts fair held last
weekend of the month on South Village
Green. Call 356-0408 or 356-0115.
Pick-your-own blueberries and raspberries at
Goodale Orchards.
Reggae by-the-Sea at Castle Hill. Call 356-4351.

Manchester: Fourth of July Parade, forms at 9 a.m. in the
morning.
Concert in the park. Call 526-7626.
Art in the park exhibits by North Shore artists
at Masconomo Park.
Booster Club's summer festival at Masconomo
Park, rides, games, food.

Rockport: Art Association lessons, programs, exhibits. Call
546-6604.
Fourth of July parade. Call 546-6575.
Coffee House music concerts at First Baptist
Church at 7:30 p.m. Call 546-6121.
Community House has on-going programs.
Call 546-6575.
Free guided walks and programs at Halibut
Point State Park. Call 546-2997.
Little Art Cinema films start at 7 p.m. and 9:15
p.m. Call 546-2548.
Music in the meadow community festival at
Millbrook Park. Call 546-6934.

Sea breeze fair at the United Methodist Church.
Call 546-2093.
Summer dance festival at Windhover
Performing Arts Center. Call 546-3611.

AUGUST

Essex:	Music festival held last Saturday this month, from noon to 7:30 p.m. at Centennial Grove. Fun and music, swimming and picnicking. Call 768-3414 or 468-6581.
Gloucester:	Eden's Edge concert at Hammond Castle. Call 283-2080.

Cape Ann community band at Stage Fort Park.
Call 281-0543.
Learning Umbrella, celebrates learning in
Gloucester and Rockport. Call 800-649-6839.
Major Exhibition II at North Shore Arts
Association. Call 283-1857.
Rocky Neck Art Gallery weeklong festivities.
Call 283-7978.
Schooner festival mayor's race for 100-foot
schooners, lots of activities. Call 283-1601.
Biggest sidewalk bazaar on the North Shore.
Call 283-1601.
Waterfront festival features U.S. and Canadian
exhibitors. Call 283-1601.

Ipswich: "Circus Smirkus" international youth circus at
Castle Hill. Call 356-4351.
Castle Hill Concert. Call 356-4351.
"Sand Blast" annual sandscape contest at Crane
Beach. Call 356-4351.

Manchester: Circus at Masconomo Park.
Manchester Players, live theater. Call 526-7626.

SEPTEMBER

Cape Ann:	Annual road race, a 15-mile foot race. Call 283-0470.
Essex:	Clam fest held second Saturday of the month, chowder tasting and fun. Call 283-1601.

Dance in the barn at Essex County Greenbelt. Call 768-7241.

Kayak trip and river cruise at Greenbelt. Call 768-7241.

Traditional boat rendezvous, a gentleman's race. Call 768-2541.

Wildlife art festival, sculptures, carvings and paintings. Call 768-6953.

Gloucester: Pipe organ concert at Hammond Castle. Call 283-2080.

Eden's Edge at Hammond Castle. Call 283-2080.

"Tea by the sea" afternoons at Beauport Museum. Call 283-0800.

Fishbox derby race for youngsters ages 8 to 14. Build their own cars and are eligible to win money for college scholarships. Call 283-6853.

Students' art exhibit at North Shore Arts Association. Call 283-7978.

Seafood festival food, boat tours, and entertainment. Call 283-1601.

Ipswich: Antique auto show and jazz band. Call 356-4351.

Apple picking, cider pressing and hay rides at Goodale Orchards.

Manchester: Ice skate swap at Community Center. Call 526-7626.

OCTOBER

Gloucester: Annisquam arts and crafts fair on Columbus Day weekend 10 a.m. to 5 p.m. Call 283-3053.

Arty party on Rocky Neck on Columbus Day. Call 283-7978.

Swing band harvest ball with "Starlighters." Call 283-7874.

Vampire night at Hammond Castle. Call 283-2080.

North Shore antiques show. Call 281-0572.

Ipswich: Halloween celebration at Castle Hill. Call 356-4351.

Horribles parade for children and adults held the night before Halloween starting at 6 p.m. in the center of town. Call 356-6644.

Manchester: Arts gala, only Manchester artists may exhibit. Call 526-7050.

Great pumpkin festival. Call 526-7626.

Rockport: Fine artists art walk and open house. Call 546-6604.

NOVEMBER

Essex: Pride Week held the week before Thanksgiving "Turkey Trot," 5-mile road race, dance, many activities. Call 768-3414.

Holiday fairs at all downtown churches held third Saturday this month. Doors open at 10 a.m.

Gloucester: Plentiful feast murder night at Hammond Castle. Call 283-2080.

Hammond Castle Thanksgiving concert. Call 283-2080.

Ipswich: Oak Hill auction at 7:30 p.m. on Friday before Thanksgiving. Call 356-1530.

Veterans' Day ceremonies at 10:30 a.m. at war memorial on Route 1A.

Manchester: Wine tasting at the Community Center. Call 526-7626.

Rockport: Chamber Music festival auction. Call 546-7391.

DECEMBER

Essex: Holiday family celebration second Friday in December. Call 283-1601.

Gloucester: Annisquam Christmas fair. Call 283-6161.

City celebrates holiday season second Saturday of the month from 2 to 4 p.m. Call 281-9781.

Santa Claus parade. Call 283-1601.

Gloucester Stage Company performs "Scrooge and Marley." Call 281-4099.

Hammond Castle holds Christmas tours and concerts. Call 283-2080.

Ipswich:	Christmas concert at Castle Hill. Call 356-4351.
	Santa comes by boat to the town wharf, first weekend. Call 356-6644.
Manchester:	Holiday events held all month: party, shopping, open house, fair, museums, Santa parade and tree lighting. Call 283-1601.
	Women's Chorus Christmas concert. Call 283-9021.
	Jingle bells walk for children and adults. Call 526-7626.
Rockport:	Christmas in Rockport includes ice sculptures, live nativity, pageant, and caroling. Call 546-6575.
	Chorus North Shore performs Handel's *Messiah*. Call 546-1740.

WHAT'S WHERE?

Note What's Where contains information not listed any-where else in this guide book; for more information and additional listings consult the index.

Bathrooms **(H)** means handicap access: **(H-24)** means 24-hour handicap-access.

Essex:	Fire & Police Station **(H-24)** on Martin Street (Route 22) in the town center.
	Town Hall, Mon.–Thurs. 8:30–4 and Fri. 8:30–noon.
Gloucester:	Police Station **(H-24)** on Main Street.
	City Hall **(H)** weekdays 9–5.
	Cape Ann Chamber, Commercial Street, end of May thru mid-Oct. weekdays 8–6, Sat. 10–6, Sun. 10–4; mid-Oct. thru end of May weekdays 8–5.
	Fitz Hugh Lane House, Rogers Street, 9–6, 7 days a week from June–Oct. Sawyer Free Library, Dale Avenue (see library hours).

Stage Fort Park Visitors Center **(H)**, Hough Avenue, end of May–end of Oct.; 7 days a week 9–6.

Ipswich: Bialek Park **(H)**, Linebrook Road, weekdays 9–2, July and Aug. only.

Memorial Building, 23 Central Street, weekdays 8–11.

Town Hall **(H)**, 30 S. Main Street, Mon. 8–7 (except holidays), Tues.–Fri. 8–4.

Manchester: Fire Station, 12 School Street, open 24-hours.

Town Hall **(H)**, 10 Central Street, building is open 24 hours, but handicap access is Mon.–Wed. 9–5, Thurs. 9–8.

Rockport: Town Hall **(H)**, on Broadway, weekdays 8–4.

T Wharf **(H)**, end of May thru Nov. daily 6 a.m.–9 p.m.; Dec.–May daily 7 a.m.–4 p.m.

Front Beach and Back Beach **(H)**, weekends Apr.–May; daily 6 a.m.–7 p.m. June thru September.

B & B Reservations will help you select the perfect lodging place for your overnight, weekly, or monthly rental. They serve those who are looking for carefully selected accommodations and do not want to risk finding a place on their own. A $15.00 fee is charged. Call 617-964-1606 or 800-832-2632.

Campgrounds Directory for Massachusetts Campgrounds. Call 617-727-3200.

Chambers of Commerce

Essex: See Cape Ann Chamber of Commerce (Essex Chapter), Gloucester.

Gloucester: Cape Ann Chamber of Commerce, 33 Commercial Street, Gloucester, MA 01930. Call 283-1601 or 800-321-0133.

Ipswich: Ipswich Business Association, P.O. Box 94, Ipswich, MA 01938.

Ipswich Chamber of Commerce, c/o Barbara Parsons, 46 Newmarch Street, Ipswich, MA 01938. Call 356-3231.

| *Manchester:* | See Cape Ann Chamber of Commerce (Manchester Chapter), Gloucester. |
| *Rockport:* | Rockport Chamber of Commerce and Board of Trade, 3 Main Street, Rockport, MA 01966. Call 546-6575. |

Fall Foliage Fall Foliage Hotline begins September 15th; foliage conditions are updated three times a week. Call 800-227-MASS.

Fishing Division of Marine Fisheries for Massachusetts Saltwater Guide tells you how, where, when, and what to catch. Call 617-727-3193.

Parks and Recreation (for details see the Recreation section in each community) Department of Environmental Management (DEM), Division of Forests and Parks, 100 Cambridge Street, 19th floor, Boston, MA 02202, for map and guide to state park system. Call 617-369-3350.

Snow Skiing Cross-country skiing is allowed in all parks and reservations in the Cape Ann area.

Transportation

Essex:	A Whitehorse Limousine, Inc. Call 768-6599. Moonlight Limousine Service. Call 768-6344.
Gloucester:	A-1 Airport Livery of Cape Ann. Call 281-8121. Atlantic Taxi. Call 281-5550. Cape Ann Transportation Authority (public bus service for Essex, Gloucester, and Rockport). Call 283-7916. Cape Ann Yellow Cab. Call 283-9393. Charlie's Cabs, Inc. Call 281-4747.
Ipswich:	Airport Connection (taxi service). Call 356-7238 or 800-371-7238.

Visitor Information (serving the Cape Ann area)

| *Essex:* | Cape Ann Chamber of Commerce (see Gloucester). |

Gloucester: Cape Ann Chamber of Commerce, 33 Commercial Street. Call 283-1601. City of Gloucester Stage Fort Park Visitors Center, Hough Avenue. Call 800-649-6839.

Ipswich: Ipswich Chamber of Commerce. Call 356-3231. Ipswich Visitors' Center (May 31–Oct.) 36 S. Main Street. Call 356-8540.

Manchester: Cape Ann Chamber of Commerce (see Gloucester).

Rockport: Rockport Chamber of Commerce and Board of Trade Visitors Information Booth on upper Main Street (Route 127) as you enter town.

Visitor Information (serving the Cape Ann area and other Massachusetts areas)

Massachusetts: Massachusetts Office of Travel and Tourism (MOTT), 100 Cambridge Street, 13th floor, Boston, MA 02202. Call 617-727-3201 or 800-447-MASS.

North Shore: North of Boston Convention and Visitors Bureau, P.O. Box 642, Beverly, MA 01915. Call 921-4990 or 800-742-5306.

(Courtesy of Todd Lyon)

THE SEA, THE LAND, AND THE PEOPLE

Millions of years ago enormous glaciers formed the Cape Ann area. As four glaciers in succession advanced and retreated from the North across the land and toward the sea, the ice was at times more than one mile thick. Finally, as the last of these great ice ages (known as the Wisconsin) retreated, the outlines of Cape Ann, the little islands, and finger-like peninsulas along the coast were exposed.

Before the glaciers, the continental shelf (two hundred miles east of Cape Cod) was a plain well above sea level. As the climate cooled, the glaciers grew and moved southward through New England carrying rocks, sand, gravel, and huge boulders from the lands in the North to their southern limits. The leading edge of the last glacier extended some forty miles beyond today's shoreline and absorbed sea water until the level of the sea fell between three and five hundred feet. When the climate warmed again and this last glacier retreated, the materials trapped in the ice remained behind as sediment. This sediment was deposited in layers (called stratified drift). For example, silt and lighter materials formed the first layer of sediment and the coarser materials were deposited on top.

Wherever large amounts of debris were deposited at the very edges of the glacier's reaches, "terminal moraines" exist. On Cape Ann visitors can see a terminal moraine at Dogtown in Gloucester (see Index for more information about Dogtown). Cape Ann's high rocky headlands and offshore reefs are overlain with huge boulders left behind by glaciers. Some of these can be observed up close at Agassiz Rock Reservation in Manchester-by-the-Sea. If you look at a map of almost any barrier beach north of Long Island, you will notice the outlines of some of this glacial debris as submerged sandbars that form the ocean floor close to the shore. During storms, great quantities of this material are brought closer to shore.

The glaciers also left behind long, narrow, tapered mounds which look like the bowl of an inverted spoon—called drumlins—such as Hog (Choate) Island in Ipswich. The constant forces of the sea continue to shape these drumlins, altering their original form and carrying the finer materials to new areas and redepositing them to develop sand spits and beaches. To this day, the effects of the Wisconsin glacier are still operating; the land continues to bounce back at the rate of about six inches every one hundred years, while the sea level rises as the polar ice cap melts.

Cape Ann's coastline is never still. The forces of tide, wave, and storm are constantly at work. At this narrow band where sea and land meet, plants and animals must adapt to changes brought about by nature and people. This struggle for survival is the only thing that remains constant. In this area, there are several ecosystems in which a great variety of plants and animals live in an interdependent relationship.

Along Cape Ann's coastline, there are rivers and estuaries which move nutrients and food, and there are the daily effects of the tides and local currents. Waves erode beaches and rocky shores; rains from heavy storms pick up and redeposit materials deeper into the open sea. In this way some places are diminished by erosion while others are nourished by deposition.

Plants and animals vary according to the average high and low tide zones along the shores. Wave disturbances, the shape and make-up of the ocean bottom, coastal currents, and tides, all influence what species of fish will choose to live in a particular habitat. The flow patterns, circulation, and mixing of fresh and salt waters in the estuaries determine the location of shellfish beds or spawning areas of clams, crabs, and lobsters.

Nature actually helps to modify the effects of waves and tides. Where the glaciers scrubbed the soil down to the very skeleton of the land—the granite bedrock seen exposed everywhere in the Cape Ann area—rocky headlands tumble down to the sea's edge. Eagle Head at Singing Beach in Manchester-by-the-Sea helps to break the full force of storm-driven waves and tides and helps to protect the beach. These same rocky headlands protruding from the shore protect the entrance to the harbor in Manchester, helping to make it safe for boats and people. The very arch of Cape Ann and the offshore islands moderate the force of ocean-born storms by breaking the intensity of waves and currents.

Established communities of plants and animals protect both the shore and the islands. Beach grasses and shrubs guard sand dunes against wind erosion. Through the efforts of coastal managers and hundreds of volunteers, new beach grasses have been planted at Crane Beach in Ipswich and Wingaersheek and Good Harbor beaches in Gloucester. Tidal marshes cushion some of the intertidal areas (between the low and high tide marks) against the full forces of storm-driven water. Healthy, growing plants provide a stable base for themselves as well as fostering a strong biologic community which will allow all plants to expand into a wider area.

The most complex ecosystem in the Cape Ann area is the estuary. An estuary is complex and may contain many ecosystems (tidal marsh, eel grass beds, sand dunes, sandy beaches, tidal flats, rocky shores, and barrier beaches). Wherever fresh water flows into and mixes with salt water, estuaries exist along the coast. One type of river estuary is most common to Massachusetts and particularly to Cape Ann. In our area, the partially mixed estuary is most common because both the influence of the tides and the seaward movement of fresh water are strong. The plants and animals living in the estuary distribute themselves according to the level of salinity.

Estuaries are critical environments for most commercial and many freshwater and saltwater species of fish and shellfish. Seasonal phytoplankton blooms make estuaries a desirable nursery for the planktonic larvae of many invertebrates (such as worms, mollusks, and crustaceans) as well as for young fish. Some species live in the estuary their entire lives, while others depend upon the estuary for part of their life cycle. About two-thirds of the important commercial fish require the estuary for spawning and as a protective environment during their early stages of development. Other important species need to move through the estuary to freshwater spawning areas. After spawning in fresh water, these young fish move back into the estuary for food and for a protective area in which to live until they grow to a certain size; then they move downstream toward the sea.

Tidal marshes exist along the entire coast of Massachusetts. The vegetation on a marsh produces food, reduces extreme temperatures, transfers moisture from the soil to the air, and adds organic material to the marsh soil. One acre of marsh produces anywhere from five to ten tons of organic matter each year, making it one of the earth's most productive ecosystems.

Tidal marshes have definite zones in which plants and animals live. If you stop to explore a tidal marsh in the Cape Ann area (see Index under Open Spaces), you will notice that the surface of the marsh is not level. There are high spots, called hummocks, and pockets, called pannes. At high tide these pockets fill with water. When the tide goes out again,

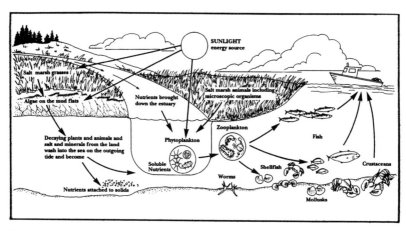

Diagram of an Estuary   *(Courtesy of the Gulf of Maine)*

Marsh Grasses: *Spartina alterniflora* and *S. patens*
(*Liz Mackie*)

the water remains in the tide pools and slowly evaporates. Salt becomes more concentrated in these pannes and a little plant called glasswort exists here. This little fleshy, leafless plant turns bright red in the fall, adding flashes of color to the marsh. Out on the tidal marsh it is easy to observe the changeover from land that is flooded daily by sea water to that which is only occasionally flooded. Two dominant plant species grow on the tidal marsh. Where the tall coarse grass (*Spartina alterniflora*), which gets flooded daily, changes over to the salt meadow cordgrass or salt hay (*S. patens*), the changeover from one zone to another takes place.

Look at the muddy surface of the marsh and notice the slicks of green and gold microscopic algae. These add to the high productivity of the marsh and are essential food sources for small invertebrate animals. These tiny algae are nitrogen-fixers, extracting nitrogen from the air and converting it into a form used by other marsh plants. At the end of the growing season the marsh grasses die back and decompose. The resulting nutrient materials are released, recycled, and returned to the soil and water where they can be reabsorbed by plants.

Many animals seek food, nesting places, and shelter in the tidal marsh and large numbers of birds are attracted year-round. Marsh hawks, wrens, sparrows, herons, egrets, owls and many more birds find food here. In fall and winter these vast acres of marshland are stopping places for migratory birds.

Eel grass beds are important because they produce food and provide a nursery for fish and other sea animals. These grasses need sunlight and grow where the currents are not too swift and the ocean bottom contains enough nutrients. Eel grass is a food source and provides a hiding place for animals that need calm waters, such as winter flounder and jellyfish. Brant geese and black ducks depend upon eel grass for food.

Sand dunes are found most often in coastal areas where there is an abundance of glacial moraine material or where coastal currents have deposited sand from distant moraine sources. Sand dunes endure considerable stress. The plants growing in the dunes depend upon fresh water for their survival and rainfall here is inconsistent. Wind erosion is constantly shifting the sand and making the surface unstable. Winds also carry salt spray from the sea and this discourages plant growth. Dunes suffer from extreme storms and waves as well as foot and vehicular traffic. When you visit areas where there are sand dunes, please obey all signs and regulations and stay on designated paths.

Cormorants off Hog Island
(Kay Ellis)

The American beach grass is the dominant plant species of the sand dune. It has an intricate network of roots which anchor the sand and hold the dune surface in place. Two particularly good beaches to observe the shaping of sand dunes as well as beach grass are Wingaersheek Beach in Gloucester and Crane Beach in Ipswich.

Sandy beaches are the least stable ecosystem. These are fully exposed to surf, wind, summer sun, and winter storms, and provide homes for few plants or animals. Some nutrients are brought onto the beach from tidal marsh runoff, eel grass ecosystems, or whatever the tide brings in. Crabs and snails emerge when the tide comes in to search for food and sea birds nest on the high beach. The endangered piping plover and least tern nest on the beach and you may see sections of beach cordoned off during nesting season so the birds are not disturbed. Some of the more common birds found along the seashore are gulls, terns, plovers, and sandpipers. You'll often see gulls shatter live shellfish on the paved parking lots by dropping them from the sky and then swooping down to eat their meal.

Shore birds   *(Liz Mackie)*

While at the beach, pick up a handful of sand. You'll notice many colors in the sand; these represent different minerals: the black particles of magnetite, the red particles of garnet (used in sandpaper), and the majority of light-colored particles of quartz. By studying these particles, a geologist finds clues to the original type of rock over which the glacier moved. The farther south you travel along the eastern seaboard the higher the percentage of shell fragments in the sand.

The tidal flat or clam flat is very common along the coast of Massachusetts. The salinity of the flats varies from less than one percent in the upper estuary (where fresh water flows into the tidal creeks, rivers, and saltwater bays) to sea water (3.5% saline) further away from the shore. The salinity of the tidal flat determines the type of plants and animals able to survive there, and since the salinity varies (due to heavy rainfall, melting ice and snow, or extreme heat and drought in summer), the animals and plants either constantly adapt or migrate elsewhere. Soft-shell clams are found on mud flats, little necks are found when flats are about equal parts sand and mud, and razor clams are found in pure sandy habitats. Other animals include various types of worms (the clam worm is prized by fishermen as bait), snails, and hermit crabs. The flats are important to the migrating shore birds, as they depend on the worms and crustaceans for food.

On Cape Ann rocky shore ecosystems are easy to identify. If you visit Bass Rocks or Eastern Point in Gloucester or drive around Cape Ann through Lanesville, Pigeon Cove, and Rockport, you will see exposed rocky headlands and man-made rock structures such as rip-rap walls (walls created by stacking stones to keep sandy banks along beaches from eroding), piers, and breakwaters. At Halibut Point in Rockport you will find one type of rocky shore, the sea cut cliff. Here the bedrock extends below the sea surface and ends abruptly at the ocean's edge. You will find many tidal pools in the rocky depressions just at or below the high tide level made up of rainwater or sea water from splashing waves. Sea urchins, blue mussels, snails, and various sea plant life exist here.

The steep grade, rapid drainage when the tide changes, and exposure during low tides cause the plants and animals at the rocky shore great stress. The changeover from one zone to the next as you move from the land toward the sea is obvious here. Notice especially how the brown "weeds" of the sea drape over the boulders when the tide is out. If you look closely you will see that they lack roots and hold on to the rocky surfaces with structures called "holdfasts." Seaweeds range in size from microscopic to ten feet long and come in a variety of shapes and colors as well as growing requirements.

A barrier beach is a composite ecosystem; that is, it is a combination of two or more ecosystems. When sand or gravel is transported by waves from a sediment source, a barrier beach is formed. It usually begins as a sand spit which grew out from and is parallel to the shore. The barrier beach becomes an island when the connection to the shore is breached by storm waves. This beach is usually long and narrow and may contain high sand dunes.

Crane Beach in Ipswich is a perfect example of a barrier beach ecosystem. This beach suffers greatly from erosion and its contours can vary considerably after storms. When heavy storms drive the sea water across Crane Beach to the lagoon behind, sand is carried to new places and forms shoals and deltas. Wherever these washover deposits land on old tidal marsh, new dunes form. New tidal marsh develops where deposits occur in the lagoon. The forces of sea and weather are constantly shaping this barrier beach ecosystem.

The first people to inhabit the Cape Ann area were the Algonquin-speaking Agawam Indians. They came to the coast during the summer to fish, clam, and farm. They knew the climate was too severe here year-round and that barrier beaches bore the brunt of the hurricanes that raged up the coast in the fall. Unfortunately, in 1616, with the arrival of European traders and explorers, eighty percent of the Indian population was killed by pestilence brought over from Europe. Hepatitis, smallpox, and influenza plagues claimed many lives.

In 1634, Masconomet, chief of the Agawams voluntarily surrendered what remained of his people to the Massachusetts Colony government. In the 1670s the Agawams made one last great effort to save their cultural integrity in New England, but their culture was eventually absorbed. Wherever traders and explorers interacted with these coastal Indians, the catastrophic demise of the Indians was so sudden that little knowledge of their culture and trade survives today. The fact remains that the Indians aided the early colonists and shared with them many valuable parts of their culture.

From the arrival of the first European settlers, the harbors, fish, and maritime trading routes provided food, housing, and income. Over time ports developed and settlements grew along the coastline. People's needs often conflicted with the coastal ecosystems, and development often placed great stress on a resilient environment.

At first the colonists allowed domestic animals to graze on the beaches and in the marshes because dense forests covered much of this area. Before long the animals had grazed and trampled the plants down to bare sand. Townspeople soon realized the destruction they had caused and enacted ordinances to protect these areas. In time small fishing villages grew up behind the dunes in the many coves and backwaters. As populations expanded, roads were developed, more elaborate homes built, and vacationers constructed cottages. Soon hotels, more houses, more roads, and endless development began to threaten this coastal area.

Along the coast of Cape Ann lie the graveyards of many ships that went down to the bottom of the sea. It was because of these disasters that lighthouses were constructed at strategic places along the shore. Lighthouse keepers kept provisions for shipwrecked sailors, but they could not patrol the coastline in search of vessels in distress.

In 1871, the Life Saving Service was established to build permanent life saving stations along the coast. These stations were stocked with emergency provisions and the most dangerous sections of beaches were patrolled around the clock. The brave men who made up the station crews often endured lonely watches in the cruelest of weather giving up their own lives to save those in distress. Finally, in 1915, the Treasury Department combined several agencies, including the Life Saving Service, into what is today's U.S. Coast Guard.

In 1979 approximately 25,500 acres were designated as an Area of Critical Environmental Concern (ACEC). Essex, Gloucester, and Ipswich are located within this district (the other towns are Newbury and Rowley). Essex Bay is one of the two water bodies included in the ACEC (the other is Plum Island Sound). The ACEC includes several rivers, brooks, and creeks as well as miles of barrier beaches protected under public or private management. Thousands of acres within this district are part of the Atlantic flyway migration route. On this site, more than 60 bird species breed, over 300 bird species have been sighted, and 75 rare species have been noted. During the spring and fall migrations, 25,000 ducks and 6,000 Canada geese pass through this corridor. The waters of the ACEC contain vast amounts of shellfish and host some of the largest runs of alewives and smelt on the North Shore.

Organizations such as the Department of Environmental Management (DEM), Massachusetts Coastal Zone Management (MCZM), Massachusetts Audubon, U.S. Fish and Wildlife Service, Trustees of Reservations, Essex County Greenbelt Association, Manchester Conservation Trust, and others both public and private are working to help protect Cape Ann's fragile coast. The interaction among the coastal ecosystems, the positive and negative effects of nature, and the interrelationships between animals and plants combine with the influences and demands of people to create a delicate balance here.

As you visit the beautiful natural areas on Cape Ann, please help preserve their quality and character by following a few simple steps.

1. Read and respect all signs; they're for your safety.
2. Respect all fences and barriers; they exist for a reason.
3. Take out whatever you bring in; leave no litter.
4. Keep pets under your control; wildlife may be near.
5. Please don't pick plants.
6. Remain on designated paths or roads.
7. Accidental fire in summer is a real danger; use caution with matches.
8. Educate your children and friends to respect natural areas.
9. If you see anyone polluting the waters of Cape Ann and its vicinity, report them to the U.S. Coast Guard by calling 800-424-8802.

In closing, here are a few cautionary notes about insects, poisonous plants and the daily fluctuation of the tides. Deer ticks inhabit the Cape Ann area. When visiting natural areas, wear light-colored clothing (the tiny dark ticks are easier to see on light colors). If you are wearing long pants, tuck them into high socks. After your hike, check yourself and your children for ticks. Have adults check each other (sometimes ticks are difficult to spot on yourself). Don't panic; not all ticks are deer ticks and not all deer ticks carry Lyme disease. If you remove the suspected tick within twenty-four hours, the disease is usually not transmitted. Should a red, ring-like rash appear at the site of the bite, followed by what seems like the flu—feelings of fatigue, headache, and stiff sore joints—see a doctor immediately. Antibiotics usually will effectively treat the disease.

Greenhead flies and mosquitoes can be aggressive from approximately the last two weeks in July until the middle of August. The greenhead (a horsefly) provides an important source of protein for young swallows, flycatchers, and kingbirds living in and around the tidal marshes. We may not appreciate the important roles that both the mosquito and greenhead play in the food chain, but fish feed on the larvae and birds depend upon these insects for food. Wearing light-colored clothing and plenty of insect repellent does discourage them.

Sometime in the 1960s a young high school science teacher, Lawrence Ulrich, studied the greenheads and noticed that they bred in salt marshes and laid their eggs in the mud, where larvae emerged anew each year. He also noticed that they were attracted to hot places and dark colors. So, he designed a wooden trap, placed it on legs and set it along the edge of the marsh. You will notice square black boxes scattered throughout the marsh river banks. These boxes help to trap millions of greenheads every summer. The flies are attracted to the dark color and fly into the boxes through a slit in the screens at the bottom. Once inside, a screen across the top makes it impossible for them to fly out again. You will notice these boxes especially along the banks of the Essex River.

Some of the drainage ditches you see cut into the marshland were dug during the 1930s in an attempt to control the mosquito population. This method proved to be fruitless, however, and the action of the tides caused the trenches to erode and cave in.

Poison ivy and poison sumac have overrun many wild areas. Learn to recognize these plants and avoid contact with them; you will be spared the agony of a reaction. Poison ivy is the guardian of the forest; it can be found in meadows, take the form of climbing vines on tall trees, and be found close to the sea on dry sandy beaches. An old saying, "leaves of three, leave them be," reminds us that poison ivy's glossy leaves cluster in groups of three. It is one of the first plants to turn brilliant colors in the fall.

Tides change! When exploring coastal areas be aware of the time and height of the tides. Some local businesses (such as banks) offer handy pocket-size tide calendars free for the asking. Almanacs and daily newspapers also list daily tide charts. The time of high and low tide varies slightly for each community.

For your safety: (1) when exploring rocky shores, obey all "NO TRESPASSING" signs; (2) use caution when walking on rocks, they are extremely slippery when wet; (3) watch the tide; when it comes in or at high tide, waves and surf are unpredictable and can be dangerous.

High tide   *(Ann Fessenden)*

THE CLAM INDUSTRY

The clam industry in the Cape Ann area depends on the soft shell clams found on the tidal flats. Although many kinds of clams exist, it is the soft shell clam which is harvested for frying and steaming. Clams live below the surface of the flat and extend their foot (on Cape Ann the foot of the clam is referred to as the neck) up through the mud and sand when the flat is covered with sea water. This is when they feed. Should you hear the expression "He (or she) is happy as a clam at high tide," you'll know what it means! When the tide is out, the flats are exposed and wherever the clams' necks have retracted, slight depressions leave clues as to their whereabouts.

When the flats are exposed, approximately four hours at each low tide, the clammers go out to dig. Low tide is followed by high tide a little more than six hours later, and each day the time of low and high tide is about forty minutes later than the day before. This pattern of tidal oscillation makes the timing of clam gathering completely predictable.

Using a clam fork, clammers scoop down where the depressions can be seen and turn the mud over to pick out the clams. Roughly thirty to forty bushels of soft-shell clams are

Low tide   *(Ann Fessenden)*

dug each year on a one-acre flat. A clammer must get a license from the local shellfish commissioner who regulates the opening and closing of the flats for digging.

Occasionally clams take in abnormally high amounts of an alga known as "red tide." This alga is usually present in small and harmless amounts, but sometimes the alga count increases to such a point that tidal waters take on a reddish cast. Government officials monitor the coast for signs of "red tide" and shut down the flats whenever they find it; because, although this alga is not harmful to the shellfish, consuming clams dug on flats where red tide is present can cause paralysis in humans.

Soft-shell clam   *(Liz Mackie)*

Long before the first settlers arrived on these shores, Indians spent their summers harvesting the shellfish. Large heaps of clam, mussel, and oyster shells have been found in several locations on Cape Ann. The clam industry began in the Essex and Ipswich area from the time the first settlers arrived in 1634 and has continued without interruption to the present day. From the late 1700s to the mid-1800s, clams were used mainly for bait and were dug, shucked (taken out of their shells), and shipped salted or fresh in barrels to fishermen in Gloucester, Boston, and Provincetown. This industry brought in considerable money to coastal communities, but it was not until the late 1800s that inland markets became important. At about this time clams began to be seen as suitable for human consumption and so began an industry of large proportions.

A clammer's only boss is the tide. Clamming is a rugged, albeit healthy, occupation. In the earliest times, clammers

Done clamming *(Courtesy of Dorothy Kerper Monnelly)*

rowed down the river every day (winter as well as summer) to reach the clam flats, bringing back a barrel of clams they had dug by hand. Today clammers have outboard motors for their boats, but the digging is still done by hand.

Franklyn Goucher, who has dug Essex clams for decades, wrote a collection of "true" *Clam Diggers' Stories*. His stories speak of the wisdom, humor, and good health enjoyed by rugged diggers of clams. At the end of his book he lists the tribulations of clam diggers: a clam digger has to suffer a lifetime of ninety years while the average fortunate person expires at seventy; when a clam digger feels a sickness coming on, he makes sure he drinks an extra three jiggers of whiskey that night and by morning, he's cured; and old clam diggers never die, they just go out with the tide!

Clamming became even more important to the local economy as the shipbuilding industry waned in Essex. With modern methods of transportation, people have been able to drive to Cape Ann anytime to eat clams at the many seafood restaurants and the clam's fame and reputation has spread to the far corners of the world. Since the first clams were dug over three hundred years ago, billions have been eaten raw, steamed, fried, baked, and in creamy New England chowder. It's worth a trip to the causeway in Essex just to smell the clams frying as you drive past the restaurants, but they're even better when you stop in for a meal!

The first fried clam is attributed to Chubby Woodman, who served them in 1916 at a little stand near the restaurant still operating today on the Essex Causeway. As the story goes, Woodman began his business in 1914 by serving clams-in-the-shell and freshly cooked potato chips until one day a friend, Mr. Tarr, suggested Chubby throw some clams into the iron fry kettle with his potato chips. By the following week, Woodman sold gallons of fried clams to eager passersby. Over the next few years, little clam shacks sprang up along the causeway.

Today the Cape Ann area is known for its excellent restaurants, which serve various kinds of seafood as well as many other favorite menu items. Whether you prefer eating seafood "in-the-rough" or in a more formal atmosphere, Cape Ann has a dining establishment waiting for you!

SALT MARSHES AND THEIR INDUSTRY

"The marshes turn green and withdraw through gold into brown, and their indolent, untouched, enduring existence penetrates your fibre. You find you must drive down toward the beach to see them once a week or it is like a week without love. The ice cakes pile up along the banks of the tidal inlets like the rubble of ruined temples." John Updike,"The Indian," *The New Yorker*, August 17, 1963.

The Indians called the marshes Owascoag, meaning the land of many grasses. As the cradle of marine life, the salt marsh blends many living worlds. The tall grasses feed and hide a variety of living creatures and the changing tides sweep through the marshes bringing in waters from the ocean to where it meets the outflowing nutrient-rich fresh water from brooks, streams, and rivers.

The hardy grasses growing in the salt marshes are the Spartina grasses. *Spartina* comes from the Greek word for cord; hence they are often referred to as cordgrass. Spartinas thrive where few plants can stay alive. They have adapted to living with their roots extended into the salty marsh and to being completely flooded periodically by high tides. *Spartina alterniflora* is a tall thick-leafed plant growing best near tidal creeks. Away from tidal currents grows *Spartina patens*, a shorter, more slender grass. The change from *S. alterniflora* to *S. patens* marks the average high tide.

In the earliest records of the division of lands for housing and planting, references are made to salt marshes. Salt marshes were owned by farmers as far inland as Georgetown and Topsfield. When the first settlers arrived, the land was heavily forested and strewn with rubble from the last receding glacier. The marshes provided farmers with land already cleared from which they could cut tons of fodder; the hay was a rich source of vitamins for their cows and they in turn provided excellent milk.

The earliest settlers used thatch or coarse salt hay grass to insulate houses and barns as well as make roofs. Even when temperatures reached twenty below zero, hay stacked three-feet deep around a house kept it warm. Many people also used salt marsh grass for mulching their gardens, to keep weeds from growing and reduce the need to water their gardens, much as Cape Ann gardeners do today.

If you look closely at the marshes, you will see ditches traversing in all directions; these were cut by hand with spades by the early settlers in order to drain the salt marsh hay areas. The ditches were cut two and one-half feet deep and eight inches wide. Later a two-bladed saw was developed to cut the ditches. The salt marsh grass was cut by scythe and harvested from June to October. Men swinging scythes could be seen dotting the landscape when the salt marshes were not flooded.

Once the grass was cut, raking, piling, and stacking followed. The hay was carefully balanced on staddles, circular foundations built of cedar stakes driven into the marsh. After the hay had been raked and piled, it was carried to the staddles on hay poles. No matter how miserable the mosquitoes, black flies, or greenheads were making the job, the load could not be put down until they had reached the staddle. Staddles were built high enough to raise the hay above the highest tide level.

Hay staddle on the marsh   *(Courtesy of Old Newbury Historical Society)*

In later years horses pulled mowing machines over the marshes. In order to keep the horses from getting bogged down in the soft marshes, they wore special wooden shoes the size of dinner plates with iron clamps to hold them to their hooves. Hand raking was replaced by the drag rake in the 1880s. A horse was driven in a zigzag pattern over the hay field dragging the rake in tow in the direction of the hay staddles. In warm weather, the stacked hay was transported by flat square boats called gundalows which had to be poled up and down the waterways to the nearest landing. The gundalows could transport up to 12 tons of hay at a time. In winter, sleds (called blue dump carts and similar in design to a dog sled, only larger) were pulled by oxen over the frozen marsh.

In 1821 a toll canal (now one of the oldest in the country) was dug through the Ipswich marshes connecting the Ipswich River with the Essex River. A half-mile cut between Fox Creek and Castle Neck River made an island out of Castle Hill which exists to this day. The canal benefited both the Essex shipyards as well as the cooperage (barrel) industry by making shipments of timber, hoop-poles, and staves from communities along the Merrimack River possible without having to go to sea.

At one time, the bridge on Argilla Road (the road to Crane Beach and Castle Hill) was nothing but a foot bridge with a toll gate. As the timber came down the Fox Creek to the Essex River, the vessels passed the toll at the Argilla Road bridge and were charged different fees according to what they were carrying. Once the railroad came to Ipswich, most of the canal business disappeared except for the gundalows laden with salt hay. Hay for sale was taken into town by wagons and weighed before being loaded on railroad cars and shipped into Boston.

Today as we look out over the acres of marshland, this industry is no longer apparent. It wasn't that long ago, however, that local landowners counted on the thick cordgrass for fodder, insulation, mulch, and thatch. We know the nutrient-rich marshes provide nurseries for sea animals, breeding and nesting places for birds and animals, and ever-changing places of natural beauty that renew the spirit of each person who stops long enough to enjoy them.

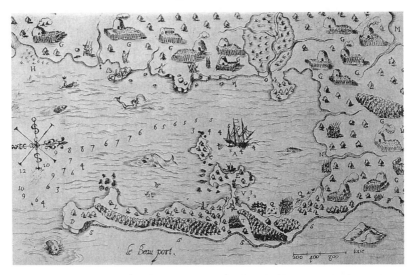

In 1605 Samuel de Champlain visited these shores and called Gloucester Harbor Le Beauport. *(Courtesy of Boston Public Library)*

ARCHITECTURAL STYLES OF THE AREA

Try to imagine the landscape around you in its natural state: plentiful virgin timber, millions of rocks of various sizes strewn haphazardly about, underbrush growing in a mass of tangles. When the first settlers came, they had to build simple, crude shelters to protect themselves from the elements, wild animals, and intruders. These structures were made from the materials around them: sod, salt marsh hay, twigs, and logs (none of these dwellings exist today). The settlers had to clear the land in order to grow food and provide pasture for their animals. The Indians who summered in the Cape Ann area lived in dwellings probably similar to the structures depicted in the old Le Beauport map and settlers most likely fashioned their first homes after these. It was only after their most critical needs had been met that they were able to think about constructing houses of timber.

As you read this chapter, please note that in all of the first-period (1640–1725), second-period (1725–1790), and third-period (1790–1830) houses, there are half, three-quarter or full center entrance houses. These also can be referred to as three-, four-, or five-bay façades, depending on the number of windows and doors dividing the house into bays. The period of a house is not determined by its form. For example, a salt-box, cape, or two-story house can be found from almost any period up to and including the present.

FIRST PERIOD (1640–1725)

First-period houses were built without regard to aesthetics. Since more than seventy percent of the first settlers came from England, the earliest New England houses (up until about 1830) mirrored styles dating back to their homeland. The Fairbanks house in Dedham is the oldest standing wood frame house in America. Few 17th-century houses remain, and those that do are usually from the last quarter of that century. Most first-period houses date from 1700 to about 1730.

The original structures were typically one large (20 feet square) room, one to two stories high, with a steeply pitched roof, and a massive oblong chimney that provided heat. Built of natural materials and ruggedly constructed, the dwellings met the needs of their owners. Frames were usually of oak (especially in the 17th century) and decorated with chamfers and well-finished off (as they were meant to be seen). The older the house, the larger and more decorative the chamfers. The foundation was made with field stones and the house sat close to the ground on its sills.

First-period houses usually consisted of a hall or kitchen/living room and perhaps a chamber above. As

First-period House   *(Liz Mackie)*

more space was needed, the structure was expanded by building an addition on the other side of the chimney so it could provide heat to each room. The new room was called the parlor and the room above the parlor chamber. These have come to be called hall and parlor houses.

In time even this did not provide enough space and a lean-to was constructed along the rear and the roof of the existing house simply continued downward at the same angle as the old roof or tilted upward slightly. It was by adding the lean-to (late in the 17th century) that the Saltbox style was born. With the addition of the lean-to, the kitchen moved to the rear. This style was called the Saltbox because it resembled the shape of the salt boxes used by our ancestors. (For an example of a Saltbox, see the Whipple House in Ipswich.)

The long, steeply pitched roof with the lean-to added on faced north, providing a sturdy windbreak, and the entrance of the house usually faced south. The outer walls were covered with clapboards (originally called "clay-board" because boards covered the clay and straw daub with which these early house walls were filled). The decorative garrison overhang (where the second story projects out over the first story by several inches) was called a "jetty," reminiscent of England. A few windows were placed where they were needed most, and since glass was expensive, windows were small by today's standards. Today none of the original diamond-paned window glasses remain; double-hung window sash came in after 1700 and usually replaced the leaded casements. Any diamond-paned casements seen in 17th-century New England houses are reproductions.

During this early period, the first Cape Cod cottage was constructed in New England. It is safe to say that the first Capes probably evolved from the crude one-room, one-and-a-half-story, steep-roofed houses with end chimneys that the settlers had known in Europe. At first this house had no style name; it was built to meet the settlers' needs. Then in the 19th century, the president of Yale College suggested it be called the Cape Cod cottage and the name stuck.

The Cape forms a compact rectangle. Even with later additions, the original structure stands out. It sits close to the ground and, like the Saltbox, generally faces south. It has an unbroken gable roof, pitched steeply enough to provide

Cape Cod cottage   *(Peter H. Gertsch)*

living space with headroom underneath. The façade is approximately eight feet high. From sills to roof peak, the house is approximately twenty feet high. It has a massive chimney that rises through the roof ridge and, in the largest Capes, is centrally located between the gable ends. It is of frame construction. The walls are clad with wooden shingles, clapboards, or both. The rather small, multi-paned, double-hung windows are placed close under the eaves. It lacks exterior ornamentation.

Whereas the Saltbox is pretty much straight forward, the Cape Cod cottage has more variations in size. Today's Capes are referred to as half, three-quarter, and full size. The full house is most common: the front door is centered in the façade, both sides of this door are flanked by a pair of windows, and the chimney is centered above the front door. The three-quarter house has a somewhat off-center chimney with one window on one side of the front door and two windows on the opposite. And in the half house, the front door and chimney are at one end and two windows are between the door and the other end of the house. Capes were built in other sizes, but these are quite rare.

Cape Ann cottage   *(Courtesy of Peabody Essex Museum)*

As the settlers' knowledge of construction grew, they found that if they put a gambrel roof on a Cape Cod cottage, there would be more head room on the top floor. This gambrel-roofed house is called a "Cape Ann" cottage because it is thought to have originated on Cape Ann.

The floor plans of the Saltbox and the Cape Cod cottage are similar; the oak timbers in the frame construction of both were held together by intricate wood joints and oak pegs. Most of both styles had double-hung wood windows with wide muntins (wooden strips which divide the panes of glass). In both, the massive chimneys are their crowning glory. They are simple but sturdy structures which dominate the entire house.

For a period of time, the Saltbox and Cape Cod cottage fell out of favor. People's fancies changed. After the Great Depression, the Cape Cod cottage became popular again. Royal Barry Wills, a Boston architect, was mainly responsible for its revival. He designed many Saltbox-style houses, but the Capes were the most popular. Wills saw the Cape as the ideal style for new home owners, but it was not until after World War II that his opinion was fully accepted. When organizations such as the National Trust for Historic Preservation and the Society for the Preservation of New England Antiquities began to generate public interest in historic buildings, Saltboxes once again became popular.

GEORGIAN PERIOD (1725–1790)

As communities such as Boston, Portsmouth, Salem, and Providence were firmly established, and trade, industry, and farming were making new Americans more prosperous, the functional house was no longer good enough. Again the colonists turned to England for inspiration. Under the rules of King George I, II, and III, Georgian architecture reigned supreme. New immigrants who were in the building trades brought style books from England with them. Brickyards in America were turning out high-grade brick, plaster had improved, and paints were mixed in a greater variety of hues. The stage was set for a building boom in this refined formal style.

Hallmarks of this design were a larger number of rooms (smaller in size but with higher ceilings), a central hall bisecting the two rooms on each side of the ground floor and again on the second floor, and a rigid regard for symmetry. The central chimney still predominated in most rural areas and vernacular houses and foundations were much higher.

Details on the exterior of the house became important and front doorways works of art. Pilasters with flutes or carvings set off these proud portals. Pediments or ornamental gables were fashioned above the door frame. Sliding sash came into style. The hipped roof was still quite steep but would be lower in the next period.

In Gloucester, the hallmark of this period was the gambrel roof, whether on a humble Cape Ann cottage or the Sargent House Museum on Middle Street. In fact, the Sargent house originally had a gambrel roof (see page 92).

FEDERAL PERIOD (1790–1830)

Although this period began with the Revolution, architecturally it began much later. The trend continued with foundations becoming higher and the roof pitch lower. Asher Benjamin's pattern books introduced this style to country builders in remote places and brought the styles of Macintire

Main Street, Essex *(Courtesy of Nancy Marculewicz)*

and Bulfinch to the remote areas of New England. This period is also referred to as "Adamesque" after the Adams brothers in England who had inspired Bulfinch.

Self-made merchants, bankers, traders, and shipbuilders—principally identified with the Federalist Party—were daring in business but conservative in attitude. This era's architectural goals were to bring comfort, dignity, and quality to all classes, whether in city townhouses, cottages, or on the farm. As Carole Rifkind says in her book, *A Field Guide to American Architecture*, "In these early years of nationhood the sense of American identity demanded an American architecture for the common man as well as the privileged."

Though American architectural styles from this period derived from the English, Americans' building materials and needs were different. Georgian proportions became more refined. Ornamentation inside as well as out was subdued and lightness of scale was keynote. Tall slender chimneys and fanlighted front doorways were hallmarks of this style; balance and symmetry were prized. The hip-roof style was introduced on an almost square house which usually had a five-bay window arrangement and the portico, or frontispiece, of the house was set in the middle. Door and window openings were beautifully scaled (often with fans and ovals). The roof balustrade was much smaller than during the Georgian years and now ran around the perimeter of the hip roof.

GREEK REVIVAL STYLE (1830–1860)

It was interest in ancient Greece as well as the Greek War for Independence in 1821 which resulted in this new architectural style in the United States. Though grand Greek Revival buildings are not as common to the Cape Ann area as elsewhere, you will still find many private homes which have the classical Greek Revival styling.

For the first time the gable end of the house was turned toward the street. Like Greek temples the houses were adorned with giant porticos typically supported by four Doric columns. Look for exterior elaboration around doorways, porch support columns, and windows. A universal feature is the pediment (a triangular space created by the sloping eaves and horizontal cornice line of the gable) with a wide band of trim beneath the cornice lines of the main roof. Where the Greeks built with stone, New Englanders built with wood and made adjustments to compensate. For example, here the exterior walls were covered in flat-matched boarding which resembled stone and were painted white. The buildings were either one and one-half stories or two stories high with a low pitch roof and insignificant chimneys. Classical correctness of style was key. This period flourished until the Civil War began. For an example of a Greek Revival building, look at the old Town Hall at the intersection of Middle and Washington Streets in downtown Gloucester.

VICTORIAN PERIOD (1840–1900)

Andrew Jackson Downing, landscape architect and author of *The Architecture of Country Houses* (1850), wrote in his House Pattern Book, "It is the solitude and freedom of the family home in the country which constantly preserves the purity of the nation and invigorates its intellectual powers." Downing preached that a building must be harmonious with the surrounding landscape and must serve a purpose. Vincent J. Scully, Jr. commented in his book, *The Shingle Style*, "Downing is important to us because he decisively established the principles of asymmetrical, picturesque design in America and thereby laid the foundation for a whole new sequence of experiments in planning and spatial organization."

Whether blue collar workers or millionaires, homeowners wanted houses which reflected their individual style; variety was in vogue. The early Victorian Period with its house pattern books stimulated the imagination of American architects. Gothic Revival was popular around the 1840s and 1850s and its influences can be seen most clearly in mansions, churches, and some public buildings. Gothic Revival houses on Cape Ann can most often be seen in Gloucester. Some distinguishing features are pointed arches, towers, steeply pitched roofs, the use of leaded stained glass, verandahs, and bay windows.

Around 1855, the Bracketed Style (also known as Italianate) became popular. This style came to America from Northern Italy by way of England; specifically, the pattern books of Andrew Jackson Downing. From highly decorative (low roof, overhanging eaves with decorative brackets, round-headed windows, and arcaded porches) to the simplest (a square house with a low pyramidal roof, bracketed eaves, and perhaps a belvedere), this was a highly adaptable style. There are many Bracketed Style houses in Gloucester.

The years 1860–1900 have become known as the "age of exuberance" as architects combined features from various styles. The mansard roof was also in vogue (taken from a roof style that had been introduced by François Mansart in Paris during the 17th-century French Renaissance). It is a double-pitched roof with a steep lower slope. Dormers are usually set into the lower portion of the roof to allow light to enter the second story.

Around 1870 the eclectic Victorian Gothic style (influenced by John Ruskin) drew from Italian, German, and English Gothic precedents. This style was used mainly for public buildings, schools, churches, and libraries.

From about 1865–1880, the Stick style (where the expression of the inner structure of the house was brought through to the exterior ornament) exhibited boards at intersecting right angles applied over the exterior clapboards to symbolize the structural skeleton. Sometimes diagonal boards were also applied to resemble half-timbering.

The Queen Anne Style is usually associated with Richard Norman Shaw (1831–1912). A contrast of materials was used in construction from brick or stone on the first floor to upper stories of stucco, clapboards or decorative shingles (tiles were used in England). Asymmetrical in form, the space flowed freely into ample rooms; the "living hall" was introduced. The hall was not only used to get from room to room, but had a living area, fireplace, and grand staircase. Huge medieval-type chimneys were common, as were gabled or hipped roofs, corner turrets borrowed from the French chateaux; banks of casement windows were used, and verandahs or balconies opened the house to the outdoors.

The first true American style that evolved out of the Queen Anne was the Shingle Style. It was here in New England that architects such as Henry Hobson Richardson and William Ralph Emerson as well as McKim, Mead, and White fully developed this style during the second half of the 19th century. (For an example of the Shingle Style, see the Essex Town Hall.) When Shaw's English tiles became difficult to manufacture in America in the 1870s, natural wood shingles were used in their place. It was a time of prosperity with many "cottages" being built in fashionable seaside communities.

In contrast to the vertical lines of the Queen Anne, the Shingle Style had horizontal lines. The entire building was covered with wooden shingles and if another material was used for porch columns or foundations, usually it was rough-surfaced native stone or fieldstone rubble which complemented the rough natural texture of the shingles. The houses were designed to fit into the irregularities of the natural landscape (see Essex Town Hall, page 57). This "age of indiscretion" led to the great modern architecture of the 20th century.

It makes sense that as architecture flourished, the need for landscape designs which complimented these structures would also be desired. It was during this time that Frederick Law Olmsted, the famous landscape architect, was at work on the Boston Parkways and several wealthy homeowners on the North Shore asked him to lay out their grounds.

The architects, McKim, Mead & White, understood what Richardson had accomplished and took the "Shingle Style" and made it an even greater work of art. The building of summer "cottages" and country houses for the wealthy gained architectural firms commissions for monuments and downtown office buildings. McKim, Mead & White's house designs were in part influenced by Japanese styles (use of open space and privacy screens), which they adapted to the American way of life. As architecture continued its progress into the 20th century, the Japanese influences are again apparent in the designs of Frank Lloyd Wright. He was influenced by Andrew Jackson Downing, Richardson, and McKim, Mead & White, and always (sometimes to the point of absurdity) strived to keep alive a sense of union between the building and the land. This fusion of dwelling and landscape has formed one of the bases for modern architecture.

After 1900, the American dream of an individually owned home with its lawn-fronted lot for every working man became a testimony to material progress and to family stability. Americans began to commute to places of business and lived elsewhere; the suburbs were born. Neighborhoods acquired distinct characteristics as expressed by the social, ethnic, and economic class of their residents.

Between 1900 and World War I, people were nostalgic and began to look backward; there was a new appreciation for antiques and hand-crafted work. Beams were now exposed in ceilings; fieldstones were used in foundations; and wrought iron lighting fixtures were appreciated. The Bungalow and American Four Square styles were born. In contrast to the Victorian Period "age of exuberance," people now wanted to get back to basics.

Today's mass-produced components have allowed for a vast volume of construction but not always structures which make best use of materials, knowledge of design, or use of the land. Ideally there should be a harmony between a house and its site. Houses are built to be lived in. Owners change and alterations are made to reflect changes in taste, and this often makes it difficult to determine a building's age, period, or style by visual observation. Often the sophisticated, high styles of city buildings are not appropriate to the countryside and only certain aspects of sophisticated styles are applied to country houses. For example, it is easy to change doorways and windows to reflect styles popular at a given time. Rooflines, moldings and trim, decorative elements, or new additions can be added to reflect the latest style.

As time passes, buildable land in desirable locations increases in value and young houses (less than twenty years old) are being torn down to allow owners to build anew. What buildings constructed during the 20th century will remain to become the architectural treasures of tomorrow?

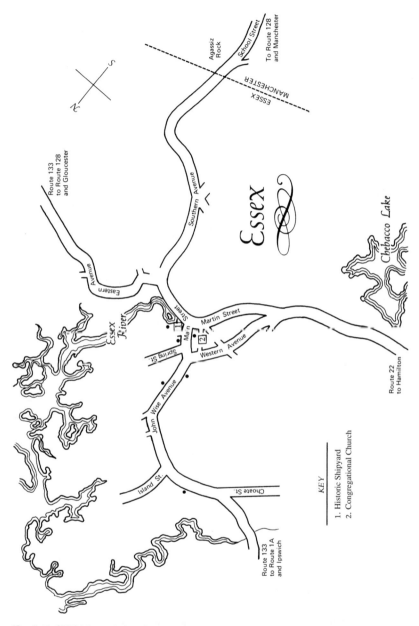

Essex

Essex River

Route 133
to Route 128
and Gloucester

Eastern Avenue

Southern Avenue

School Street

To Route 128
and Manchester

Agassiz
Rock

ESSEX
MANCHESTER

Main Street

Spring St.

Martin Street

Western Avenue

John Wise Avenue

Island St.

Choate St.

Route 22
to Hamilton

Chebacco Lake

Route 133
to Route 1A
and Ipswich

KEY

1. Historic Shipyard
2. Congregational Church

(Courtesy of J.W. Murray & Associates)

Historic Shipyard   *(Tom O'Hara)*

Essex

HISTORY

As you drive along the causeway in Essex you will see an abundance of antique shops and seafood restaurants. Essex is certainly a well-visited town thanks to these attractions, but what many people don't realize is that the town boasts a rich history that goes beyond antiques and clams.

SHIPBUILDING

The people of Essex thrived on shipbuilding for centuries. Ipswich (of which Essex was once a part) granted land for the purpose of building vessels in 1668. The first boats were built for transporting people and supplies and for fishing. The "Chebacco" (so called because it was the original name of Essex) was a 30-foot long boat which was practical for these uses. Then came the "Pinkie," a 30-ton vessel pointed at both ends, with primitive rigging and standing room only in the center. As fishermen moved farther away from shore, the vessels grew in size and sturdiness.

Legend has it that the first Essex boat was built in 1660 by a member of the Burnham family in the garret of an old house; a window and wall are said to have been removed to take the boat out of the house. It isn't until the 1850s that records provide more information on shipbuilding in Essex.

Due to the rough landscape in the Essex area, farming wasn't a viable option for most of the first settlers. The access to the coast through the Essex River, however, led the early settlers to become involved in coastal and inshore fishing as a means of getting by. Essex was fortunate to have vast woodland areas that provided timber for building fishing vessels.

In 1852, fifteen shipyards were operating in Essex. By the time of the Civil War, almost all the available land was being used to build ships. Various types of vessels were built—sailing vessels, steamers, three-masted coasters, fishing schooners, and yachts. Hundreds of these vessels were being sent down the narrow winding river that led into the Ipswich Bay. Once-a-week launchings were common all year round. From 1850 to 1853, 169 vessels went down the river.

By the 1920s crowds of people came to witness the launchings of these beautiful vessels. The launchings became fewer, but the boats were bigger than ever! The largest was the *Vidette*, a steam collier weighing 810 tons. Large vessels such as these were quite a challenge to launch. Some would get stuck in the mud until the next high tide allowed them to squeeze through the narrow channel.

Some 4,000 vessels were built in Essex shipyards. The craftsmanship of the vessels was highly praised and envied by sailors all over the globe. Some of the vessels are on display at museums across North America and were designed by legendary naval architects, such as Edward Burgess, George M. McClain, and Bodoin Crowninshield.

If you are interested in learning more about shipbuilding in Essex, local historian Dana Story has written several fine books filled with photographs documenting this history, from

Gertrude L. Thebaud, last of the Gloucester fishing schooners, Launched March 17, 1930, from Story Shipyard in Essex. 115.8 ft. long, 25.2 ft. broad, 12.2 ft. deep, weight 137 tons. *(Courtesy of Essex Shipbuilding Museum)*

the minute intricacies of construction to many of the actual launchings from his family's historic shipyard.

Today the shipbuilding industry of Essex is still practiced by a few remaining builders. The town is very proud of its history and honored the industry with the opening of the Essex Shipbuilding Museum in 1976. The Essex Historical Society runs the museum, which is housed in an 1835 Federal-style schoolhouse at 28 Main Street. On display are artifacts from shipbuilders from Essex's past. The society also has a second location at 66 Main Street, which is the original one-acre historic site (the Story Shipyard), on a 1668 land grant from the town of Ipswich. The *Evelina M. Goulart*, an Essex-built vessel is on display here and visitors can witness the art of shipbuilding. The society provides a year-round program of tours, slide shows, lectures, and more (see **Places of Interest** for more information).

CONGREGATIONAL CHURCH

The town and the church were as intertwined as threads of cloth; there was no separation of church and state as there is today. Town committee meetings and Sunday morning church services were held in the same meetinghouse. The first book used to teach reading and writing was the Bible and instruction was done in the church and at home. The meetinghouse was located strategically at the center of the community, with the burial ground nearby and the earliest houses were built in its proximity.

At one time Essex was part of Ipswich. Before 1677 the people of Essex had to go to Ipswich to worship, to bury their dead, and to attend town meetings. The distance of four to seven miles was over a rough road surrounded by forests in which wolves, bears, and other wildlife roamed. Only the wealthiest people had transportation and most had to cover the distance—through winter snowstorms, spring mud season, and summer heat waves—on foot. When they arrived for church services, no seating was available to them and they had to stand (sometimes for hours) before returning home. The "Chebacco" people had to stand, either because the Ipswich church (built in 1646) had become overcrowded or because the people of Chebacco did not pay their share of the taxes. At any rate, the Chebacco people felt socially inferior, and for two years the Ipswich selectmen stalled the inevitable.

By 1679 the sills were laid and timbers were ready to build the first meetinghouse in Chebacco. While the General Court deliberated, three Chebacco women (Madames Varney, Goodhue, and Martin), without the knowledge of their husbands and under advisement of two Chebacco men, went to Gloucester and Manchester (towns not under the legal restraint of Ipswich) to get the manpower needed to raise the meetinghouse. The General Court ordered the Chebacco people to appear. The case was eventually dismissed, a committee was formed in Chebacco to resolve the problem, and it was decided the meetinghouse should be finished. At a town meeting held February 15, 1681, Ipswich accepted the General Court's order and discharged Chebacco from any further church taxes; however, town taxes continued to be paid to Ipswich until Essex became incorporated in 1819. At the meeting in 1681, the boundary line of Chebacco was determined as well as the granting of one acre for a graveyard.

THE REVEREND JOHN WISE (1652–1725)

The first meetinghouse in Essex was built near the home of the famous first pastor, John Wise. (You will find an historic marker at the site of the John Wise House located on John Wise Avenue, Route 133, between Essex and Ipswich.) He became famous for being the first to oppose the idea of "taxation without representation."

In 1687, Sir Edmund Andros, governor of the colony and an obnoxious tyrant, levied a tax of one penny per £ on property holders without giving taxpayers a say in the matter. Ipswich held a special town meeting to appoint assessors to apportion the newly imposed tax; Reverend John Wise and several other prominent men held their own meeting and decided to oppose the appointment of assessors for raising this money. At the special town meeting, John Wise gave a speech where he stated that "taxation without representation is tyranny," convincing those at the meeting to vote unanimously not to appoint assessors. Several other towns in the colony followed suit.

John Wise was the original American political philosopher; a colonial character of the noblest kind. His confidence and outspokenness inspired revolutionary leaders to fight for equal and fair rights for all. Maidee Proctor Polleys wrote in her 1952 essay entitled, "The Founder of American Democracy," that the Reverend John Wise spoke words that later made Thomas Jefferson famous. Twenty-six years before Jefferson was born, John Wise said, "All men are born free, and nature having set all men upon a level and made them equals no servitude or subjection can be conceived without inequality." In 1776 Thomas Jefferson declared, "All men are created equal."

Upham, in his *History of the Salem Witchcraft*, said Wise "had a free spirit and was perhaps the only minister in the neighborhood or country who was discerning enough to see the erroneousness of the proceedings [witchcraft trials and hangings] from the beginning." Upham refers to two incidents. In 1692 Wise and his parishioners signed an address to the General Court on behalf of Chebacco's John Proctor, who was jailed in Salem for allegedly practicing witchcraft and awaited execution. Their efforts failed and Proctor was hanged. In 1703 Wise showed courage by declaring "there is great reason to fear that innocent persons suffered." This time an act was passed that resulted in several convictions being declared null and void. Though his deeds have all but been forgotten, John Wise's services live on in what Americans cherish as the greatest achievements of democracy.

MEETINGHOUSES

The first meetinghouse was of log construction, approximately 36 feet by 42 feet, and held roughly fifty people. The first three Chebacco meetinghouses all faced east–west. The main entrance was at the opposite end of the pulpit and the pulpit was the dominant feature of the building. A center aisle ran between the pews. In the front rows, there were long pews which had backrests and toward the back of the meetinghouse were short pews without backrests (less important people sat here). The church and village leadership sat in reserved pews that were paid for and maintained by their occupants. The women did not sit with the men. One's seat in the meetinghouse demonstrated one's status or humility, and once someone had "paid" for their pew by paying a fee or granting land or property, that seating was permanent. One can imagine the disagreement over seats! Visit the "Old Ship" in Hingham, Massachusetts, which was built in 1682 (and has undergone many alterations over three centuries) to see a first-period New England meetinghouse.

A serious disagreement arose in the second meetinghouse built in 1716, when the "Separate Society" was formed after George Whitefield's New England preaching tours. The Separatists built the third meetinghouse on the site of the present-day Congregational Church in 1753, and for forty years these two meetinghouses existed a few hundred yards apart. As the disagreement continued, the doors and windows of the second meetinghouse were nailed shut due to actions taken against the minister, Nehemiah Porter. When John Cleaveland, the pastor of the fourth church of Ipswich, agreed to preach for half a year in the second meetinghouse and the other half in the third meetinghouse, reconciliation began. Reunification came in 1774. Both meetinghouses continued to be used according to the same yearly schedule until the fourth meetinghouse (the present Congregational Church) was constructed in 1793. At that time, the other two were torn down.

MUSIC

It is in these early New England churches around mid-18th century that music for the public was introduced. In Essex efforts were made to secure seats "for a number of persons . . . that are skillful to lead in singing." It seems strange to us today that no musical instruments were found in these early meetinghouses; rather, one of the deacons would "line out" (sing in his own way) a hymn (psalm) and the congregation would repeat it. Each sang in his own way, and it must have made an odd noise with everyone singing as their hearts inclined. Singers usually sat in the part of the gallery that faced the pulpit; in years to come, this became where the organ was placed.

The first church organ was purchased in 1854 and was placed in the balcony at the south end of the sanctuary; in 1890 it was moved to the balcony at the north end. The original pipe organ had to be pumped by hand by young boys of the church who were hired to do this at the back of the organ. The present organ was installed in the early 1920s.

PAUL REVERE'S BELL

The 827-pound bell hanging in the present-day Congregational Church belfry was cast by Paul Revere in 1797. The inscription on the bell reads "Revere, Boston 1797." The bell was not acquired until four years after the building was constructed and was hauled from Boston on an oxcart and then hoisted into the tower. The tower was a separate structure attached to the south end of the meetinghouse.

The tonal quality of the bell is said to have been achieved by blending one hundred silver dollars, an abundance of silver spoons, and silver jewelry. All of the silver was contributed by the people of Chebacco Parish. The church steeple was struck by lightning in 1859 and 1973, but the bell never sustained damage. Its silvery tone has called worshippers to church on Sunday mornings for almost two hundred years.

For years the bell was rung at specific times throughout the day to mark the time for men working in the shipyards and farms. By 1894 the bell had become considerably worn where the tongue struck, and from this time forward, it was saved for special occasions such as funeral processions, the death of presidents, and the requiem for soldiers of three wars. It was rung feverishly as a fire alarm, to call the people to the ballot box and town meetings, and jubilantly on the Fourth of July.

Of all Paul Revere's foundry products (his foundry in the North End of Boston cast stoves, cannon, ship fittings, and other goods) his bells are perhaps best known today. Bell casting was just a small part of his foundry operations but it became one of his most enduring enterprises. Of all the bells cast by Paul Revere before he retired in 1811 at the age of 76, only 23 are still in existence. All other bells are credited to his sons and grandsons. The first church bell cast by Paul Revere was cast in Boston in 1792 and still rests in the auditorium of St. James Episcopal Church in North Cambridge, Massachusetts.

ANCIENT BURIAL GROUND

For the first fifty years, Essex inhabitants bore their dead five miles to bury them in the graveyard on High Street in Ipswich. In 1680 Ipswich granted one acre of land to Essex for a burial place. Seventeenth-century New England graveyards were typically municipal property and not directly connected with any church. The roughly rectangular T-shaped graveyard is not easily visible from Main Street, with most of the area being behind the Shipbuilding Museum. The oldest graves are clustered along the pathway leading from the stone entrance gate straight to the table tomb of Reverend John Wise. Even after Essex separated from Ipswich and was incorporated in

Hearse House, Ancient Burial Ground *(Courtesy of Nancy Marculewicz)*

1819, it still continued to use the graveyard until 1852, when a new cemetery was consecrated on Spring Street. The old Chebacco graveyard is notable for several reasons.

As you enter the graveyard through the stone gate the Hearse House is on the left. This small white building still contains hearses, caskets, excavating tools, and other implements necessary for maintaining a graveyard. Rare 1860-vintage summer and winter sleigh hearses and ice-preserving caskets (zinc-lined caskets which held ice to help preserve the deceased) are stored inside. Eight or more bodies had been disinterred from their original graves by Dr. Thomas Sewall over a period of time. The bodies were placed in a common grave under the Hearse House.

On the right as you enter the graveyard through the old stone gate are two underground tomb structures with iron doors. The one nearest the street was the town's receiving tomb, which was used for temporary interments during the winter months when the ground was frozen. The one adjacent was constructed in 1813 for Colonel Jonathan Cogswell, who was a descendant of one of the founders of Essex as well as a Revolutionary War officer. The Dodge tomb (a low mound) is visible as you walk further into the graveyard as well as from the entrance door of the museum.

In this cemetery lies the first pastor of the first church in Essex, Reverend John Wise (1652–1725). John Wise was the fifth of twelve children and the only one who received a Harvard education; in 1673, he graduated in a class of four. In 1680 John Wise came to Chebacco after helping his two previous churches through splits. He apparently had gained a reputation as either a good fighter or a peacemaker, because he was called to Chebacco only to face a similar situation.

Reverend Wise's remains were interred near the center of the graveyard. In 1815 a copy of the original inscription (below) was cut in slate and elevated upon four granite pillars. It is believed that other family members may also be buried beneath this spot.

> *Underneath lies the body of the*
> *Rev. John Wise, A.M.*
> *First Pastor of the 2d Church of Ipswich.*
> *Graduated at Harvard College, 1673.*
> *Ordained Pastor of said Church, 1681.*
> *And died April 8, 1725.*
> *Aged 73.*
> *For Talents, piety and learning,*
> *he shone as a star of the*
> *first magnitude.*

The Reverends Theophilis Pickering and John Cleaveland, second and third pastors respectively of the First Church in Chebacco (also known as the Second Church of Ipswich) are also buried here, as well as Nathanial Rust, first schoolmaster in Chebacco, Thomas Low, Deacon of the Second Church from 1683 to 1712, and many Revolutionary War soldiers (marked SAR). The oldest stones in the cemetery are for John Burnham (January 11, 1708) and Job Giddings (February 27, 1708).

Graves of the 1600s through early 1800s were marked by headstones and footstones, with the deceased laid to rest facing east to rise again at dawn on Judgment Day. The footstones are smaller, lack descriptions, and usually contain one's initials and year of death.

The Essex stones represent examples of the animated vernacular work of Essex County carvers (John Hartshorne, Robert Mulliken, Jonathan Worster, and Joseph Marble), as well as those of the sophisticated Boston carvers. For an ex-

Town Hall and T.O.H.P. Burnham Library   *(Courtesy of Nancy Marculewicz)*

ample of an Essex County carved stone by John Hartshorne (1650–1738), see Thomas Andrews' (1718) grave. For an example of a Boston stone carved by the Lamson family stonecutters in Charlestown in the early 1700s, see Capt. Jonathan Cogswell's grave. The Boston stones are of high-quality slate (which appear almost new), while the Essex County stones are carved gray schist (granular stone which weathers poorly).

ESSEX TOWN HALL AND MEMORIAL LIBRARY

Despite the bitter weather on February 15, 1894, the people of Essex came out to dedicate the new Town Hall and Memorial Library building on Martin Street. Seventy-five years had passed since Essex was incorporated; it was a special year. The town government moved out of the space used at the Congregational Church and into a glorious new building. The threads which had bound church and state together were finally separated.

Thomas Oliver Hazard Perry Burnham (otherwise referred to as T.O.H.P. Burnham) made this building a reality. When the people of Essex didn't have the necessary funds to build a hall, a committee went to Boston to seek his financial help. T.O.H.P. Burnham was a native of Essex who had made his fortune at the Old Corner Bookstore. Unfortunately, Mr. Burnham wasn't as enthusiastic about the project as they were; he was gruff and asked them to leave.

When Mr. Burnham passed away, he left provisions in his will to finance the construction of the new Town Hall & Public Library and to purchase books. Townspeople added the necessary additional money to complete the construction. The pasture stones used on the first story of the building were given by Essex people in memory of a person or place; they are referred to as "Memorial" stones, and the stories above are of wood with dark mahogany-colored shingles. Rather large stone posts extending out from the main entrance of the building support a porch.

Here are a few additional interesting facts. Frank W. Weston of Boston was the architect who designed the building. The first public timepiece is part of the rounded tower which rises above the main entrance along with the brick chimneys. The bell inside the clock tower weighs 2,000 pounds. The ship on the weathervane commemorates the 400th anniversary of Christopher Columbus' voyage to the new world; it is a tiny replica of his flag ship, the Santa Maria.

The interior of the Town Hall originally had a large audience room seating between 500 and 600 people. With its large stage flanked by dressing rooms on either side, this auditorium was perfect for the many concerts, plays, dances, parties and town meetings held here. With the passage of time, the town needed additional office space; and in 1965 the space which had been used for entertainment purposes was converted into much-needed office space. Though the space inside the building has once again become inadequate, the character of the exterior of the building has remained constant over the years. The structure still serves as the Town Hall and Public Library over 100 years later.

On the eastern side of the Town Hall is the soldiers' monument. Through the efforts of the Sargent Woman's Relief Corps 114, its cost of $2,000 was met by fairs and subscriptions. The base of the monument is of Rockport granite, the shaft and figure of Niantic, Rhode Island, granite. The monument was dedicated on May 30, 1905 to the Grand Army of the Republic and the 186 "loyal sons" of Essex who gave their lives fighting in the Civil War (1861–1865), also known as the War of the Rebellion.

PLACES OF INTEREST

Ancient Burial Ground on Main Street is the "burial place of the original American political philosopher," Reverend John Wise (1652–1725), who said all men are born free and equal, and who inspired revolutionary leaders to fight for equal rights for all. Difficult to see from the street, the cemetery is located behind the Shipbuilding Museum (see the **History** section).

Antique shops are everywhere in Essex. The "antique capital of America" has more shops per square mile than any other community its size. Leave your car behind the fire station on Martin Street at Memorial Park and walk to the many attractions and shops (see the **Antiques** section).

T.O.H.P. Burnham Public Library is at 30 Martin Street. Dedicated in 1894, this building designed by Frank Weston of Boston is an example of the Shingle style architecture popular at that time. The stones used on the first story of the building were given by local people in memory of a person or place; they are referred to as "Memorial" stones (see the **History** section). Call 768-7410.

> **Winter Schedule:** Mon.–Fri. 1–5; Mon. and Wed. evenings 6–8:30; Sat. 9–noon.

> **Summer Schedule:** Mon.–Fri. 1–5; Mon. evenings 6:30–8:30.

> Residents may obtain **free passes** for the Museum of Science, the New England Aquarium, and Museum of Fine Arts.

Cogswell's Grant (Society for the Preservation of New England Antiquities) will open to the public in

Interior of 1735 Cogswell house   *(Courtesy of Society for Preservation of New England Antiquities)*

1998. The 135 rolling acres that surround the house have been farmed continuously since 1636, when it was granted to John Cogswell. The house was built in 1735, apparently using some beams from the original Cogswell family home.

Bertram K. and Nina Fletcher Little were among the country's most celebrated and widely respected collectors of Americana—works of painters and artisans who supplied art and furnishings for the people of rural New England—what the Littles called "Country arts." They strived to purchase objects with a history they could trace.

In 1993 the Littles left this property to SPNEA. The combination of landscape, architecture, and collections is sure to make Cogswell's Grant one of the country's greatest, and most personal, house museums. For more information about Cogswell's Grant and other properties, contact SPNEA headquarters: Harrison Gray Otis House, 141 Cambridge Street, Boston, MA 02114 or call 617-227-3956.

Congregational Church (1793) is at 28 Main Street. Before 1677, the Essex people attended services in Ipswich (see the **History** section). Several changes and additions have been made over the years to this building (the fourth church). A Paul Revere bell, cast in 1797, hangs in the church steeple.

In 1842 the meetinghouse underwent considerable changes. The sanctuary had been on the ground level with entry through the Main Street door; a new sanctuary was created by laying a floor sixteen inches below the old "gallery girth," giving the sanctuary a height of seventeen feet and the vestry below a height of eight feet. The original 1793 pulpit from which the Reverend John Wise preached was moved to where it is today. Forty-seven pews had been on the floor and twenty in the galleries above; these were moved into the present sanctuary. You will notice that the numbers originally placed on the backs of the pews are still there, though they do not correspond with their present placement.

In 1846 the north porch was removed and the present addition was added on to allow for indoor "privies" and stairs to the sanctuary and the minister's study. Major renovations made in 1852 included the removal of the tower and dome on the south side and an addition to the building along the entire south end. A pyramid and spire were erected above the addition as housing for the Paul Revere bell. The present-day narthex with its twin staircases leading to the second-story sanctuary is located in this addition. These renovations made possible a much-needed large vestry. In 1852, the carriage sheds were added to the north side. Until the town hall was constructed in 1893, the selectmen had a small office located in the southeastern corner of the large vestry (the church's historic corner).

The Essex River is a tidal river visible from many vantage points as it meanders through acres of pristine marshes on its way to the Atlantic. The river can be enjoyed by canoe, sea kayak, sailboat, or motorboat. Boating down the Essex River through the unforgettable salt water estuary (not reachable by car), you will see Hog Island, Crane Beach, and Crane Wildlife Refuge, as well as the areas where over 4,000 fishing schooners were built and launched (see the **Recreation** section).

Choate House on Hog Island   *(Photo by the author)*

"The Island 'Mid the Marshes"

The Island 'mid the marshes waits for you;
Its winding road o'ergrown with tangled vine
Leads past the pasture in a wavering line
Up through the fields, just as it used to do.

Do you remember how the river's blue,
A sparkling path, those tall, old trees gleamed through?
Do you remember, when each summer came
We used to have those "sings" at fall of dark?
The dim fields filled with flickering fireflies' spark;
Familiar songs–can you recall each name?
Are "Annie Laurie"—"Old Black Jo" the same?

Can you forget the gentle rise of hill
Where stood the farmhouse, facing sand-duned sea?
Ah, wondrous years of childhood; years to be
Never forgotten, wander where you will.
May their dear memories your whole life-time fill—
The Island 'mid the marshes waits you still!

(from Candles of Memory *by Agnes Choate Wonson, 1925)*

62

The Essex Shipbuilding Museum is at two locations, 28 and 66 Main Street. Opened by the Essex Historical Society in 1976, the museum honors the town's long history of shipbuilding. The 1835 Federal-style schoolhouse at 28 Main Street contains exhibits covering 300 years of shipbuilding through a hands-on collection of tools, photographs, 20 rigged ship models and builders' half models (the second floor contains archives available to researchers by appointment). The 66 Main Street location is adjacent to the acre of land granted by the town of Ipswich in 1668 and is on the riverfront where shipbuilding flourished for over 300 years. At the shipyard, visitors can see the Essex-built schooner *Evelina M. Goulart* as well as more exhibits.

Framing Exhibit of Schooner *Rob Roy*   *(Courtesy of Essex Shipbuilding Museum)*

The administrative offices of the Essex Historical Society and Shipbuilding Museum, Inc. are also located at the 66 Main Street location. In 1996 work was begun on the new 65-foot schooner, *Lannon*, which should be finished by summer 1997. Plans are under way to develop new building projects which will follow the *Lannon's* launch in 1997. The museum's ultimate goal is to have some phase of a vessel construction process underway at all times. For hours of operation and complete information about year-round programs, tours, slide shows, and lectures, call 768-7541.

Essex Waterfowl Museum is located at 66 Main Street near the Essex Shipbuilding Museum in the rebuilt paint shop. On display are hand-made working birds, contemporary decoys and their anchors, Indian artifacts, and clam harvesting tools. Open Saturdays and Sundays (call 768–6953 for hours or to visit by special appointment).

John Wise House on John Wise Avenue near the Cape Ann Golf Course was the home of the first pastor of the Congregational Church in Essex (see the **History** section). This is a private home and is not open to the public.

Places of Worship

CATHOLIC

St. John the Baptist Church, 52 Main Street. Call 768-6284. Sunday service at 8 a.m. and 10 a.m.; Saturday service at 4 p.m. (summer Sat. at 5 p.m.); CCD class at 8:45 a.m. September–May.

CONGREGATIONAL

Congregational Church, 29 Main Street. Call 768-7855. Service and Sunday school at 10:30 a.m. Nursery provided all year; summer service and Sunday school (beginning 4th Sunday in June) at 9:30. Annual church fair with luncheon and silent auction on 3rd Saturday in November.

METHODIST

United Methodist Church, 18 Eastern Avenue. Call 468-3106. Sunday service at 9:30 a.m.; children's Sunday school at 10:30 a.m., September–June.

NON-DENOMINATIONAL

Fair Haven Chapel, 180 Western Avenue. Call 768-6601. Sunday service at 10 a.m., followed by 11:15 prayer service for adults and Sunday school for children; mid-week Bible Study Tuesday at 7:30 p.m..

UNIVERSALIST

First Universalist Church, 57 Main Street. Call 768-3690. Sunday service at 10 a.m..

Antiques

Although antique shops existed in Essex from about 1900, the first recorded antique shop in Essex was St. Stephen's Antiques, which Simon Adisjarin opened in 1932. Mr. Adisjarin was an Armenian immigrant and antique dealer who came up from Boston. His business no longer exists.

In 1940 Leo Landry opened an antique shop and auction business in Salem's historic Hamilton Hall specializing in appraisals, auctions, and the buying and selling of fine antiques from estates on Boston's North Shore and throughout New England. As the firm grew, it moved to Essex, where it continues today as **L.A. Landry**, owned by Robert Landry.

Lucille Blackwood started her shop, Gabriel's Horn, at 3 Southern Avenue in 1961. Later she moved her shop to Martin

Street and finally to the brick house on the corner of Southern and Eastern Avenue. Her specialties were Chinese porcelain, and European and English china. As her knowledge grew, she lectured and taught antiques to business people, college students, and professional organizations. In the late 1960s she began Blackwood Auction Company. Women auctioneers were rare and she often found antique oriental rug merchants questioning her knowledge and ability to run this successful business. In 1970 she started the North Shore Antique Dealers' Association, which sponsored the first antique show in Essex. Dealers from all over the North Shore came to exhibit their finest items at individual booths set up inside Woodman's Hall. This organization was supplanted by the **Essex Antique Dealers' Association** in 1996 to promote the industry by holding various functions during the year as well as advertising throughout the region and the nation. For more information call 768-7922. One son, Michael March, continues to run **Blackwood-March Antiques** at 3 Southern Avenue, buying, selling, and auctioning antiques.

In 1953 Edward Saltzberg, a dealer from Ipswich, bought the old schoolhouse at the corner of Western Avenue and Martin Street for the sum of $1,200. Here he stored and refinished antiques. Over time, he placed items on consignment in Essex at Christian Molly at 165 Eastern Avenue. In 1965 Saltzberg purchased the old forge at 1 Southern Avenue as well as Christian Molly. For several years, Edward and Lucille Blackwood ran their respective shops almost directly across the street from each other. Through their shared interests, they came to know one another and eventually married and had a son, Richard. Until Edward's death in 1995, he ran the Christian Molly and did antique appraisals, bought the contents of attics and cellars, and collected Americana and American paintings. Today Richard follows in his father's and mother's footsteps as he continues in the antique business (albeit at 1 Southern Avenue in the old forge building) while renting out the 165 Eastern Avenue location to **Antiquarians**.

Soon others realized that reasonable rental property was available in Essex either for selling antiques or serving fried clams. During the 1950s the second-hand market became flooded with goods; people wanted new, modern furnishings and discarded their old claw foot tables and chairs as well as oak sideboards and bureaus. As many people migrated towards the Pacific, they either loaded perfectly usable articles into the family car and drove them to the local dump or sold them.

In 1952 the **White Elephant Shop** opened at 32 Main Street. Bill and Ruth Toivainen bought the building in 1950 thinking it had "possibilities" and moved into the roomy apartment on the second and third floors. The ground-floor duplex store had been a meat market and grocery store. Like many others, the Toivainen's wanted to leave the winter climate of New England for the sunshine of California. After trying to sell the building for two years without success, they finally decided to place an ad in the newspaper and put their unwanted items in the vacant shop on the ground floor. As Ruth recounts, "Results were good; everything sold—except the building!"

People frequently commented to Ruth that their building was a great set-up for a second-hand store or antique shop. Finally, without any cash outlay on her part, Ruth opened a shop to sell goods on a consignment basis. She ran the shop for nineteen "heart-swelling" years and was closely watched by locals, who thought the business strange and doubted it would succeed. The shop flourished and the idea of moving

White Elephant Shop   *(Courtesy of Rick Grobe)*

to California faded away. In 1971 the shop was sold to Alberta and Lawrence Shanks. The present owner, Rick Grobe, has run the local landmark since 1985.

During the late 1970s and early 1980s inflation and operating costs increased, forcing smaller shops to find ways to cover their overhead or go out of business. The first group shop, **Chebacco Antiques**, was formed so that dealers could share expenses. Today other groups (such as **Ro-Dan Antiques**, **Main Street Antiques**, and **Joshua's Corner Antiques**) have found this method of operation beneficial.

Dana Guarnera of **Ro-Dan Antiques** has an interesting background. In 1938 his grandmother, Dorothy Roach, opened "Sea Song" near the end of Bearskin Neck in Rockport as a place to display her collection of Oriental art; and to her delight, Sea Song brought many pleasant hours as well as a profit. Dana's mother, Aldora, was an artist who ran a gallery, "Pinxit," at the entry to Bearskin Neck from 1964–1978. It was in this gallery that Dana, who loved antiques, put items on display in and around his mother's artwork. This combination of art and antiques seemed to show everything off to its best advantage. Dana also worked for a combination art/gift shop, the "Bell, Book & Candle," which was owned by Robert and Judy Randall. By 1970 Robert and Dana opened **Ro-Dan**, a separate antique shop in Essex. At the time they rented space from Lucille Blackwood at what is today the **Brick House Antiques**. The name Ro-Dan is a combination of Ro from Robert Randall and Dan from Dana Guarnera. In the 1980s Robert became ill, and after he passed away, Dana bought Robert's share from Mrs. Randall. In 1988 Dana purchased the old Hotel Essex at 67 Main Street, where he buys and sells "anything that will turn a profit."

People often ask how Essex came to have so many antique shops. If one considers the location of Essex, between Boston and Newburyport, it might explain how this has proved advantageous for the growth of this industry. Though dealers will lament that they can't find the "really good stuff" any more, the many early period houses existing in the area have provided them a seemingly endless bounty of merchandise. You cannot find another one-mile stretch of road with more than 50 dealers and 35 separate shops. Essex is the "Antique Capital of America."

ANTIQUE DEALERS

If you are interested in antique hunting, you will find an abundance of antique shops here. Some specialize in merchandise from specific periods; others have an eclectic mixture of old and not-so-old objects and furnishings. You will find a range from small "fine antiques and objects d'art" shops to cooperative dealerships, as well as barns and old houses with several rooms of old things. No matter what your interest, there are shops with something for everyone. Here is a list.

Americana Antiques, 48 Main Street. Call 768-6006.

Antiquarians, 165 Main Street. Call 768-4545.

Antiques & Elderly Things, 199 Western Avenue. 17th–19th American and European antiques. Call 768-6328.

As Time Goes By Antiques, 63 Main Street. Call 768-7479.

Auntie Lil's Antiques, 63 John Wise Avenue. Call 768-7550.

Blackwood March Antiques, 3 Southern Avenue. Call 768-6943.

Brick House Antiques, 166 Main Street. Call 768-6617.

A.F. Brosch Antiques & Restorations, 143 Main Street. Call 768-7949.

Chebacco Antiques, 38 Main Street. Call 768-7371.

John D. Cushing Antique Restoration, 113 Martin Street. Call 768-7356.

Emmons & Martin Antiques, 1 Martin Street. Call 768-3292.

Essex Antiques & Interiors, 166 Eastern Avenue. Call 768-7358.

Friendship Antiques, John Wise Avenue. Call 768-7334.

Golden Egg Antiques, 140 Main Street. Call 768-3922.

Howard's Flying Dragon Antiques, 136 Main Street. Call 768-7282.

Joshua's Corner Antiques, 2 Southern Avenue. Call 768-7716.

L.A. Landry, 164 Main Street. Call 768-6233.

Main Street Antiques, 44 Main Street. Call 768-7039.

Ellen Neily Antiques, 157 Main Street. Call 768-6436.

Neligan & Neligan, 144 Main Street. Call 768-3910.

North Hill Antiques, 155 Main Street. Call 768-7365.

163 Main Antiques, 163 Main Street. Call 768-3411.

Rider J.E. Antiques, 164 Main Street. Call 768-7441.

Ro-Dan Antiques, 67 Main Street. Call 768-3322.

The Scrapbook, 34 Main Street. 15th–19th century antiquarian maps & prints. Call 768-7922.

South Essex Antiques, 166 Eastern Avenue. Call 768-6373.

Susan Stella Antiques, 166 Main Street. Call 768-6617.

Tradewinds Antiques, 63 Main Street. Call 768-3327.

Waller, APH & Son, 140 Main Street. Call 768-6269.

Alexander Westerhoff Antiques, 144 Main Street. Call 768-3830.

Walker Creek Furniture & Art Gallery, 59 Eastern Avenue. Call 768-7622.

White Elephant Outlet, John Wise Avenue (Route 133). Call 768-3329.

White Elephant Shop, 32 Main Street. Call 768-6901.

Zakas Antiques, 149 Western Avenue. Call 768-0045.

Art

The Essex River has captured the attention of artists for years. As you drive along Route 133 through Essex on your way to and from Gloucester, you pass what many now refer to as Motif #2 (see photo on page 80). Adjacent to Eben Creek, across from Farnham's Restaurant, is an old weathered house with a wraparound porch. Seagulls often perch on its roof and chimney tops and time and tide have gradually worn away its paint and often challenged its very foundation. Artists set up their easels and spend hours on a lovely day capturing the beauty around this site. For a few short weeks in spring, the wild lupines bloom in the abandoned field near the house, and in autumn the marsh is dressed in glorious shades of orange, yellow and brown, with dabs of red provided by the tiny glasswort plants. In summer the sea lavender appears on the marsh blooming in fragile shades of purple. The shift of tides, change

Art in the Barn *(Courtesy of Essex County Greenbelt Association)*

of seasons, passing light of day, and ever-changing sky and landscape blend together to create a scene that is never the same twice. It is no wonder artists and writers continue to be drawn to Cape Ann and vicinity.

Close by is the headquarters of the Essex County Greenbelt Association (ECGB), where "Art in the Barn" is held each June. The headquarters is directly off Route 133 at 82 Eastern Avenue. The barn in which this popular annual event is held was the former studio of Allyn Cox, a muralist who spent his summers here (see **Recreation** section). From all over the North Shore artists come to display and sell their works—pottery, watercolors and oil paintings, sketches and drawings, wood carvings, nature photographs, sculptures, and prints. They donate half the proceeds to help ECGB purchase and maintain land in Essex County to preserve as open space. Art in the Barn is a lovely way to spend a summer afternoon and Greenbelt's gardens and grounds are open for all to enjoy. While you're at Art in the Barn take time to stroll down to Clamshell Landing for a view that will long stay in your memory. If you are interested in exhibiting your art or would like more information about Art in the Barn, call ECGB at 768-7241.

GALLERIES

Antiquarians, 165 Main Street. Call 768-4545.

Rider J.E. Antiques, 164 Main Street. Call 768-7441.

ARTISTS (BY APPOINTMENT)

Nancy Marculewicz, artist, 57 Eastern Avenue. Call 768-6288.

Susan Guest-MacPhail, artist and print-maker, 7 Eastern Avenue. Call 768-7653.

To reach someone on the Essex Cultural Council call 768-7111 or 768-6531.

Music

The *Essex Echo* on July 20, 1894 told of the "great picnic of the season, the fireman's muster . . . at Centennial grove;" people came by car, carriage, and train. Firemen and their engines came from as far away as Brunswick and Androscoggin, Maine. The weather was warm and some people drank "liquid refreshment stronger than water which made them rather noisy . . . but as a rule all passed off in fine shape and a very pleasant day was spent."

A century later, on August 27, 1994, the first Essex Music Festival was held at Centennial Grove on Chebacco Lake. Anne White (Sweet Loretta) and husband Bob Wilhelm (Mad Dog Earl) planned this event thinking a hundred people might come; four hundred flocked to the all-day festival of bluegrass, country & western, blues, and folk music provided by several vocal and instrumental groups.

The musicians worked together with the community to hold this event to earn money to "bring back the grove" (sand for the beach, new steps to the water, building renovations, and etc.). The town committee wanted people to come to the grove to enjoy the beauty of this lakeside environment. Some brought picnics, spread their blankets, and set up chairs; for those who didn't, the Essex Lions made hot dogs and hamburgers available. People sat and listened to the music and children swam and played on the beach. It was a delightful time.

A year later, the event was repeated. Musicians from the North Shore provided their own original music with a familiar, down-to-earth sound. Add to that food, swimming, and families relaxing at Chebacco Lake, and you have the kind of event everyone looks forward to year after year. Cheap Champagne (Robert Wilhelm, Anne White, and Joan and Alan Pinkham) hosted the second successful event. Six hundred people came! By the Third Annual Music Festival, there was a new music workshop stage and folk guitar, banjo, special blues duo, Irish music, and jug band song workshops became part of the program. A magic performance by "Magic Happens" (Richard Nunziato of Ipswich) was added to the full day of music and fun.

Each year the crowds grow at the grove and the bands play on. So, don't miss the 1997 fourth annual festival with Cheap Champagne (quirky original tunes), Tamarac (music you know and love), Old Cowboy Death (country sound with fiddle, hand drum, guitar and stand-up bass), Old Cold Tater (bluegrass and more), and other groups to entertain you. Bring a picnic or enjoy refreshments provided by volunteers. Admission is free but a small donation is suggested to help "bring back the grove." Please leave pets at home. Centennial Grove is located off Route 22 in Essex. For information call 468-6581.

CHEAP CHAMPAGNE

Robert Wilhelm and Anne White are husband and wife as well as Mad Dog Earl and Sweet Loretta. Together with Raw Silk (Alan Pinkham) and The Blue Diva (Joanna Pinkham) they founded the band and musical revue called Cheap Champagne. With that "sitting-around-the-table jug band blues aura about them," their audience spans all ages. They play in places like the Hart House in Ipswich, the Rhumb Line in Gloucester, and the Red Barrel Pub in Essex. Earl and Loretta also play as a duo, and as a trio called "The Night Crawlers," with the multi-talented Herb Broadbent. For more information call 468-6581.

DAISY NELL

Daisy Nell is a native of Essex who grew up in and around boats; as an adult, she has worked on ships, taught maritime history, and sung songs about the sea. For a long time Daisy Nell has been associated with several historic wooden vessels, including the schooners *Adventure* and *Mimi*. As a mate on various vessels, she has led tours of "Cape Ann by the Sea," whale watching expeditions, and hands-on sail training.

She researches and seeks out traditional folk songs with universal themes that touch us all. Daisy Nell has memorized over 200 songs which she has performed at private engagements, coffeehouses, and the Mystic Seaport Maritime Music Festival, where she's been featured for the past ten years. She brings alive the history of the sea. A variety of programs is available to teachers, schools, and other organizations. For more information call 768-7630.

MUSIC AT EDEN'S EDGE (MEE)

Fifteen years ago, a small group of musicians joined together to present a summer concert series to a diverse audience across eastern Massachusetts. Over the years, MEE has developed a prominent presence on the North Shore in terms of both chamber concerts for the general public and outreach programs to underserved audiences. Under the leadership of founder and artistic director, Maria Benotti (violinist, violist and teacher), the group is the Artist-in-Residence at Hammond Castle. The Summer Chamber Music Series is held on Friday evenings in the Great Hall. The castle offers a unique ambiance and superior acoustics. Once home to John Hays Hammond (one of the world's foremost inventors in radio and TV), the castle was a gathering place for many of the intellectual and artistic luminaries of the 1930s, including George Gershwin and Sergei Rachmaninoff.

Since 1990, MEE has reached out to introduce live chamber music to almost 10,000 schoolchildren on the North Shore through free Youth Chamber Concerts. This unique program allows musicians and young people to interact through small group workshops that prepare students for assembly hall concerts. For information about these and other programs, please write to Music at Eden's Edge, 94 John Wise Avenue, Essex, MA 01929.

ONE WORLD COFFEE HOUSE

Performances take place year-round at the First Universalist Church on Main Street every Saturday evening at 8 o'clock. Desserts are available. A donation is requested to cover the cost of the music and to help the church. A Folk Music Festival is held in February. For current information call 768-3690.

WALKER CREEK BAND

At the far end of Concord Street is a little bridge spanning Walker Creek; it is here that Robert Hanlon and his neighbors first got together to play in a backyard talent show in 1983. They've been playing their favorite rock 'n' roll music together ever since. Their folk music is designed for dancing, celebrating, and forgetting your troubles—you can't hear their music and sit still! Walker Creek Band has played for benefit dances for the Open Door/Cape Ann Food Pantry to combat the problem of hunger on Cape Ann as well as other benefits. The band members include Robert Hanlon (bass), Harold Wyman (vocals and lead guitar), John Lovell (piano), Bill Collins (rhythm and slide guitar), Joe Simcox (vocals and electric viola), John Matson (vocals, harmonica and conga drum), and Peter Van Ness (drums). The band plays for weddings and parties. For information, contact Robert Hanlon, 57 Eastern Avenue, or call 768-7622.

 *Recreation*

BEACHES

Centennial Grove is located at the end of Centennial Grove Road on Chebacco Lake. Parking by permit only. Swimming, picnic tables, and fishing. Call 768-7111.

Clammer's Beach located at Conomo Point, a town landing for clamming only. Resident parking only.

Front Beach at Conomo Point Landing, a town landing for seasonal use only. No parking.

Agawam Boat Charter's *Sachem*   *(Courtesy of Ted Marshall)*

BOATING, CRUISES, MARINA

Agawam Boat Charters, 21 Pickering Street. Private and semi-private cruising on the *Sachem* with USCG-licensed Capt. Ted Marshall. For day and hour rates call 768-1114.

Kayaking on the Essex River
(Courtesy of ERBA)

ERBA (Essex River Basin Adventures), PO Box 270, is located at the historic shipyard location of The Essex Shipbuilding Museum. Will provide sea kayaks and expert guides to take you down the river or to other spectacular vistas. Call 768-3722 or 800-KAYAK-04.

Essex Marina, 35 Dodge Street. Slip rentals, sales, service, and storage. Call 768-6833.

Essex River Cruises, 35 Dodge Street. Discover the estuary, salt marshes, islands, barrier beaches, sand dunes, and wildlife as you relax aboard the *Essex River Queen*. Daily narrated cruises, private charters, or island tours Call 800-748-3706 or 768-6981.

Perkins Marine, 82 Main Street. Boat slips, ramp, storage, transportation, and machine shop. Call 768-7145.

Essex River Queen (Courtesy of Cliff Amero)

Pike Marine, 80 Main Street. Sales, service and marine store. Call 768-7161.

Public Launching Ramp, located off Main Street next to the historic shipyard. Sticker parking for residents only. All others may launch boat here and park behind the fire station at 24 Martin Street. Call 768-7111.

Sloop Boat Charters, 141 Main Street. Sail on the *Chrissy*, a fully restored Friendship Sloop, with Capt. Harold Burnham. Up to six people can sail for a minimum of three hours, a full day, or overnight. Call 768–7035 for rates and reservations.

FISHING AND HUNTING

Fin & Feather Shop, Main Street. Summer hours Mon.–Fri. 8–7, Sat. 6–6, Sun. 6–5; winter hours vary. Sells canoes, fishing and hunting gear, duck decoys, bows and arrows. Call 768-3245.

Wilderness Adventures, 219 John Wise Avenue. Offers hunting and fishing trips on Cape Ann and worldwide, and sporting clays from August–November. Open Mon.–Fri. 8–5:30, Sat. and Sun. 9–noon. Call owner Alan Guminski at 768-3338.

Friendship Sloop *Chrissy*
(Courtesy of Harold Burnham)

GOLF AND TENNIS

Cape Ann Golf Course, 99 John Wise Avenue. A public 9-hole course with breathtaking views of the marsh, estuary, and Hog Island. Open from daybreak to dusk daily, from the time the snows melt in Spring until it falls again. Call 768-7544.

Town of Essex public tennis courts are located at Memorial Park behind the fire station. Open daily from spring until snowfall. Call 768-7111.

HORSEBACK RIDING

Castle Neck Farm, 106 Choate Street. Horses are available for riding, hunting, and jumping lessons. Specializes in English riding style and offers private boarding. Open daily year-round from 7:30–5:30. Call 768-7998.

Meadow Ridge Farm, Inc., 105 Southern Avenue. Horses are available for lessons

Cider Pressing at the Cox Reservation *(Courtesy of Essex County Greenbelt Association)*

in dressage and combined training, and private boarding and a training stable are also available. The barn is open Mon.–Fri. 7–9, Sat., Sun., and holidays until 6 p.m. Call 768-7842.

OPEN SPACE, PARKS, AND PLAYGROUNDS

Centennial Grove, located at the end of Centennial Grove Road on Chebacco Lake. Swimming, picnic tables, and fishing. Permit parking only. Call 768-7111.

The Cox Reservation (Essex County Greenbelt Association headquarters) is located at 82 Eastern Avenue, on 31 acres of saltmarsh farmland along the Essex River. It was once the summer home of artist Allyn Cox. Mr. Cox painted murals on commission in his studio-barn. At the Reservation, visitors will find several trails offering magnificent vistas of scenery that are virtually untouched by the passage of time. Stand at Clamshell Landing and gaze across the river to Cogswell Grant, a first-period farmhouse with barns surrounded by rolling fields and woodlands. Look down river at the white sands of Crane Beach and the glacier-formed drumlin called Hog Island. A copy of "Passport," Essex County Greenbelt's pocket guidebook to all of their properties in Essex County, is available for a small fee. Ask about ECGB scheduled guided walks. Call 768-7241.

Eagles Nest Playground is on Western Avenue, next to the Essex Elementary

School. The children of Essex helped to design this wooden play area in 1987, and their parents and the citizens of the town built it.

Memorial Park, centrally located behind the fire station off Martin Street. Includes three baseball diamonds, a tennis court, and outdoor playground equipment.

Stavros Reservation (a property of The Trustees of Reservations) is located on Island Road (off Route 133). A short trail leads to the top of White's Hill, offering a marvelous panoramic view of the Essex River salt marshes and Hog Island. A great spot to see birds, have a picnic, or sketch. Limited street parking. If you have time, walk to the end of Island Road and enjoy the salt marsh views.

 *Lodging*

Prices were verified at the time of publication. For the most current information contact the lodging places directly.

Essex River House Motel, 132 Main Street located on the Essex River, open April–October. AC, cable TV; within walking distance of restaurants, antique shops, and attractions. Off/mid/high season rates from $59 to $84. Call 768-6800.

George Fuller House Bed & Breakfast Inn, 148 Main Street. 1830 Federal-style house with seven uniquely furnished guest rooms with private baths. Relax on the porches or in the common rooms and enjoy a complimentary country breakfast. Close to restaurants, shops, and attractions. Rates range from $90 to $125 double occupancy; open all year. Call 768-7766.

George Fuller House Guest Room   *(Courtesy of Bob and Cindy Cameron)*

Restaurants

Dining out has become a pastime. The wide assortment of seafood available on Cape Ann is served in a variety of settings, from elegant dining rooms with ocean views to picnic tables and lobster in the rough. Along with freshly caught seafood, you will find many ethnic restaurants (Portuguese, Chinese, Italian, Mexican, Cajun, Greek, and others) serving tasty dishes. Whether you're in the mood for a seventeenth-century, first-period dining room with a walk-in fireplace or a fishing shack draped with fish nets and buoys or a modern dining room with large picture windows facing a real working harbor or scenic shoreline, you're sure to find more than one favorite spot. Don't forget to try the "bread of the fishermen," baked fresh several times a day in Gloucester, or the endless variety of locally made ice cream and the home-made donuts and pastries.

Cape Ann Pizza, 65 Eastern Avenue. Pizza, subs, roast beef, salads, and dinners. Open 10–10 daily. Call 768-3925.

Conomo Cafe, 112 Main Street. Serving "unique menus" indoors or out, directly on the Essex River. Opens at 11:30 daily most of the year. Call 768-7750.

Essex Pizza and Restaurant, 235 Western Avenue. Pizza, pasta, subs, and dinners; delivery available. Call 768-3227.

Essex Seafood, 143 Eastern Avenue. Fish market, fried seafood and take out. Open 9–9 daily. Call 768-7233.

Fortune Palace II, 99 Main Street. Fine Chinese cuisine; great lunches and dinners and great service. Call 768-3839.

Burnham House—Motif #2 *(Nancy Dudley)*

J.T. Farnham's, 88 Eastern Avenue. Serves lunch and dinner. Famous for its fried clams, eat in or take out. "Seafood with a View." Open March–November at 11. Call 768-6643.

Jan's Encore, 233 Western Avenue. Full menu offering a variety of "affordable excellence." Features Louisiana-style cooking, too. Open year round for lunch and dinner. Call 768-3599.

Jerry Pelonzi's Hearthside, 109 Eastern Avenue (Route 133). Dine in the warmth of a 1680 New England farmhouse. Enjoy lobster, fresh seafood and 40-ounce prime rib and desserts and bread baked on the premises. Call 768-6002.

Lewis' Restaurant, 234 John Wise Avenue. Fresh seafood, beef, and chicken. A great value for your dollar. Call 768-6551.

Periwinkles, 74 Main Street. Serves the "freshest fish in Essex" for lunch and dinner. Opens daily at 11:30. Call 768-6320.

Red Barrel Family Pub, 171 Eastern Avenue. Features live entertainment every other Wednesday evening, fish and chips made with fresh haddock and daily specials. They dig, shuck, and serve their own clams! Opens at 4 o'clock Wednesday–Sunday. Call 768-7210.

Road Kill Cafe, 65 Eastern Avenue. "Food and booze with a sense of humor." Opens at 11:30 daily year round. Call 768-7686.

Tom Shea's, 122 Main Street. Fine seafood in a relaxing atmosphere with a view of the Essex River. Call 768-6931.

Village Restaurant, 55 Main Street. Voted "North Shore's best seafood restaurant" from 1987 to 1996. Opens at 11:30 daily; closed Mondays. Call 768-6400.

Woodman's Lobster Pool, 125 Main Street. Established in 1914. *Yankee Travel Guide* calls it the "best local food in MA!" For clambakes and catering call 768-2559; for the restaurant call 768-6451 or 800-649-1773.

Woodman's   *(Chris Gurshin)*

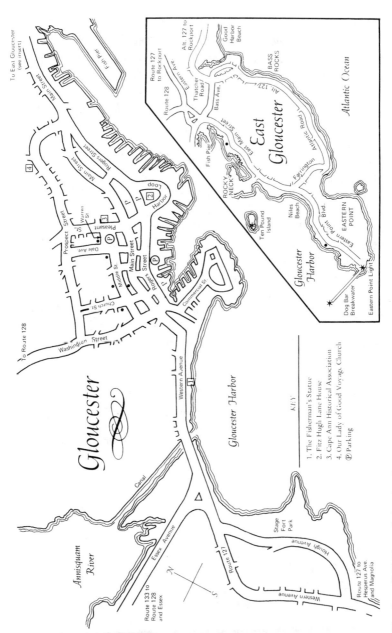

(Courtesy of J.W. Murray & Associates)

Gloucester Fishermen   *(Tom O'Hara)*

Gloucester

HISTORY OF GLOUCESTER

CAPE ANNE

On July 16, 1605, the French explorer Samuel de Champlain landed on these shores and met the Indians' living here. He named the promontory where he landed the "Cape of Islands." Later, Captain John Smith landed on this promontory and called it "Tragabigzanda" for a fair Moslem to whom he owed a debt of love and gratitude. As a memorial to three Turks he allegedly beheaded in a conflict at the city of Arianople, he conferred the name "Three Turks' Heads" upon the three islands (Milk, Thacher, and Straitsmouth) lying off the extreme point. These names were quickly superseded.

In 1614, Captain Smith made a map of the eastern coast of the United States and presented it to Prince Charles. The prince approved the name of "New England" and called the fair headland "Cape Anne" in honor of his mother, Anne of Denmark.

In 1623 Cape Anne became the first permanent settlement of the Massachusetts Bay Colony with fourteen men under the authority of Reverend John White from Dorchester, England. At this time, Cape Anne was the only fishing station in Massachusetts. The Dorchester company dropped anchor in Gloucester harbor and set up their stages (fish-drying platforms) on "Fishermen's Field." (At Stage Fort Park there is a bronze plaque affixed to the giant rock commemorating this historic event.)

The Puritans represented some of England's best and wealthiest families and brought spirit and culture with them to this wilderness. They came by the highest authority in the land, that of the king. Their purpose was to make a home in this new land and bring with them what they needed to work the land and sea; this was not a trading post. The people had authority under their charter to construct churches, build school houses, and appoint civil and religious officers.

Roger Conant joined the Massachusetts Bay Colony and was elected its first Governor. He remained here as ruler of the people until he went to Naumkeag (Salem) in 1627 and was superseded by John Endecott. The people did not come all at once to settle this area: some came in 1623, then others in 1628, and by 1630 there was a great emigration of 12 to 13 vessels from England. In 1630 the actual charter was brought over from England on the *Arbella* (see Manchester-by-the-Sea's **History** section). Finally, in 1642 Cape Anne was named Gloucester, after the city in England.

GLOUCESTER

The ocean breeze is with you wherever you are in the city of Gloucester. It blows as you wind your way around the harbor, the coastline of East Gloucester, and the rocky shores of Magnolia. As you meander by the salt marshes of West Gloucester, the inlets of Annisquam, and the quarries of Lanesville, the crisp salt air awakens your senses.

Gloucester grew from a collection of hamlets, including Annisquam, Lanesville, and Riverdale. In the early days, the heart of Gloucester was Meetinghouse Green, just north of the Ellery House and the Babson Homestead (where Grant Circle is today). For seventy-five years the only meetinghouse in Gloucester was located here and attendance was mandatory for all residents. The Green was a practical place for the first settlement since the land was fertile and level for farming, it was close to the Annisquam River (where a canal was dug in 1642 so vessels no longer had to circle the Cape), and a freshwater brook was nearby.

In 1642 at Cape Pond Brook, the first mill was built by William Ellery. In 1644 a grist mill for grinding corn and a mill to pre-shrink homespun wool were built on the same brook a short distance away (the Tidewater Mill in Riverdale). These two small falls on Cape Pond Brook were an important factor in locating the original settlement. The James Babson place (32 acres) was the first property granted by the early settlement in 1658. (See **Places of Interest:** Rockport.)

During the first 100 years of Gloucester's settlement about eighty homes were constructed in the parish. These homes were typical first-period dwellings (see **Architectural Styles of the Area**). The settlement on the high grounds became known as the "Commons Settlement" and it was accessible to most of the coastal points. (This land was later to become Rockport, Pigeon Cove, Lanesville, Annisquam, and the harbor.) The Commons Road, in what is today known as "Dogtown" (see **Places of Interest:** Dogtown), was the original road from Annisquam and Riverdale to Rockport.

As the Commons grew in population, the people petitioned the General Court of Massachusetts in 1738 to allow them to establish their own church. Since twenty percent of Gloucester's "best families" lived in the Commons Settlement and owned ten percent of Gloucester's land, the petition was granted in 1751. The people no longer had to travel to the Green to attend church.

Gloucester's history has been tied to the fishing industry since the first English fishermen set up fishing stages along Gloucester's shore in 1623. Fish houses, wharves, and drying racks were built on the inner shores of the sheltered harbor. Other fishing outposts sprang up in Annisquam, Folly Cove, Hodgkins Cove, Plum Cove, Pigeon Cove, and along Sandy Bay in Rockport.

For several generations, Gloucester rivaled Marblehead as America's number one fishing port. But after the embargo from the War of 1812 and a gale on the Grand Bank on September 19, 1846 that claimed eleven schooners and sixty-five men and boys, Marblehead never regained her prominence. From this point on, Gloucester was regarded as the premier fishing port in New England and the world.

The development of a salt fish trade with Spain and the West Indies in the 1700s added to Gloucester's fisheries and helped establish the port as a major fishing center in the North Atlantic. The 1800s saw the rise and fall of the halibut fishery. American fishermen employed the French system of trawl-line fishing. This new system replaced single-hook fishing from one large vessel with multi-hook fishing from dories. This method of fishing increased the dangers to fishermen and resulted in many lost lives. Many a dory lost sight of the mother vessel during squalls and snow storms and was never seen again. In the mid-1800s, fishing for mackerel with hooks was replaced by purse seines, and by 1851 the city boasted 241 schooners in the mackerel fishery alone.

Gillnetting was introduced in the late 1870s. The nets were set and hauled by hand from dories. This method of fishing was not very popular until 1908, when five or six small gillnetters, fully equipped, arrived in Gloucester from Michigan. A mechanical lifter enabled men to set and haul the nets directly from the vessel and proved to be successful.

The modern fishing vessels that we see today, called otter trawlers, were first used in New England in 1905. Coal-and steam-driven engines supplemented the power of the wind and the advent of the internal combustion engine completed the metamorphosis. With this new-found power came the most important change of all, and that was in the way men fished—*from using hooks to using mobile nets.* Today, diesel engines give vessels the power to tow large nets along the ocean bottom. Although this technique was the beginning of modern fishing, many believe it was also the beginning of overfishing.

1925 saw the decline of the salt fish trade with the development of quick freezing by Gloucester's Clarence Birdseye; he later sold his business to General Foods Corporation. Packing and distributing frozen fish is now one of Gloucester's major industries. Gorton's of Gloucester is a well-known processor of frozen fish. Gorton's uses the catch from foreign vessels (from Newfoundland and Nova Scotia as well as from Greenland and other countries) that are now a common sight in the harbor.

The depression of the early 1930s was a difficult period for Gloucester. However, the situation changed for the better when redfish (formerly discarded as "trash fish") was discovered to have filleting qualities and a taste similar to that of freshwater perch. This paved the way for Gloucester's "golden era of fishing." In one week in June 1944, more than 9,500,000 pounds of fish were landed at Gloucester wharves. Total landings for the month were 33,577,000 pounds, of which 18,259,000 pounds were redfish. Even with today's fishing fleet and sophisticated navigational equipment, Gloucester vessels can't compete with the abundance of that era; today's landings of 3–5 million pounds each month fall far short of bygone days. Gloucester currently hosts about 200 vessels in the ground fishery and 100 in the lobster fishery.

Today fishery managers are taking important steps to save the fish. Spawning areas south of Nova Scotia, near the Canadian–U.S. border, have doubled and tripled in size and are closed to all extended net and dredge fishing. Also, large portions of Georges Banks are closed to net fishing. Gloucester's unique proximity to major fishing grounds such as Georges and Stellwagen Banks, combined with its deep sheltered harbor, will always make it a major player in fisheries along the eastern seaboard.

Over the years Gloucester fishermen left the shelter of this harbor to face the uncertainties of the sea. One such man was Alfred "Centennial" Johnsen, the first man to sail solo across the Atlantic with "not even the company of a dog." In his sixteen-foot sailing dory he sailed from Gloucester (on a dare!) on June 15, 1876, and arrived in Liverpool, England, sixty-seven days later. The trip was not uneventful: his boat capsized and sharks followed alongside him, but he frightened them away with a knife he fastened to a pole.

Many brave fishermen lost their lives to the sea. In a gale on February 24, 1862, 120 men drowned at sea. During 1873, thirty-one Gloucester fishing vessels and 174 fishermen were lost. In 1879, the sea claimed twenty-nine fishing vessels and

249 of Gloucester's sons. Between 1880 and 1897, Gloucester lost 264 of its fishing vessels and 1,614 men. Since the founding of the fishing industry in Gloucester over 10,000 men have been lost at sea! Truly, fishing has been a dangerous profession for Gloucester natives. The Fisherman Statue on Stacy Boulevard overlooking Gloucester harbor is a memorial to these brave men. Inscribed on its base is the first line from Psalm 107:23:

> *"They that go down to the sea in ships,"*
> *1623–1923*

For more than 350 years the women of Gloucester have gazed seaward. In 1969, the Gloucester Fishermen's Wives Association (GFWA) was formed as a non-profit organization to protect and promote Gloucester's and New England's fishing industry as well as improve the quality of life for fishermen's families. It is the first organization of its kind to bring together conservationists, businesses, government, artists, clergy, educators, fishermen, and the broader community. GFWA championed the concept of a 200-mile Exclusive Economic Zone (EEZ) to allow the United States to protect and manage local fisheries for the benefit of coastal communities. Since 1969, GFWA has fought oil drilling on Georges Bank and won, developed a *Fishermen's Wives Cookbook* of new gourmet recipes for less familiar species of fish, supported establishment of the Stellwagen Bank Marine Sanctuary, opposed ocean dumping of toxic waste, and more. At present GFWA is working with other organizations to provide affordable health insurance for fishing people.

Soon the wives, mothers, sisters, and daughters of Gloucester fishermen will have their own memorial, the Fishermen's Wives Memorial. Sculptor Morgan Faulds Pike is designing a sculpture made of bronze with a base of Cape Ann granite that will stand twelve feet high on Stacy Boulevard, just south of the Blynman Bridge. The sculpture will commemorate the faith, diligence, and fortitude of the women of fishermen and mariners everywhere. If you would like to contribute to the building of the sculpture, contact The Gloucester Fishermen's Wives Memorial, Inc., 11–15 Parker Street, Gloucester, MA 01930, or call 282-1401.

PLACES OF INTEREST: DOGTOWN

Before the settlers came, this area was heavily forested. They cleared the land, built homes, and grew crops. Originally part of the Commons Settlement, this area prospered from 1650–1750.

Dogtown represents the growth, decline, and disappearance of a community. It offers lessons in the brief economic cycles of people as well as the much longer cycles of nature. As the early community turned from logging and farming to fishing and shipbuilding, people moved closer to the harbor and shore. Some men became sea captains and voyaged around the world, trading in China, India, and the East Indies. These men built fine houses near the harbor, on Middle, Washington, and Pleasant Streets. Dogtown homes were rented out to the poor. Widows of sailors often lived here and kept dogs for protection; hence the area became known as Dogtown. Some residents earned a living by selling blueberries; others by fortune telling and other gypsy ways. Over time, the area became run down. Another reason for the decline was the major change in traffic flow. When the bridge was built at Goose Cove, roads were constructed along the shore, and the main road that ran through Dogtown to Rockport was no longer important.

As you visit Dogtown, reflect on what life must have been like when some of Cape Ann's finest families lived here. It is hard to imagine this desolate, rock-strewn acreage with its forty abandoned cellar holes and overgrown paths as a flourishing community. You'll be reminded that every person's life has a beginning and an end and that everyone faces one certainty: change.

As the people left, nature took over and the area is once again rich in bird and animal life. About forty species of trees grow here and you will see many wildflowers in season and, of course, blueberries—millions of them. Gloucester native Roger Babson was fascinated with Dogtown and hired unemployed Finnish granite quarry workers during the Great Depression to carve inspirational messages on some of the huge boulders. You will see boulders with messages such as "Be Clean," and "Help Mother." Babson said he was writing a book with words carved into stone rather than printed on paper.

Geologists will be interested in knowing that Dogtown is the southernmost extent of the glacial ice sheet, a terminal moraine. Cape Ann is where glacial deposits are most evident. Boulders two to six feet in diameter are piled on top of one another over an area one-half mile long by several hundred feet wide. Artists and writers have been moved by Dogtown. Thomas Dresser wrote in *Dogtown: A Village Lost in Time,* "Dogtown is an artist's inspiration, a hiker's haven, a naturalist's preserve, an historian's archive, and a school child's classroom."

Northwest of and adjacent to Dogtown is the Norton Memorial Forest. Since there is no public parking nearby, it is best to hike in from the south or east. Over fifty years ago this area was a barren hillside when Frederick H. Norton, the late MIT professor of metallurgy and ceramics, started preparing the land for a tree farm. With the help of friends and neighbors, catbrier was rooted out. Over time, Professor Norton built roads and walking paths. He raised seedlings in his own garden before transplanting them onto the hillside, and planted 100,000 trees on his tree farm. Of his many accomplishments (as a scholar, teacher, scientist, author, and a man who had a profound influence on the world of ceramics), Professor Norton considered the Forest his finest work. In 1972, this area received The National Tree Farm Award as the best Massachusetts Tree Farm. In 1975, the over 100 acres of woods and trails were given to The New England Forestry Foundation so it could be maintained for perpetual use as conservation land.

In 1985 the Dogtown Advisory Committee (under the auspices of Gloucester's Conservation Commission and the Department of Public Works) was established to preserve the natural and cultural features of Dogtown, protect the watershed areas of the reservoirs, and develop a land management program to maintain Dogtown as a safe, clean, quiet place for passive recreation. **Never go to Dogtown alone, and never without a map!** It is easy to become disoriented (there are many blueberry pickers' trails which lead nowhere). Maps are available from the Dogtown Advisory Committee, the Gloucester Conservation Commission, Essex County

Greenbelt, and the City of Gloucester Welcoming Center at Stage Fort Park.

To reach Dogtown, from the Grant Traffic Rotary head north on Route 127, Washington Street, toward Annisquam and Pigeon Cove. Drive about one mile to the Mill Pond causeway in Riverdale. Bear right on Reynard Street and follow it to the end. Turn left on Cherry Street and proceed north to the entrance to Dogtown on the right up a steep drive, Dogtown Road; public parking is on both sides of Dogtown Road before the two gates. There are other points of access to Dogtown; however, no public parking is available. Dennison Street and Revere Street are **NOT** entrances; use these only as exits in case of emergency. Please respect the privacy of landowners near Dogtown Common.

PLACES OF INTEREST: CENTRAL GLOUCESTER

"Gloucester is fair, yes wondrous fair for artist's brush or poet's pen; yet still its wealth beyond compare is in its race of sturdy men."
—Fred W. Tibbets, *Historical Sketch of Gloucester*, 1916

In Gloucester, the Historic Trail is marked by a red line painted on some of the sidewalks; this line will lead you to the city's landmarks. For more information and a map, stop by the city's Visitors' Welcoming Center at Stage Fort Park or contact the Cape Ann Chamber of Commerce. Central Gloucester encompasses the institutional, commercial, and early residential core of the city. Within this historic district is a concentration of eighteenth and early-nineteenth century buildings (especially on Middle Street); many date back to 1840 or before. The clapboard houses with gambrel and hipped roofs are close to the street and are set off by granite curbstones, steps, and walks.

The Sargent House Museum is at 49 Middle Street. The house was built in 1782 and was the home of Judith Sargent Murray (1751–1820), a philosopher, writer, and activist, and

The Sargent House Museum (1782)   *(Courtesy of The Sargent House Museum)*

her husband, the Reverend John Murray (1741–1815), founder of Universalism in America. He achieved the first ruling in this country for freedom of religion. Here Judith Sargent Murray composed many essays that challenged the new nation to extend equal access to education and economic opportunity. In Gloucester she penned letters only recently discovered which offer an eyewitness account of 18th-century American history. Today, this important historic home of American patriots, sea merchants, religious and community leaders is among the finest remaining examples of high-style Georgian architecture in the area. The House is open from June 1 to October 15, Friday–Monday from noon to 4; there is a small admission fee for non-residents. For information about programs and tours, call 281-2432.

Independent Christian Church, Unitarian Universalist is at the corner of Church and Middle Streets. The church has the distinction of being the first Universalist Church in America. Under the leadership of John Murray, interested members of the First Parish Church separated and formed the

Independent Christian Church in 1779. The 1806 building was designed by Jacob Smith. Sunday services are at 10 a.m.; child care and Sunday school are available. Call 283-3410.

Isabel Babson Memorial Library is at 69 Main Street. Roger Ward Babson (1875-1967), an economist and financier, founded the library in 1961 to honor his ancestor, a midwife, who had come here from England in 1637. She lived in a log cabin which stood on this site. The library remains devoted entirely to family topics, from prenatal life through grandparenting and the golden years. It is open Monday–Friday, from 10 to 4. Call 283-5624.

Thomas Sanders House (Sawyer Free Library) is at 84–86 Middle Street. In 1831, the Gloucester Lyceum was founded as a lecture society. Some well-known celebrities who spoke at this literary institution were Henry David Thoreau, Ralph Waldo Emerson, and Oliver Wendell Holmes. With a gift from Samuel Sawyer in 1872, the Lyceum became the Gloucester Lyceum and Sawyer Free Library. In 1884 Sawyer purchased the 1764 house of Thomas Sanders and renovated it for library use. In 1934 Frederick L. Stoddard (assisted by Howard A. Curtis) hand painted murals depicting scenes from Gloucester's history directly onto the uneven plastered walls which give the artwork an antique appearance and harmonizes with the age of the building. In 1980 Mr. Curtis helped restore the mural decoration in the main hall of this building and painted new murals in the Anderson Room. In 1976 the addition to the Sawyer Free Library at 2 Dale Avenue, designed by local architect Donald Monell, was opened. The Sawyer Free Library at 2 Dale Avenue is open:

Winter Schedule: Mon.–Thurs., 8:30–8; Fri. and Sat., 8:30–5; Sun. (Sept.–May), 1–5.

Summer Schedule: Mon.–Thurs., 8:30–8; Fri., 8:30–5; Sat., 8:30–1.

Residents may obtain **free passes** for the Children's Museum, Isabella Stewart Gardner Museum, John F. Kennedy Library, Museum of Fine Arts, Museum of Science, New England Aquarium, Peabody Essex Museum, Cape Ann Historical Society, and Gloucester Stage Company. For more information, call 281-9763.

City Hall is at 9 Dale Avenue. The 1869 building was designed by the Boston firm of Bryant and Rogers and replaced an earlier version destroyed by fire the previous year. The building dominates the area by its size, tall tower, and rich decoration. Inside are hand-painted murals depicting local historical scenes as well as other artwork. As you go up the staircase (by the Warren Street entry), you will see the names of fishermen and mariners who were lost at sea between 1874 and 1978 inscribed on the walls. The Gloucester Archives contain vital records from 1634 to the present, and are open Monday–Friday, from 9 to noon.

The Cape Ann Historical Museum at 27 Pleasant Street was founded in 1873 as the Cape Ann Scientific and Literary Association. Its mission is "to foster an appreciation of the quality and diversity of life on Cape Ann past and present." Its first headquarters, the Captain Elias Davis House, built in 1804, was purchased in 1923. The six furnished rooms in the home contain fine 19th-century fine furniture and decorative arts representative of domestic life in Cape Ann during the 1800s. The 1969 addition has imposing brick walls and arches echoing those of the Sawyer Free Library. The museum contains a world-renowned collection of paintings and drawings by Gloucester native maritime artist, Fitz Hugh Lane (1804–1865) as well as Winslow Homer, Maurice Prendergast, Frank Duveneck, and others. There are sculptures by Paul Manship, George Aarons, and Walker Hancock. On display are decorative arts, and a fine collection of fisheries and maritime exhibits. The museum is open Tuesday–Saturday, from 10 to 5 (group tours available; call first). Admission is charged; members and children under 6 are free. The museum is located one block north from Main Street and a short block east of City Hall and the Sawyer Free Library. Limited parking adjacent to the Museum; metered public parking nearby. Call 283-0455.

The Fitz Hugh Lane House is located off Rogers Street at Harbor Loop. As a toddler, Fitz Hugh Lane ate some poisonous seeds in the garden; this caused paralysis of his legs. As a child his artistic talent was obvious, and he later received his art education in Boston. Lane designed and built this house, fashioned after the House of Seven Gables in Salem.

The northwest room was his studio and once offered a panoramic view of Gloucester harbor. His extreme accuracy and attention to detail have made his paintings a valuable record of vessels afloat in the 1800s. At the foot of the hill on the Rogers Street side is the 18-foot granite threshold of the First Baptist Church, which once stood at Middle and Pleasant Streets. This stone was taken from a Rockport quarry and hauled to Gloucester by forty-two pair of oxen on a specially made cart (for photo, see **History** of Rockport).

Old Town Hall (1844–1845) is at the intersection of Middle and Washington Streets. It is a striking building with the simple, bold, classical detail of the Greek Revival style. It was originally designed in the temple form with a columned portico on the east facade only. In the early 20th century a second portico was added onto the north facade when the building became the home of the American Legion.

The Joan of Arc Statue is a bronze statue standing outside the American Legion Hall on Washington Street. Summer resident Anna Vaughn Hyatt Huntington used an actual fire department horse named "Frank" as her model.

Blackburn Tavern is at the intersection of Washington and Main Streets and was built by James Tappan in 1810. This Federal-style building was the only commercial building on the street to survive two 19th-century fires. The most heroic figure in the annals of Gloucester fisheries is Howard Blackburn. He was a Nova Scotian halibuting out of Gloucester on the Schooner *Grace L. Fears* in January 1883 when he and his dorymate Tom Welch were separated from the schooner by a gale sixty miles off Newfoundland. Welch froze to death. Blackburn knew his bare hands would freeze and he curled them around the oars so they would freeze in the shape of their grasp. Without food or water and with his dead mate onboard, he rowed to the coast for five days. No records exist which equal such fortitude at sea. When Blackburn arrived in Newfoundland he was near death, but a family cared for him and he returned to Gloucester in the spring. He lost fingers, half of each thumb, and most of his toes. A public subscription was raised for him and he entered the saloon business on Main Street. Not to be beaten by his disability, he went on to cross the Atlantic alone on two occasions.

Our Lady of Good Voyage Church is at 142 Prospect Street. For over 100 years this has been the church of the Portuguese-American fishermen and their families. The church is modeled after a mission church in the Azores of Portugal. Its twin blue towers house the first cast-bell carillon in America, brought to the church through the efforts of A. Piatt Andrew. The twenty-five bell carillon was cast by the John Taylor and Company Foundry of Loughborough, England; the same company cast our nation's Liberty Bell. Six more bells were later added to the carillon, making thirty-one bells. Between the twin towers is a statue of the Virgin Mary gently holding a schooner, symbolizing her protection of the fisherman. Each year at Pentecost the Portuguese hold a Festival of the Crowning of Our Lady of Good Voyage, a practice brought over from Portugal dating back to the 14th century, when Queen Isabella crowned one of her loyal subjects for a day. Captain Joseph Mesquita began this event in Gloucester in 1902, after his vessel *Mary P. Mesquita* collided with the Cunard Steamer *Saxonia* off George's Banks. All but one of his men were rescued from his sinking schooner. You can hear the carillon every Tuesday in July at 7 p.m. Sunday morning services are at 7:00, 8:30, 10:00, and 11:45. Call 283-1490.

Beauport, Sleeper-McCann House (Society for the Preservation of New England Antiquities) is located at 75 Eastern Point Boulevard in East Gloucester. Beauport, built in 1907, was the summer home of the collector and interior designer Henry Davis Sleeper and served as a showcase for his professional skills. Built on the rocks overlooking scenic Gloucester Harbor, this house is a labyrinth of rooms decorated to evoke different historical or literary themes and contains extraordinary collections of 17th- and 18th-century furnishings. Summer programs include afternoon teas, evening concerts, and sunset tours. The house is open Monday–Friday from May to September, 10–5; daily from September to October, 10–5; closed on Memorial Day, July 4th, and Labor Day. Tours run on the hour and on the half-hour in July and August, with the

Beauport, Sleeper-McCann House (1907) *(Courtesy of the Society for the Preservation of New England Antiquities)*

last tour at 4 p.m. Admission is charged; SPNEA members and Gloucester residents are admitted free. For group rates, educational programs, and special events, call 283-0800.

The Patrons' Museum and Educational Center is at 122 Thatcher Road. The basic philosophy of The Patrons' Museum is to teach people of all ages who artists are, how they grow and develop, and how very important their influence is on our lives, not just for today but for all time. In the Charles Tiernan Memorial Gallery, the museum features a historical perspective collection of artists who have been art teachers on Cape Ann over the past 150 years. There is also a significant Mural of Gloucester Harbor (c. 1950) by Ken Gore and an extensive photographic collection of the museum's founder, Bradley Smith. The Patrons' Museum is located halfway between Good Harbor Beach and Long Beach on Route 127A. No admission fee is charged. Open May–December, Monday–Friday, 1–5; Friday–Sunday evenings, 7–10. Call 281-6437.

Man at the Wheel (Fisherman Statue) *(Nancy Dudley)*

Man at the Wheel (Fisherman Statue) was sculpted by Leonard Craske at his Rocky Neck studio and placed on Stacy Boulevard overlooking Gloucester Harbor in 1923, commemorating the 300th anniversary of the city. Dressed in oilskins and leaning against the wheel, his eyes gaze intently across a storm-tossed sea. "They that go down to the sea in ships," from the Book of Psalms, is inscribed at the base of this bronze monument, remembering the rugged character and courage of the fishermen who have braved the open ocean. For many years in mid-August tribute was paid to the fishermen who had died. Thousands would gather at the edge of the harbor and with prayers, music, and a roll call children would cast wreaths and garlands on the water. For a time this tribute was not held. In mid-August 1997, citizens of Gloucester will once again gather at the harbor to remember their fishermen.

Blynman Bridge (the "Cut" Bridge) by the harbor was named after its engineer, Richard Blynman, who was also Gloucester's first minister. The communities of Gloucester and Rockport are on an island separated from the mainland by the Annisquam River. When the first settlers arrived, the Annisquam River did not flow through from one side of Cape Ann to the other and vessels faced treacherous voyages around the Cape. In 1642, the people realized the need to make this "cut" to create a canal and built a bridge.

"Dunfudgin" Landing is where the currents of the Annisquam River change, in the vicinity of Gloucester High School. Here is a park, boat ramp, playground, sports field, and free parking. When the people who used to cut and harvest the salt marsh hay had poled their loaded gundalows against the tide and reached this point, they would catch a fair tide and say "we're done fudging."

Eastern Point Lighthouse and **Dog Bar Breakwater** are located off Eastern Point Boulevard. The lighthouse provides a welcome signal announcing the entrance to Gloucester Harbor; it was originally built in 1832 and rebuilt in 1890. Next to the lighthouse, which is owned by the United States Coast Guard, is a public parking lot. The breakwater was built at the location of a treacherous sandbar. It is fun to walk out to the end of the breakwater, but there are no safety railings and the footing is uneven; use caution and carefully watch young children.

Ten Pound Island is located inside Gloucester Harbor. A lighthouse was constructed on the island in 1821 and rebuilt in 1881. It served the maritime community until 1965, when the keeper's house was razed and the tower abandoned. Winslow Homer, one of America's greatest artists, stayed on

Eastern Point Light (1832) *(Lighthouse Preservation Society)*

the island with the keeper's family in 1880 while he painted more than 100 of some of his most famous works of art. On Stacy Boulevard near the Fisherman Statue is a plaque presented by The Lighthouse Preservation Society in commemoration of America's Lighthouse Bicentennial (1789–1989). Through the efforts of concerned citizens under the leadership of The Society, the tower on Ten Pound Island was restored and relit in 1989. The Lighthouse Preservation Society has been the catalyst for the preservation of lighthouses up and down the nation's coasts. For more information, please contact The Lighthouse Preservation Society, 4 Middle Street, Newburyport, MA 01950. Call 499-0011 or 800-727-BEAM. CATA (Cape Ann Transportation Authority) runs a water shuttle service daily with stops at several harbor locations including Ten Pound Island where visitors can get off and explore. Call 283-2112.

Stage Fort Park on Hough Avenue is where the Dorchester Bay Company established its first "stages," or fish-drying platforms, in 1623 and then mounted a cannon on the point to protect the platforms. Fort Conant, named after 1625 Governor Roger Conant, remained in service through the Civil War. The Fort was the actual sight of a battle during the Revolutionary War (1775) when the British sloop *HMS Falcon,* captained by John Linzee, chased a West Indies trading ship into Gloucester Harbor. The British intended to burn the stages and the town, but were met by the local militia led by Captain Joseph Foster. The cannon ball fired by the *HMS Falcon* at the steeple of the First Parish Church during this battle is on display at the Cape Ann Historical Museum. The Fort is still there for you to explore. In addition, Stage Fort Park provides a playground with a giant dump truck slide, pirate ship to climb, a sea serpent, mini-rotunda, and more. There are picnic tables, two beaches, a ball field, and lots of parking. Gloucester's Visitors Welcoming Center is located inside the fieldstone building. Be sure to stop here for information or just to enjoy sitting in the shade of the verandah with wraparound ocean views. There are bathroom facilities in the lower level. A restaurant is close by. The Tony Gentile Bandstand is the location for free summer concerts.

Cape Ann's Sea Serpent *(Liz Mackie)*

A Sea Serpent was sighted off Ten Pound Island in 1817 with a belly as large as a good-sized barrel and a mouth two feet wide, out of which shot a forked tongue. The 100-foot-long serpent was seen on several occasions along the Massachusetts coastline by about 200 "reputable" citizens. Records exist that the Indians saw a sea monster here as early as 1638 (see **History** of Rockport section). As you look out over Gloucester Harbor watch for the sea serpent—he may come back!

The *Adventure* is a 121-foot, all-wooden, two-masted fishing schooner built in Essex in 1926. For twenty-seven years she was used for fishing the outer banks of the North Atlantic. She is the only National Historic Landmark vessel in Essex County as well as the last of Gloucester's great fishing schooners. This unique floating museum is open Saturdays and Sundays for guided tours. Admission is free; however, donations are appreciated. A full breakfast is served by a volunteer crew every Sunday morning from 9 to noon; suggested donations are $6 for adults and $4 for children. A ship's store is on board; all proceeds from the breakfasts and sales from the ship's store are used for restoration and maintenance. As a living symbol of this region's proud maritime history, the vessel is host to a wide variety of cultural and educational events which are held during the summer. The vessel is berthed at the Gloucester Marine Railways at Harbor Loop. Come and enjoy an *Adventure*! Call 281-8079.

The State Fish Pier (built in 1937) is reached via Rogers Street to Parker Street. This very large pier with a boat landing and fishing area has public rest rooms and free parking. At one time there were two islands in Gloucester harbor (Ten Pound Island and Five Pound Island); this pier is part of what was once Five Pound Island. These islands were named for the price paid for them by the original settlers.

PLACES OF INTEREST: ANNISQUAM

The name Annisquam is derived from a proper family name, Annis, which means "island." (Squam means "pleasant or peaceful harbor.") In 1662 Charles Annis came from Ireland to Newburyport and later built his home on the Annisquam River, which is how the area got its name. However, Annisquam was first settled in 1631 by Abraham Robinson and a group of men who were sent from Plymouth to set up fishing stages and flake yards. What began as a summer operation with time grew into a settlement.

The Village Church was built in 1728 with approval from the General Court. Originally this third parish encompassed the region from Goose Cove to Halibut Point and Sandy Bay, which is now the town of Rockport. The first minister of the Annisquam Village Church was Reverend Benjamin Bradstreet; but the Reverend Ezra Leonard, who came in 1804, was most admired by his parishioners. The memory of the Reverend Leonard is alive in Annisquam today: the community's main street is called Leonard Street; the Leonard School, which is now the Annisquam Exchange, still stands; and the men's club is called the Leonard Club.

Before long Reverend Leonard became interested in the teachings of Reverend John Murray (see **Places of Interest**: Central Gloucester) and rejected orthodox Calvinism for the doctrine of universal salvation. Reverend Leonard started a school, taught navigation to young men who wanted to be sailors, authored a farmers' and mariners' almanac, and was a generous man. He remained among his parishioners until his death in 1832.

People believe that after the strict tenets of Calvinism were set aside for the freedoms found in Universalism, the stage was set for creativity. Artists, writers, and musicians began to express themselves openly and the area's natural beauty gave them many subjects for their expression. The first church was replaced in 1830 by the present building designed by James Dennison. In 1957 the Village Church became a member of the International Council of Community Churches, thereby crossing all denominational, racial, class and theological barriers.

Civil War Monument at Mt. Adnah Cemetery *(Courtesy of the Annisquam Historical Society)*

Annisquam Harbor Light overlooks Wingaersheek Beach. The present structure replaced the original on Wigwam Point in 1897.

Civil War Monument at Mt. Adnah Cemetery. This tin soldier monument is one of only five remaining in the United States today. It was erected and dedicated in 1890 in memory of the soldiers and sailors of 1861–65, who gave their lives fighting in the War of the Rebellion.

Stone Seat, located in Chester Square, is a natural granite "chair" that was quarried on Cape Ann and brought here by George Clough.

Annisquam Footbridge for a long time was a toll bridge that could be opened to let tall boats through. Several years ago the bridge needed to be repaired to make it safe for vehicular traffic; the citizens of Annisquam decided to make the bridge accessible only to foot traffic and let the cars drive "all the way around" and enter the town by the Annisquam Church. As a result, Annisquam has become even more peaceful.

Annisquam toll bridge   *(Courtesy of the Annisquam Historical Society)*

Annisquam Market and Restaurant, 33 River Road. Open May–October for breakfast, lunch, and dinner daily. Mariners and those arriving by road may dine on the harborside deck or in the dining room. Lobsters fresh or cooked; convenience store and fuel for boats. Call 283-3070.

Annisquam Boat Livery, 25 River Road. Provides rental of boat slips, sea kayaks (by the hour), and boat rides to Wingaersheek Beach. Concession on premises. Open Memorial Day–Columbus Day; Call 283-0522 or 283-0764.

The Annisquam Exchange is located in the old Leonard School at 32 Leonard Street. On the first floor are antiques, hand-made items, home-made condiments, and collectibles. The Exchange is open June 10–September 10, Monday–Friday, 10–4:30, and Saturdays, 10–noon. Call 281-0358.

The Art Gallery is located on the second floor of the Exchange and contains works created by former or present residents of Annisquam. On permanent display is a collection of etchings and paintings by George Wainwright Harvey (1855–1930). Mr. Harvey was a self-taught painter. For thirty-six years Mr. and Mrs. Harvey maintained adjoining studios at 47 River Road. Mrs. Martha Hale Rogers Harvey (1862–1949) was

Annisquam Artists at the Shore   *(Courtesy of the Annisquam Historical Society)*

one of the finest photographers of her period. Her vast collection of excellent photographs is on display at the Annisquam Historical Society. Call 283-0667.

Annisquam Historical Society was established in the early 1940s when Mrs. Lelia Norwood Adams wished to create a museum to permanently display memorabilia of her ancestors, including Captain Andrew Harraden, Captain Jonathan Harraden, and Nathaniel Harraden (who had been the sailing master of the *U.S.S. Constitution*). With the support of several Annisquam residents, the Historical Society was started in the old firehouse, "Hose 8." Many local historic items as well as genealogical information can be found here. Visitors may purchase reproductions of photographs taken between 1885 and 1920 by the renowned photographer Martha Hale Harvey. Open June to September, Mondays from 2 p.m. to 4 p.m. and Thursdays from 7 p.m. to 9 p.m. or by appointment year-round. For information or to arrange research time, call 283-1426.

Village Hall is located on Leonard Street directly next to the Exchange and Historical Association buildings. The Village Hall, built in 1829 as a Baptist Church to provide a place of worship for those who did not wish to follow the teachings of Universalism, is the center of social and civic life in the community. Today the hall is used for various community activities including the traditional "Sea Fair," which is held each July. The "Sea Fair" is held on the Village Green in front of the Hall (weather permitting) and has a "wax works" as well as a "clothesline" for displaying local art for sale, and a luncheon is served. In the evening (by reservation) dinner is catered and served on the Annisquam Bridge. The annual Annisquam Arts and Crafts Show is held at the Village Hall on Columbus Day weekend featuring artists and artisans from throughout New England. An activities calendar is published July 1. For Village Hall and Arts and Crafts Show information call 283-3053.

The Village Library is located in the Village Hall. In this well-stocked library you will find the classics, books from the best-seller list, and children's selections. During the winter months tea is served using a restored tea service which had been stolen years ago. After it was found badly dented in the Medford marshes, it was brought to Boston, where it was restored to its former luster, and now is once again in use. Open Mondays from 3 p.m. to 5 p.m. year-round and Thursday evenings from 7 p.m. to 9 p.m. during July and August. There is a small fee to join the library. Call 281-1401.

In 1837 the Female Benevolent Society was formed by Eunice and Anstice Fellows (two sisters who were teachers). Today it is known as the **Annisquam Sewing Circle**. It is the oldest society of its kind in New England and has met here continuously for 160 years. Annisquam ladies have worked to supply needed goods during six wars. The Holiday Fair in December is a tradition; the ladies serve a home-cooked chicken luncheon, sell evergreen decorations, and hand-made items. For more information call 283-6161.

PLACES OF INTEREST: MAGNOLIA

Located on the western shores of Gloucester, Magnolia is a quiet village named for the wild *Magnolia virginiana* tree, which once grew abundantly in the swampy wood-

Magnolia Beach includes private property; a small portion of this beach is publicly owned. Parking and a boat landing are available on Shore Road for residents with stickers.

Hammond Castle Museum is at 80 Hesperus Avenue. This "medieval castle" was actually built between 1926–1928 by inventor John Hays Hammond, Jr. (not a member of the Hammond Organ family), an inventor who has over 400 patents to his credit. The castle is on a rocky cliff overlooking the Reef of Norman's Woe in Gloucester Harbor. Built of mostly Rockport granite in the Gothic-Renaissance design, this castle looks like those of Europe during the 16th century. Part of it represents a French fortified tower of the 12th century.

The most impressive room in the castle is the Great Hall, 100 feet long and 25 feet wide, with a domed ceiling 60 feet above the tiled floor. Hammond designed this hall for his organ, which has 10,000 pipes, four manuals, and 144 stops, and which took twenty years to build. A series of concerts is held in the Great Hall during the year. The castle is open from Memorial Day to Labor Day, daily from 10 a.m. to 4 p.m. Directions: from Manchester-by-the-Sea take Route 127 to Magnolia. Turn right onto Raymond Street. Go through Cole Square on Norman Avenue (which becomes Hesperus Avenue) until you see the Museum on your right and a large parking lot. From Gloucester, the Museum is also reached by taking Route 127 to Magnolia. From Route 127, turn left onto Hesperus Avenue and the Museum will be on your left. Admission is charged. Hours vary; call 283-2081.

From the Museum grounds you look directly at Norman's Woe. Goodman Norman and his son were the first to settle on this headland and its outlying islet. No record remains to explain how the rock originally got its name or what catastrophe it might perpetuate; its origin is lost. Henry Wordsworth Longfellow's ballad, *Wreck of the Hesperus*, vividly describes

THE SHIPWRECK.

Wreck of the Hesperus *(New England Legends and Folklore)*

a shipwreck in all its dreadfulness. Longfellow composed his ballad by combining several events of a gale in the winter of 1839 which strewed this coast with wrecks. He read of these disasters and of the loss of one vessel named the "*Hesperus*," and a woman found washed upon the shore in Gloucester lashed to a piece of wreckage. He combined several images with Norman's Woe as the setting to write the ballad.

Ravenswood Park (a property of The Trustees of Reservations) was established in 1889 by Samuel E. Sawyer. Here the Sweetbay magnolias still grow in the swampy woods. The hermit of Ravenswood, Mason A. Walton, lived here for many years and wrote a book about his experiences, *A Hermit's Wild Friends*. A bronze plaque on a huge boulder on Bond Hill marks the spot where his home once stood.

Located off Route 127, Western Avenue, Ravenswood at one time was the site of a house where people who had smallpox were isolated during the years of the Revolutionary War. The "Old Salem Road," which was the main road from Salem to Cape Ann, once passed through this park. Countless boulders strewn about the landscape by the last glacier are covered by mosses and lichens. Today more than 500 acres with several miles of well-maintained trails provide woodlands for the public to enjoy year round (a great place to walk, ride a bike, take photographs, or cross-country ski). A trail map for Ravenswood Park is posted at the park entrance and is available at Stage Fort Park Visitors Center in Gloucester. Parking is free; the park is open daily year-round, from sunrise to dusk.

Our Lady of Good Voyage
(attributed to Angelo Lualdi), 1915, painted wood.
CAPE ANN HISTORICAL COLLECTIONS.
27 Pleasant Street, Gloucester, MA 01930.

CAPE ANN HISTORICAL
ASSOCIATION
Board of Managers
Saturday, June 9
9:30 a.m.

Sarah Robbins
5 Aileen Terrace
Gloucester, MA 01930

POST CARD

USA 20

Antiques

Annisquam Exchange & Art Gallery, Leonard Street. Call 281-0358.

Antiques, 1095 Washington Street. Elizabeth Enfield, Proprietor. Call 546-2434.

Bananas Vintage Clothing, 78 Main Street. Call 283-8806.

Beauport Antiques, 43 Main Street. Call 281-4460.

Bella's Used Furniture (consignment and rugs), 47 Main Street. Call 283-2221.

Burke's Bazaar, 512 Essex Avenue. Call 283-4538.

The English Bookshop (old books), 22 Rocky Neck Avenue. Call 283-8981.

Gloucester Used Furniture and Antiques, 161 Main Street. Call 281-3116.

Jean Leowenart, 9 Lexington Avenue (Magnolia). Call 525-3656.

Jer-Rho Antiques, 352 Main Street. Call 283-5066.

Main Street Arts and Antiques (group shop), 124 Main Street. David Cox, Proprietor. Call 281-1531.

Oz Antiques, 1091 Washington Street. Andrew Bonaventura, Proprietor. Call 283-7906.

Salt Island Antiques (varied older merchandise), 269 Main Street. Call 283-2820.

Tally's Trading Post, 108 Eastern Avenue. Call 283-8662.

Ten Pound Island Book Co. (old rare books; specialties in art and architecture, maritime books, and local history), 108 Main Street. Call 283-5299.

William Greenbaum Fine Prints (fine antique prints), 1074 Washington Street (Lanesville). Call 283-0112.

Art

"The primary impulse in the Arts is to give permanence to the fleeting moment, to bid it stay, because we cannot bear to lose it."
—Paul Manship, Sculptor (1885–1966)

Fishtown Artspace at 1 Center Street offers artists in the Cape Ann region a comfortable and supportive environment in which they and their art can flourish. Artspace provides musicians, visual artists, dancers, actors, writers, filmmakers, and videographers with low-cost rehearsal and performance space, equipment, musical instruments, and opportunities to exhibit their work. Through "Core Public Art Programs," teenagers and adults are encouraged to develop their creative talents. Open year-round, seven days a week from 9 to 9. For more information call Shep Abbott at 283-1381.

Future Art-Kids of Cape Ann is located at 122 Main Street. Young artists—from pre-schoolers to teenagers—create under the caring instruction of Patti Dugan. She offers an impressive list of subjects and materials: portraits, advertising, pencil drawing, pastel and acrylic painting, mobiles, plaster carving, and more. Parents are enthusiastic about Dugan's relaxed style and the friendly atmosphere, which boosts their children's self-esteem and helps them express themselves. Young people exhibit their work there and at other locations. The program is also open to young artists in the surrounding communities. For more information call 281-4884.

The Learning Umbrella promotes the cultural richness on Cape Ann. For more information call Gloucester Visitors Welcoming Center at 800–649-6839.

North Shore Arts Association is at 197 Rear E. Main Street (East Gloucester).

Gloucester's first formal public exhibition was in 1909 featuring the works of over twenty-five recognized American artists residing on Cape Ann. News spread that a major art colony was growing here. Artists were discovered working in dark lofts, old outhouses, chicken coops, and other poorly lighted, cramped spaces discarded by the fishermen. An exhibition center near Rocky Neck was sorely needed. In 1922 the present location of the North Shore Arts Association was purchased. Overlooking the inner harbor and Smith Cove in East Gloucester, the property offers artists and visitors breathtaking views of the historic fishing village of Gloucester. Today the Association houses one of the largest collections of art in New England.

Each June the Association opens a major members' exhibition; other revolving exhibits, including paintings, sculptures, and graphics by some of the country's finest artists, run concurrently throughout the summer and into fall. The North Shore Arts Association celebrates its 75th Anniversary in 1997 and will present a three-week show in retrospect, "Emile Gruppe and his Contemporaries." The annual fundraiser auction is held in July and the Association closes for the season in October. For information on weekly sketch groups, workshops, exhibits, and many programs, call 283-1857 or 800-943-2255.

Rocky Neck Art Colony is at 77 Rocky Neck Avenue. This is the oldest official art colony in America. Over the years several well-known artists painted on Rocky Neck: John Singer Sargent, Winslow Homer, Fitz Hugh Lane, Edward Hopper, and Childe Hassam, to name a few. Augustus W. Buhler (1853–1920) became famous for his paintings of Gloucester fishermen, including his depiction of a "Man at the Wheel," which became Gorton's trademark. This symbol of Gloucester was the inspiration for Leonard Craske's famous Fisherman Statue by the same name, which was created at Craske's studio on Rocky Neck (see photo, page 98).

Rocky Neck Art Colony was and is a collection of working artists. Limited by the season and influences of changing times, this colony continues to reflect the unique character of each artisan. The artists are stimulated and energized by those who came before them, by one another, and by the gallery visitors—and certainly by the sound of sea gulls, smell of salt air, sight of harbor scenes, and that wonderful natural light! Since the rustic studios are located on piers jutting over the harbor and are only habitable in the summer, most of the work on display in the galleries is created on site. People come

View of Rocky Neck from East Gloucester (pre-1900) *(Courtesy of Cape Ann Historical Society)*

from all over the world to visit the galleries. Most of the galleries are open seven days a week from 10 to 10, with special events scheduled throughout the summer (see **Calendar** section). Free parking is available as you enter the "Neck" immediately off East Main Street. For more information, call 283-7978.

ROCKY NECK ARTISTS AND GALLERIES

Jack Braudis Studio Gallery. 281-4573.

Aphia Carman Gallery. 281-1070.

Gallery Five (Martha Ingalls).

Gallery Seven (J.F. Weiler Photos). 281-6443.

Paul George, Rocky Neck Avenue.

Bernard Gerstner Gallery. 283-0196.

The Goetemann Gallery. 281-6128.

Emile A. Gruppe Gallery, 11 Wonson Street. 283-2720.

Ward Mann Gallery. 281-3628.

Jane McDonald Gallery. 281-3718.

The John Nesta Gallery. 283-4319.

Dorothy B. Primm Gallery. 283-4496.

The Quilted Gallery, 77 Rocky Neck Avenue. 283-7978.

Carol St. John Gallery, Rocky Neck.

Side Street Jewelry. 283-3791.

Armand Sindoni Gallery. Rocky Neck.

Helen Wessel Studio. Call 283-6490.

MORE ARTISTS AND GALLERIES (LISTED GEOGRAPHICALLY) : EAST GLOUCESTER

AB Macomber Pottery Co., 211 E. Main Street. 281-0354.

Donna M. Amero (stained glass), 51 Eastern Point Road. 283-0903.

Gallery of Fine Arts (featuring 50 area artists), 279 E. Main Street. 283-9106.

Ken Gore, 186 E. Main Street. 283-4438.

CENTRAL GLOUCESTER

Barbara Donnelly Gallery, 19 Harbor Loop. 282-1333.

Bodin Historic Photo & Fine Art, 82 Main Street. 283-2524.

Paul Frontiero (marine artist), 13 Bertoni Road. 283-3196.

Gallery Studio. 281-7885.

Good Harbor Gallery, 60 Main Street. 281-3118.

Local Colors (cooperative gallery, fine arts and crafts),142 Main Street. 283-3996.

Barry Marshall (seascapes, landscapes, and marine art), 119 Main Street. 282-7822.

Menage Gallery, 134 Main Street. 283-6030.

Pleasant Street Galleries (inside Brown's Mall). 282-0334.

Ria Lehman Design (original jewelry), 5A Starknaught Heights. 281-6033.

Jon Sarkin Creative Designs, 186 Main Street. 282-0334.

Sawyer Free Library (Lobby Gallery), 2 Dale Avenue. 281-9763.

Swigert Studios (contemporary art and photography), 119 Main Street. 283-1715.

West End Gallery (open April–Nov.), 33 Main Street. 282-4896.

LANESVILLE

John Black Studio & Gallery (landscape paintings and silk-screen prints), 1062 Washington Street. 281-0951.

Melancon Anni & Pottery, off High Street. 281-4202.

MAGNOLIA

Susanne M. Champa Studio & Gallery (photography), 33 Lexington Avenue. 525-2134.

Willis & Clarke Gallery, 2 Lexington Avenue. 525-4404.

RIVERDALE

Marty Morgan (pottery for home and garden), 428 Washington Street. 281-3347.

For information about arts-related grants, contact the **Gloucester Cultural Council**, which distributes funds to individuals and organizations in this community. Call 283-3797.

Music, Theater, & Dance

CAPE ANN COMMUNITY BAND

The Community Band plays a traditional program of marches, light classics, popular, and patriotic music. The Antonio Gentile Memorial Bandstand Summer Concert Series is one of the best entertainment bargains in the area. Sponsored by the City of Gloucester, a different musical group is featured every Sunday evening and occasionally on other summer evenings. Come with a picnic and dance on the grass at Stage Fort Park while the sun sets over Gloucester Harbor. Music ranges from Dixieland, rock, and folk, to bluegrass and concert band, with performances by Herb Pomeroy, Amy Gallatin, John Michaels, and others. Admission and parking are free. Call 281-0543.

CAPE ANN SYMPHONY

There are two versions as to how the Cape Ann Symphony began. One is that Sam Gordon grew tired of driving his wife Helen (a gifted violinist) to Lynn for rehearsals with the Lynn Philharmonic and thought there must be enough musicians on Cape Ann to form a decent orchestra. Those who knew the couple well, however, imagined that he started the symphony as a fitting present for the woman he adored.

In 1952 the Gordons founded the Cape Ann Symphony. Sam played first trumpet and managed the orchestra, while Helen served as concertmistress. Most of the members come from the North Shore area; the youngest are Matthew Repucci, age 16 (trumpet), and Nathan Cohen, age 17 (violin). The 1996–1997 season marks the 45th anniversary of the orchestra. For information or tickets (ticket holders may bring those under 18 free of charge) call 281-0543.

CAPE ANN SYMPHONY YOUTH CHORUS

The thirty-nine middle and high school students of the Youth Chorus are chosen from six North Shore communities and perform under the direction of Anne Connolly Potter, a Rockport teacher who organized the chorus eight years ago at the Symphony's request. The Youth Chorus is a treble chorus for alto and soprano voices and performs for the Cape Ann Symphony's annual holiday concerts as well as approximately twenty concerts a year in a wide range of venues. For information or tickets, call 281-0543.

Cape Ann Symphony Youth Chorus   *(Courtesy of Cape Ann Symphony)*

DANCERS COURAGEOUS

The studio is located at 124 Main Street and was founded by dancers Carl Thomsen and Dawn Pratson. Carl's classes reflect his classical and jazz background, and Dawn's are influenced by her background in movement education, music, contemporary dance, and improvisation. The studio offers adults lessons in Tai Chi Chuan, Yoga, ballroom, street dance, and ballet. Carl created a special children's program (Power Moves™) to get boys especially active in dance classes, and both Carl and Dawn teach this program to boys and girls aged 3 and up. Creative Arts Therapy is a program for children and adults with emotional, learning, or rehabilitation needs. Dawn also directs the Cape Ann women's singing group, 'leven, which sings primarily a cappella. For more information, stop by the studio or call 283-2525.

GLOUCESTER STAGE COMPANY

Founded by award-winning playwright Israel Horovitz, the theater company is located in an old Gorton's warehouse near Rocky Neck at 267 East Main Street. The season runs from April to New Year's Eve and audiences have enjoyed performances in this intimate setting since 1979. The annual summer season is the focal point of GSC's mission of developing and producing new plays which are directly related to the working class, fishing-based community of Gloucester. After these plays have premiered here, they travel to audiences across the country and around the world. The autumn season provides a cultural resource for the year-round residents of Cape Ann.

Take a Flying Leap, a Gloucester Celebration of Arts and Education, is a partnership with Gloucester High School and O'Maley Middle School. Real Theater for Real Kids is a resource for families and children aged eight to fourteen years. The Student Intern Program invites area high school and college students to participate as interns at the theater. The Samuel Beckett Playwrighting Fellowship offers one to three promising young playwrights the opportunity to spend the summer in residence at GSC. For more information, a schedule, or reservations, call 281-4099.

HAMMOND CASTLE (see Places of Interest)

The castle is at 80 Hesperus Avenue. The sounds emanating from the 10,000 organ pipes during concerts given in the 100-foot long Great Hall are impressive. In addition to organ concerts, there are a summer chamber music series on Friday evenings and other musical performances. For an events schedule for February–December, call 283-2080 for recorded information.

OLD COLD TATER

This popular group began twenty years ago in a little cabin on the salt marsh of Farm Creek when several musicians came with their instruments to explore their shared interest in folk, blues, and jazz. They had discovered Bill Monroe's powerful blend of these elements and were inspired to combine their talents to produce bluegrass—America's unique art form. From small gatherings to major festivals throughout the Northeast, Old Cold Tater has performed side-by-side with the world's best bluegrass bands. The "Taters" range and variety of musical expression has grown, but they have not forgotten their roots. They enjoy playing in coffeehouses as well as at outdoor community concerts, such as at the Gentile Bandstand at Stage Fort Park, Cape Ann's Schooner Festival, Goodale Orchard's Strawberry Festival, and the Ipswich River Festival. For bookings, cassettes, or information, write to Box 3, Gloucester 01930 or call 283-7302 or 768-7173.

THE STARLIGHTERS

Lovers of swing have been romanced by The Starlighters for more than 30 years. Join in the revival of listening and dancing to the big band music from the masters of the 1930s to 1950s. The band plays at the Harvest Ball, held at the Elks Lodge on Bass Rocks in October. This dance benefits Action, Inc., whose mission is to assist elderly and low-income residents to achieve greater self-sufficiency. The Starlighters perform for weddings and other private and public celebrations throughout New England. Call 283-1797.

⛵ *Recreation*

We caught a 16-pounder in the Bluefish Derby *(Courtesy of Winchester Fishing Co.)*

BAIT AND TACKLE SHOPS

Fisherman's Outfitter at 3 Parker Street. Specializes in outfitting commercial, offshore, and surf fishing with all necessary equipment and live and frozen baits. Call 281-0858.

Gleason's Fish and Lobster at 42 Eastern Avenue. Reasonable prices for fresh fish and lobster; bait and tackle for fishermen. Open daily. Call 283-4414.

Winchester Fishing Co. at 18 Washington Street. Boat and marine supplies as well as custom-made lobster traps. Call for details about the Striped Bass and Bluefish Derby. Open daily. Call 283-0757.

Yankee Bait and Tackle at 79 Essex Avenue. Deep sea fishing. Specializes in custom rods, reels, live bait, and tackle outfitting. Open daily. Call 281-2204.

BEACHES

Cressy Beach is inside Gloucester Harbor at Stage Fort Park on Hough Avenue.

Good Harbor Beach is off Route 127A. Sandy barrier beach, concession, and bath house. Parking fee.

Half Moon Beach is at Stage Fort Park on Hough Avenue.

Niles Beach on Eastern Point Road is privately owned (leased to the city). Sandy shoreline with swimming and on-street parking for residents only. Use public trolley.

Pavilion Beach is at the easterly end of Stacy Boulevard inside the harbor. Sandy shore for swimming, public boat launching ramp, walkways, seawall, and on-street parking.

Wingaersheek Beach is off Route 128 (Concord Street exit) via Atlantic Street. Sandy beach and salt marsh with boating, restrooms, concession, and visitor center. Parking fee.

BICYCLES

Harborside Cycle, 48 Rogers Street. Sales, service, and rentals for all makes and models. Call 281-7744.

Joe's Bike Shop, 76 Rogers Street. Specializes in repairing and rebuilding bikes. Pick-up and delivery available. No rentals. Call 283-2552.

BOATING AND CRUISES

Essex River Basin Adventures, offers tours on a new Essex-built fishing schooner, *Thomas E. Lannon*, that sails out of Gloucester. View the working harbor, islands and lighthouses. For location and reservations call 768-3722.

Gloucester to Provincetown Boat Express, Rose's Wharf, 415 Main Street. Take a day cruise from Gloucester to Cape Cod and you're sure to see whales along the way. Spend four hours in Provincetown. For reservations call 283-5110.

Harbor Tours, Inc. is on Harbor Loop by the Coast Guard Station. Offers two tours: (1) A 1-hour Lobster Tour of the harbor on a lobster-style boat includes hauling traps, live demonstrations, and starts at noon daily, July–Aug. (2) A 2-hour Lighthouse Tour around Cape Ann to view six lighthouses starts at 2:30 p.m. daily, July–Aug. In May, June, and after Labor Day, these tours are on weekends only. Call 283-1979.

Kayak Cape Ann, 27 High Street. Specializes in scenic guided tours of Glouces-

ter Harbor, Ipswich Bay, and Norman's Woe. Lessons are given before each session. 4-hour, 6-hour, and overnight trips from novice to expert. Call 282-1370.

Moby Duck Amphibious Tours, 75 Essex Avenue. Take a narrated tour of Gloucester by-land-and-sea in a U.S.C.G.-certified amphibious vessel with panoramic views. Tickets and departure at Harbor Loop. Call 281-3825.

Sun Splash Boat Rental, 233 E. Main Street. Power or sail boat rentals for fishing, exploring, diving, or just relaxing. Call 283-4722.

BOWLING

Cape Ann Bowling Center, 53 Gloucester Avenue. Twenty candlepin lanes available. Open Monday–Saturday from 9 a.m. to 11 p.m. and Sunday noon–11 p.m. Call 283-9753.

CINEMA

Gloucester Cinema, 74 Essex Avenue. Three theaters with daily shows at a great price. For a current schedule call 283-9188.

DEEP SEA FISHING

Capt. Bill and Son's, Star Fisheries at Harbor Loop. Comfortable ships, courteous and knowledgeable crews; night fishing trips available. Reservations suggested; call 283-6995.

Capt. Tom Lukes Shark Safaris, Star Fisheries at Harbor Loop. Their modern fishing vessel, *Nicole Renee*, will show you whales and seabirds in their natural habitat. Call 281-5411.

Yankee Fleet, 75 Essex Avenue. Winner of 16 Massachusetts fishing derby awards and 3 international fish and game world records. Full-and half-day trips. Reservations suggested, Call 283-0313.

FISHBOX DERBY RACE

This race is held in September and is sponsored by a non-profit organization to provide local youth with an opportunity to strengthen family relationships. Boys and girls aged eight to fourteen may enter, and parents or neighbors can help build the cars. Cars are entered in one of two categories: "free-style" or "modified." All

of the great prizes are contributed by local businesses. All donations cover the race-related expenses and the balance is placed in a scholarship fund for the young participants who are eligible to apply. For more information or to help on a committee, write to Fishbox Derby Inc., PO Box 1752, Gloucester, MA 01930 or call 283-6853.

FITNESS CENTERS

Cape Ann YMCA, 71 Middle Street. Nautilus and free-weights, indoor pool, basketball and racquetball courts. Winter hours are: Mon.–Fri., 5:30 a.m. to 9:30 p.m.; Sat., 8 a.m. to 5:30 p.m.; and Sun., 8 a.m. to 3 p.m. For all programs and summer hours, call 283-0470.

The Fitness Zone, 37 Blackburn Industrial Park. Free-weights and cardiovascular equipment available. Open all year

Fishbox Derby Race   *(Courtesy of Dan Conrad)*

Mon.–Fri., 5 a.m. to 9:30 p.m.; Sat., 7 a.m. to 6 p.m.; Sun., 8 a.m. to 5 p.m. Call 281-5761.

MARINAS

Bickford Marina, Inc., 31 Rocky Neck Avenue. Call 283-0404.

Brown's Yacht Yard, rear 139 E. Main Street. Full service yard, gas and diesel fuel, complete engine service, seasonal dockage, transient dockage and moorings, and marine supplies. Call 281-3200.

Cape Ann Marina, 75 Essex Avenue. Over 100 boat slips, a full-time dockmaster, the highest quality marine fuels, and a fully-stocked marine store and shop. Call 283-2112.

Gloucester Marina, 30 Marsh Street. Ramps and boat docks, summer slip rental, winter storage; mechanics can repair any outboard motor. Call 283-2828.

OPEN SPACE, PARKS, AND PLAYGROUNDS

Bass Rocks is on Atlantic Road in East Gloucester. This is a scenic drive with several roadside pull-offs and views of the rocky coastline, surf, and Thacher Island with the "Twin Lights" lighthouses.

Benjamin Smith Playground is located on Main Street, East Gloucester. Free parking.

Cripple Cove Landing is a small park and boat landing area adjacent to Benjamin Smith playground. Pier, picnic tables, and free parking.

Eastern Point Wildlife Sanctuary is a property of the Massachusetts Audubon Society. Take Eastern Point Road to this rocky shoreline with a salt marsh and wooded area. Audubon members only.

Fitz Hugh Lane House is off Rogers Street in downtown Gloucester. A small park with benches and harbor views.

Flat (Wonson) Cove Landing is near Rocky Neck Park and Landing. A boat landing area on a sandy beach and mud flats with street parking only.

Fresh Water Cove Landing is off Western Avenue (Route 127) on Dolliver Neck. A rocky shore with a boat landing and fishing spot; street parking only.

Gloucester Landing and boardwalk is about two blocks away from Gus Foote Park.

Gordon Thomas Park is on Rogers Street with benches and harbor views.

Gus Foote Park is a very small park on Rogers Street.

Parks at Fort Point can be reached by taking Commercial Street out to "the Fort." This park has a scenic harbor view, playground, basketball court, tot lot, and benches.

Rocky Neck Park and Landing is reached by taking Main Street toward

Eastern Point. This is a rocky shore with a scenic view and free parking. Walk to Rocky Neck shops, restaurants, and art galleries.

St. Peter's Park (includes Samuel Gilbert Landing) is located on Rogers Street. A wharf, ramp, float, and slips for lobster boats. Free parking with a short walk to nearby restaurants and downtown shopping and sightseeing.

Solomon Jacobs Park is off Harbor Loop. A harborfront park and commemorative plaque.

OPEN SPACE, PARKS, AND PLAYGROUNDS IN NORTH GLOUCESTER

Brown's Mill Landing is located off Washington Street near Reynard Street. A park, plaza, and area for boat landing and swimming (high tide only); extensive mud flats at low tide. Free parking.

Corliss Landing is reached by taking Wheeler Street to Corliss Street to reach this small beach and boat landing area along a rocky shore with picnic tables and free parking.

Folly Cove Landing is off Washington Street (Route 127). This is a rocky shore and boat landing located on the town line of Rockport and Gloucester. Limited parking.

Goose Cove (a property of Essex County Greenbelt) is reached by taking Washington Street (Route 127). This rocky shore and salt marsh area is a great place to hike and study nature. Free parking for several cars.

Green Landing (site of original Meetinghouse Green) is adjacent to Route 128 near the Grant Rotary. This is a salt marsh and small grassy area with access on foot to water beside monument with plaque. Usable for small boats at high tide only. Parking nearby.

Head of Lobster Cove Landing is reached by taking Washington Street (Route 127). A rocky shore and boat landing area with a seawall, pier, and grassy field; on-street parking.

Hodgkins Cove Landing is reached by taking Washington Street (Route 127). Located near the UMass Marine Station. A rocky shore for swimming and fishing with a boat landing area near a small basin. Free parking.

Lane's Cove Landing is reached by taking Washington Street (Route 127). A protected boat basin with mud flats at low tide; marina, pier, ramps, sheds, and storage facilities. Free parking.

Long Wharf Landing is reached from the Concord Street exit off Route 128. Take Atlantic Street to reach this pier, plaza, rocky shore, and salt marsh area for swimming, fishing, and boating. Free parking.

Ralph O'Maley Middle School in the Riverdale section of Gloucester. A park with some salt marsh areas, a playground, and sports fields. Free parking.

Stoney Cove Reservation (a property of Essex County Greenbelt) is adjacent to Route 128N before the exit for Crafts Road. This historic spot is a rocky shore and salt marsh area for hiking. Free parking.

West Landing is reached by taking Wheeler Street to this rocky shore and breakwater, fishing pier and boat landing area. On-street parking.

SCUBA DIVING/RENTALS

Cape Ann Divers, 127 Eastern Avenue. Suits, masks, fins, and state-of-the-art diving equipment, for snorkeling or more serious divers. Call 281-8082.

WHALES

From all over the world people are coming to Cape Ann to see the whales. You are 99.9% guaranteed to see whales or the next trip is free. From May to October vessels leave Gloucester harbor for Stellwagen Bank and/or Jeffreys Ledge; but the prime time for whale watching is July through mid-September. The only way to appreciate these magnificent giants erupting from the ocean is by experiencing it yourself. So, bring your camera, a jacket, sunglasses, and wear rubber-soled shoes and you will hear, "Thar she blows!"

Besides the most commonly seen whale species, humpback, fin, and minke whales, you are apt to see Atlantic white-

"Thar she blows!" *(Courtesy of Seven Seas Whale Watch)*

sided dolphins, harbor porpoises, harbor seals, an occasional pilot, blue, or sperm whale, basking sharks, and ocean sunfish. The reason there are so many whales in these waters is that southeast of Cape Ann is Stellwagen Bank, and to the north is Jeffreys Ledge. The ocean currents sweep up against the rim of these plateaus and contain the primary food sources for the whales: krill (a small, shrimp-like crustacean found abundantly in cool and cold waters; also an important food for other marine animals and birds); plankton (a vast and abundant supply of tiny plants and animals found at or near the ocean's surface; the base of the ocean's food chains); the small schooling fish known as the sand lance; mackerel; and herring.

The humpback whale is the focal whale for Cape Ann research organizations. It is the most acrobatic and slow moving and therefore the easiest one to study. The fin whale (second-largest of all whales and the largest one found here) is called the "greyhound" of whales because it is fast moving and comes to the surface only for brief spurts. The minke whale is the smallest of the baleen whales and gives off no spout. It is most like a dolphin when it surfaces. Humpback whales are about 45–50 feet long and weigh an average of 30 tons; females are larger than males. During the winter months they travel south to warmer waters where they mate and give birth to their young. Whales are warm-blooded mammals, not fish, and the calf is nourished by its mother's milk for about a year. The calf comes north with the mother at about three or four months of age and stays with her until (and sometimes through) the migration south again. Whales travel in small groups and remain together for hours or days, but do not remain together in "families."

Humpbacks can remain under water for forty-five minutes and will dive to depths of 600–800 feet. Since Stellwagen Bank is only 100–150 feet below the ocean surface, a humpback whale is only a short distance under water; this helps to make this shallow area ideal for watching them. Here in the colder waters off Cape Ann, whales communicate by clicking, burping, chirping, and moaning under water. When they surface they "blow," or exhale the warm air from their lungs before taking in the fresh, cool air. Today there are about 10,000–20,000 humpback whales, 50,000–70,000 fin whales, and over one million minke whales worldwide.

Researchers continue to study the behavior of whales; there is still much we don't know. People have become more environmentally conscious about the oceans as home to many creatures of the sea. If you would like to receive whale research information, adopt-a-whale, purchase photographs, and/or receive teaching materials for the classroom, speak with the naturalist aboard your whale-watch vessel or contact the Cetacean Research Unit, P.O. Box 159, Gloucester, MA 01930, or call 281-6351.

WHALE WATCHING EXCURSIONS

Cape Ann Whale Watch, Rose's Wharf at 415 Main Street. See the largest creatures on earth with the world's leading research team, the Whale Conservation Institute. Call 283-5110.

Capt. Bill and Sons, Star Fisheries on Harbor Loop. Capt. Bill's boasts the best whale-sighting record over the past 18 years. You're assured of seeing whales and dolphins. Call 283-6995.

Nantucket Whale Watch, 100-ft. vessel with basic accomodations for up to 50 passengers. Leaves 75 Essex Avenue on Monday at 9:30 p.m., arrives at Straight Wharf in downtown Nantucket early in the a.m. Spend the day on Nantucket and return via sunset cruise at 7:30 p.m. arriving back in Gloucester early the next a.m. Call 800-942-9464.

Seven Seas Whale Watch at Seven Seas Wharf on Rogers Street. Take a four-hour adventure to observe the most beautiful creatures on earth in their natural habitat. Open May 1 to mid-Oct. Trips leave at 8:30 a.m. and 1:30 p.m. daily. For reservations call 283-1776.

Yankee Fleet at 75 Essex Avenue has conducted marine recreational trips for the past 50 years. For reservations and information call 283-0313.

Lodging

Prices were verified at time of publication; for the most current information, contact the lodging places directly. When you arrive in Gloucester go to the Visitors' Welcoming Center at Stage Fort Park on Hough Avenue. The center is open from May to October.

Anchorage Motor Inn, 5–7 Hawthorne Lane (E. Gloucester). 14 rooms overlook the harbor; walk to beach. Complimentary continental breakfast. $60–$95 (efficiency w/full kitchen). Call 283-4788.

Atlantis Oceanfront Motor Inn, 125 Atlantic Road (E. Gloucester). Rooms have magnificent ocean views; no-smoking rooms available. Heated pool; oceanfront breakfast restaurant. Call 283-0014 or 283-5807.

Back Shore Motor Lodge, 85 Atlantic Road (E. Gloucester). Scenic views of Twin Lights on Thacher Island; small restaurant on premises. Open year-round. Call 283-1198.

Bass Rocks Ocean Inn, 107 Atlantic Road (E. Gloucester). Oceanfront mansion listed in National Registry of Historic Places. Rooms with 19th-century antiques, complimentary breakfast buffet, wide-screen TV, billiards, and heated pool. 48 large guest rooms with cable TV, private baths, patios and balconies. Call 283-7600.

Blue Shutters Inn, 1 Nautilus Road (E. Gloucester) directly across from beautiful Good Harbor Beach. Spectacular views. Open year-round. Call 281-2706.

Cape Ann Marina Resort, 75 Essex Avenue (Route 133). Five-Star All Season Resort. 53 attractively furnished waterview rooms with large windows and private balconies, color TV, pool, restaurant, game room, conference facilities, and a whale watch "at your door." Call 283-2112 or 800-626-7660.

Cape Ann Motor Inn, 33 Rockport Road directly on Long Beach. Rooms have balconies; some efficiencies. Room rates vary according to season from, $54 to $98. Open year-round. Call 281-2900, or 800-GO 4-VIEW.

Captains Lodge Motel, 237 Eastern Avenue. 47 large rooms with cathedral ceilings. Low weekly or monthly rates; telephones, color TV, pool, and tennis. Coffee shop for breakfast, lunch, and snacks. Call 281-2420.

The Colonial Motor Inn, 28 Eastern Point Road (E. Gloucester). All rooms have private baths and TV; continental breakfast. Beach nearby; walk to Rocky Neck Art Colony. $45–$60. Open year-round. Call 281-1953.

Fairview Inn, 52 Eastern Point Road (E. Gloucester). Quiet, comfortable, reasonable prices; family-owned and operated for five generations. The "grand dame of Gloucester's tourist colony, graciously welcoming summer guests since 1842." Authors Louisa May Alcott and Rudyard Kipling summered here. Nestled away from the road; a short walk to Niles Beach and Rocky Neck Art colony and restaurants. Call 281-1758.

Good Harbor Beach Inn, 1 Salt Island Road (directly on Good Harbor Beach). Family-style accommodations, color and cable TV, private baths; rooms have balconies or patios. Open April–Oct. Call 283-1489.

Gray Manor Guest House, 14 Atlantic Road (E. Gloucester). Brief walk to Good Harbor Beach. Rooms with private baths and some with private decks; color TV, coffee in the morning, picnic tables, outdoor grills. 3-night minimum stay in season. Room rates vary according to season from $42–$55 to $57–$62; efficiencies $425 per week. Call 283-5409.

Harborview Inn, 71 Western Avenue. Decorated by *Better Homes & Gardens*. Directly across the street from America's oldest scenic harbor. Rates are $79–$139 and include continental breakfast; beach discount passes available. Call 283-2277 or 800-299-6696.

Manor Inn, 141 Essex Avenue. A 20-room Victorian style house and a 16-unit motel. Peaceful setting; many rooms overlook the Annisquam River. Generous complimentary breakfast. Rates from $39–$100 depending on season. Open May–Oct. Call 283-0614.

Ocean View Inn, 171 Atlantic Road (E. Gloucester). Resort and conference center, located on the "Back Shore." Beautifully landscaped grounds. 70 large rooms; restaurant for breakfast, lunch, dinner; two swimming pools; packages from $69. Open year-round. Call 283-6200, or 800-315-7557.

The Samarkand Inn, 1 Harbor Road (across from Good Harbor Beach). Moderate rates in and out of season; complimentary light breakfast. Open year-round. Call 283-3757.

Sea Lion Motel, 138 Eastern Avenue. Motel and furnished cottages. Lovely view and well-kept grounds; private and relaxing. Heated pool and shuffleboard; walk or drive to beautiful Good Harbor Beach. Call 283-7300.

Tara Guest House, 13–19 Shore Road (Magnolia). Cozy 1886 house with ocean views. Full breakfasts; menu varies daily. $70 double, $50 single. Open year-round. Call 525-3213.

Vista Motel, 22 Thatcher Road (E. Gloucester). Located on a knoll overlooking Good Harbor Beach, marshes, and Twin Lights. Modern accommodations; suites and efficiencies available; heated pool; nominal charge for continental breakfast. Open year-round. Call 281-3410.

Wentworth House, 107 Bass Avenue (E. Gloucester). Cozy rooms, moderate prices. Close to Good Harbor Beach; complimentary light breakfast. Open April–Nov. Call 283-3989.

The White House, 18 Norman Avenue (Magnolia). Conveniently located off Route 127. Large (no-smoking) rooms with baths; most have porches or balconies. Complimentary continental breakfast. Short walk to private beach. Open year-round. Call 525-3642.

Williams Guest House, 136 Bass Avenue (E. Gloucester). Across the dunes from Good Harbor Beach, surrounded by tidal water and salt marsh. Guest rooms from $42–$47 off-season and $62 in season for double; apartments with double bed $450–$500 per week; small cottage is $500 per week; apartments $64–$67 per night. Complimentary light breakfast. Call 283-4931.

Wingaersheek Motel, 46 Concord Street (W. Gloucester). Route 128 to Concord Street exit. Clean, comfortable, and attractive rooms; cable color TV; some units have kitchenettes. Family-oriented accommodations, moderately priced. Guest permits to Wingaersheek Beach; pets welcome. Open year-round. Call 281-0100.

CAMPGROUNDS

Camp Annisquam Campground, Stanwood Point (W. Gloucester). Route 128, take Exit 14, turn right on 133, go 1¼ miles, turn left on Stanwood Avenue and go over RR Crossing. Olympic pool, recreation room, boats, fishing, showers, picnic tables, electricity and water for R.V.'s. Rustic rooms and cottages also available. Call 283-2992.

Cape Ann Camp Site, 80 Atlantic Street (W. Gloucester). Take Exit 13 off Route 128, go northeast on Concord Street, and turn right onto Atlantic Street. Located on 100 acres of woodlands overlooking salt water inlets. One mile to Wingaersheek Beach. 300 trailer and tent sites. Open May 1–Oct. Call 283-8683.

Massachusetts Camp Grounds Directory. Call 617–727-3200.

 Restaurants

Amelia's, 2 Thatcher Road. Open year-round for lunch and dinner. Fresh seafood, soups & chowders made daily, home-made Italian food, take-out or eat in. Call 281-8855.

Bass Rocks Ocean Inn, 107 Atlantic Avenue (E. Gloucester). Fine New England dining, breakfast, lunch, and dinner. Call 283-7600.

Bistro at 2 Main, 2 Main Street. Open for dinner at 5:30 p.m. Closed Mondays. Creative contemporary cuisine. Call 281-8055.

Boulevard Ocean View Restaurant, 25 Western Avenue. Portuguese entrees: Paella a Valenciana, Mariscada, Carne de Porco Alentegana, and beer and wine. Call 281-2949.

Cameron's Restaurant, 206 Main Street. Open year-round for lunch and dinner; breakfast on Saturdays and breakfast buffet on Sundays. Lounge entertainment Thursday–Saturday; function room, catering. Call 281-1331.

Captain Carlo's Seafood, Harbor Loop. Fresh fish market and indoor/outdoor dining in the rough on the working waterfront. Seafood and lobsters. Call 283-6342.

Captain Hook's Family Restaurant, 406 Washington Street (Riverdale). Open

Monday–Thursday, 10 a.m.–9 p.m.; Friday and Saturday, 10 a.m.–10 p.m.; Sunday, 10 a.m.–9 p.m. Seafood, subs, pizza, party platters; full liquor license. Call 282-HOOK.

Captain's Lodge Coffee Shop, 237 Eastern Avenue (Route 127). Open year-round. Breakfast and lunch Monday–Friday; breakfast only on weekends. Voted #1 breakfast restaurant on the North Shore third year in a row. Call 283-8022.

The Causeway Restaurant, 78 Essex Avenue. Open 6 days year-round for breakfast, lunch, and dinner; Sunday breakfast only and buffet from 7 a.m. to noon. Daily specials, seafood, and pastas. Call 281-5256.

Charlie's Place Restaurant, 83 Bass Avenue (E. Gloucester). Open year-round 6 days for breakfast, lunch, and dinner; Sunday closes at 3 p.m. Family-style fried and baked seafood specialties. Call 283-0303.

The Cupboard of Gloucester, Hough Avenue. Open April–Oct., daily 11 a.m.–9 p.m.; take-out or eat in. Nightly specials from hot dogs to prime rib. Call 281-1908.

Destino's Subs & Catering, 129 Prospect Street. Open year-round, daily from 6 a.m. to 10 p.m. Soup and salad bar with all eat-in submarine sandwiches. Lisa Joyce is a 2½ ft. sub. Call 283-3100.

Dockside Restaurant & Lounge, 77 Rocky Neck Avenue (Rocky Neck). Grilled seafood, pasta, and pizza at reasonable prices. Entertainment nightly, can accommodate yachts up to 120 ft.; overnight hook-ups available. Call 281-4554.

Jim's Bagel & Bake Shoppe, 24 Washington Street. Open at 5 a.m. All pastries baked on premises. Call 283-3383.

Dragon Light, 226 Washington Street. Open year-round, Mondays at 4 p.m., Tuesdays–Saturdays at 11:30 a.m., and Sundays at noon. Family-style Cantonese and Szechuan food. Call 281-1150.

Espresso Ristorante & Pizzeria, 151 Main Street. Open year-round, 11 a.m.–10 p.m. Italian dishes at their very best; fresh veal, shrimp, pizza, pasta; eat in or take-out. Will deliver hot food to your door. Large buffet menu for family or business affairs. To order call 283-0600 or 281-0500.

Evie's Rudder, 73 Rocky Neck Avenue (Rocky Neck). Open April–October. During June–Aug. open Monday–Friday at 4 p.m. and weekends at noon. North Shore's most unusual menu. Specialty is "Shrimp Farcis." Provide spontaneous entertainment; will do private parties. Call 283-7967.

Flav's Firehouse, 1072 Washington Street (Lanesville). Serves breakfast starting at 7 a.m. on weekends. Call 281-0903.

Glass Sail Boat Cafe, 3 Duncan Street. Open year-round from 7 a.m. to 4 p.m.; daily specials, sandwiches, soups, muffins, coffees. Also a specialty food market and store. Call 283-7830.

(Courtesy of Gloucester House Restaurant)

The Gloucester House, Rogers Street at Seven Seas Wharf. Open year-round at 11:30 a.m. Closed Thanksgiving and Christmas. Casual dining overlooking harbor and fishing fleet. Children's menu, health-conscious menu items, outdoor cafe. Call 283-1812.

Gloucester Ice Cream Co., 89 Bass Avenue (E. Gloucester). Open in season. Call 281-3099.

The Good Harbor Cafe, 127 Eastern Avenue. Open year-round. Lunch and dinner Monday–Friday, 11 a.m.–9 p.m. Breakfast, lunch, and dinner Saturday and Sunday, 8 a.m.–9 p.m. In summer breakfast, lunch, and dinner from 8 a.m. to 9 p.m. Home-made bread and hand-tossed pizza. Call 281-3777.

Grange Gourmet, 457 Washington Street (Riverdale). Open year-round 7 a.m.–7 p.m. on Monday–Saturday, and 7 a.m.–2 p.m. on Sunday. Food-to-go for beach or boat. Fresh home-made chowder and soups, fresh croissants, and gourmet coffees. In-season garden dining. Call 283-2639.

The Gull Restaurant, 75 Essex Street. Open in season for breakfast, lunch, and dinner; full liquor license. Freshest seafood and lobster with a water view. Call 283-6565.

Halibut Point Restaurant & Pub, 289 Main Street. Open year-round from 11:30 a.m. to 11 p.m. Excellent chowders and daily specials. Call 281-1900.

Harbor's Point Ice Cream, 29 Western Avenue. Open in season. Call 283-1789.

Holy Cow, 80 Pleasant Street. Open year-round, noon–11 p.m. in summer; closed on Tuesdays in winter. Mix your own penny candy; all kinds of frozen desserts, including a totally sugar-free hot fudge sundae. Call 283-6011.

Ice Cream Gallery, 39 Rocky Neck Avenue (Rocky Neck). Featuring "Junction Ice Cream." No phone; just stop by.

Il Porto, 40 Railroad Avenue. Open for dinner at 5 p.m. Fine northern Italian specialties in a relaxed atmosphere. Pastas, veal, seafood. For reservations call 283-9732.

Imperial Marina Restaurant, 17 Rogers Street. Open at noon. No lunch buffet on Sunday and no dinner buffet on Monday, full liquor license. Call 281-6573.

J.D. & Meyers Best Friends, 24 Lexington Avenue (Magnolia). Open year-round at 11:30 a.m. Lunch and dinner, fish, chicken, pasta, sandwiches, and chowders. Full liquor license; entertainment Wednesday–Saturday. A sports bar and restaurant. Call 525-2225.

Jade Restaurant, 242 Main Street. Open year-round for lunch and dinner at 11:30 a.m. Chinese and Czechuan food. Call 281-3262.

Jalapeno's Mexican Restaurant, 86 Main Street. Open at 11 a.m. Brunch on Sunday. Authentic regional Mexican menu; live entertainment in season, take-out available. Call 283-8228.

Lennie's Sub & Deli, 8 Railroad Avenue. Open at 10 a.m. year-round. Pizza, subs, dinners, seafood, and salads. Call 281-3575.

Leonardo's Pizzeria, 273 Main Street. Closed Sundays. Open at 11 a.m. all other days. Pizza and more, eat in and take out. Call 281-7882.

LobstaLand, Rt.128, Exit12, Crafts Road. Open for breakfast, lunch, and dinner. Fresh lobsters, seafood, great chef's specials; full liquor license. Call 281-0415.

Long Beach Dairymaid, 2 Thatcher Road. Open in season. Call 281-1348.

Magnolia Breakfast Nook, 16 Lexington Avenue (Magnolia). Open for breakfast only at 6 a.m. Has been in Magnolia forever! Call 525-3895.

Magnolia House of Pizza, 35 Fuller Street (Magnolia). Open year-round at 10 a.m. Best-quality, all fresh ingredients and home-made sauces on hand-made pizza, gourmet calzones. Meats roasted on premises, chicken piccata, shrimp scampi, and more. Call 525-3030.

Maria's Pizzas, 35 Pearl Street. Open year-round at 4 p.m. Pizza, seafood, and Italian dinners in a casual, family atmosphere; take-out or eat in. Call 283-7373.

McT's Lobster House & Tavern, 25 Rogers Street. Open for lunch and dinner year-round. Fresh seafood, ribs, steak, chicken, fantastic pastas, and a full liquor license. Dine on the largest deck overlooking the working waterfront. Call 282-0950.

Mike's Pastry & Coffee Shop, 37 Main Street. Open Tuesday–Saturday, 8 a.m.–4:30 p.m.; Sundays, 7:30 a.m.–noon. Closed Mondays. Super Italian strawberry shortcakes and rum cakes, plus lots of fresh Italian cookies and other pastries. Call 283-5333.

Milena's Submarine Sandwiches & Seafood, 324 Main Street. Eat in or take out; hot and cold sandwiches, seafood, homemade chowder, haddock sandwiches, shrimp subs, and hot chopped chicken chunks. Call 281-4212.

North Shore Whole Health Center & Cafe, 2 Lexington Avenue (Magnolia). Cafe open from 7 a.m. to 2 p.m. Full juice bar, light refreshments, sandwiches and soups. Whole Health Center programs from 7 p.m. to 9 p.m. and classes at various times throughout the day: stress reduction, yoga, tai chi, dance, holistic fitness. Call 525-4848.

The Ocean Edge Restaurant, 171 Atlantic Road (E. Gloucester). Open year-round at the Ocean View Inn. Breakfast, lunch, dinner. Fresh seafood our specialty. Elegant turn-of-the-century restaurant. Call 800-315-7557.

Passports, 110 Main Street. Open for lunch Monday–Saturday, 11:30 a.m.–2:30 p.m. Open for dinner at 5:30 p.m. International cuisine and catering. For reservations call 281-3680.

Patio Restaurant of Magnolia, 4 Lexington Avenue (Magnolia). Open for lunch 11:30 a.m.–5 p.m. on Monday–Friday. Dinner served daily; full liquor license, reasonable prices. Call 525-3230.

The Penalty Box, 427 Washington Street (Riverdale). Open at 6 a.m. year-round for breakfast and lunch. In summer serves food until 3 p.m., and 21 flavors of ice cream until 9 p.m. Call 282-4625.

The Pilot House, Corner Rogers and Porter Streets. Open 11 a.m.–10 p.m., Monday–Saturday; 4 p.m.–9 p.m. on Sundays. Barbecued meats on open flame; full lunch and dinner menu; daily specials, full liquor license. Call 283-0131.

Pond Road Cafe, 7 Pond Road. Open year-round, Monday–Saturday, 6 a.m.–2 p.m.; Sundays, 7 a.m.–1 p.m. Breakfast and lunch; reasonably priced good food. Call 281-3008.

Pronto Pizza, Pasta & Subs, 2 Highland Street. Open at 11 a.m. Monday–Saturday and at 4 on Sunday. Featuring fine Italian food and pizza, free delivery. Call 283-0900 or 283-4296.

Rhumb Line Restaurant, 40 Railroad Avenue. Open year-round at 11:30; brunch on Sundays. Casual dining, full liquor license, live musical entertainment every evening. Tuesday evening is fun night with seasonal prizes such as whale watch or ski lift tickets. Call 283-9732.

Sailor Stan's Drift-In, 24 Rocky Neck Avenue (Rocky Neck). Open April–Dec. at 7 a.m. Breakfast and lunch; good food at a good price. Call 281-4470.

The Savory Skillet, (in Brown's Mall) 186 Main Street. Open year-round, 7 a.m.–3 p.m. Breakfast and lunch; home-made soups and sandwiches, and daily specials; take-out or eat in. Call 281-4042.

Schooners, 50 Rogers Street. Fresh seafood, chicken, beef, pasta; affordably priced, casual atmosphere. Call 281-1962.

Sebastian Pizza, 56 Washington Street. Open daily year-round at 3:30 p.m. Hand-made, scrumptious pizzas. Call 283-4407.

Steve's Family Restaurant, 24 Railroad Avenue. Open daily year-round from 10 a.m.–11 p.m. Subs, calzones, seafood, steak, salads, and children's menu. Call 283-4227.

Studio Lounge & Deck, 51 Rocky Neck Avenue (Rocky Neck). Open daily from 11:30 a.m. On-the-water dining in Gloucester's historic seaside artist's community; outside dining and cabana bar; luncheon, dinner specials; entertainment nightly at piano bar. Call 283-4123.

Taormina Ristorante, 56 Raymond Street (Magnolia). Open daily at 5 p.m. year-round. Return to the basics with great food, freshest ingredients using authentic Italian recipes. Dining room with ambiance, old hand-hewn beams, fieldstone fireplace, and classic old-world Italian interior design. Perfect for special parties; handicap accessible. Call 525-4900.

Thyme's on the Square, 197 E. Main Street (E. Gloucester). In winter open at 5:30 p.m. Thursday–Saturday, and Sun-days for brunch 11 a.m.–2 p.m. Cozy atmosphere, sophisticated menu. For spring, summer, and fall hours, call 282-4426.

Two Sisters Coffee Shop, 27 Washington Street. Open year-round, daily 6 a.m.–1 p.m. Breakfast and daily home-cooked luncheon specials, different special each day. Weekends open from 6 a.m.–noon. Call 281-3378.

Valentino's Pizza Restaurant, 38 Main Street. Open at 11 a.m. daily. Voted best pizza, 1991–1995 by *North Shore Magazine*. We deliver: call 283-6186.

The White Rainbow, 65 Main Street. Closed Mondays. Open year-round, weekdays 5:30 p.m.–9:30 p.m., Saturdays 6 p.m.–10 p.m. Sunday brunch 11:30 a.m.–2:30 p.m. Fine dining, stuffed chicken breast with garlic and herb cheese, filet mignon, and more. Live entertainment on Thursday and Friday. For reservations call 281-0017.

Windjammer Restaurant, 116 E. Main Street (E. Gloucester). Open Monday–Thursday at 11:30. Friday and Saturday open until 11 p.m.; Sunday brunch. Closed Christmas. Casual dress, children's menu; cozy family dining with nautical decor. Call 281-7212.

The Yellow Sub Shop, 71 Pleasant Street. Open Monday–Saturday 7 a.m.–10 p.m. Closed Sundays. Hot and cold subs, soups and chowder, salads, and mini subs perfect for the small appetite; take-out or eat in. Call 281-2217.

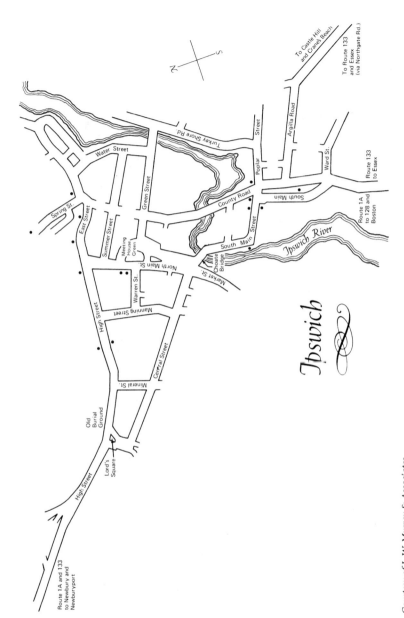

Ipswich

Courtesy of J. W. Murray & Associates

Whipple House   *Courtesy of Nancy Marculewicz*

Ipswich

THE HISTORY OF IPSWICH

Artifacts found at Bull Brook during the last century prove that Palaeo Indians lived in Ipswich as early as 8500 B.C. These nomadic people would come here during the warmer months to hunt, fish, dig clams, and gather wild plants and berries. The land, rivers, and ocean provided this native population with everything they needed, and millennia later Indians were still making use of this bountiful land.

By the time the Europeans came in the early 1600s, the Indians called the area Agawam. The Indians cultivated the land, grew corn and potatoes, and used fish for fertilizer. The Indians hunted deer and other smaller animals for food and clothing. They built temporary homes with hay from the salt marshes and used pine and spruce to make tools and canoes. The Agawams shared their skills with the early settlers, saving them from starvation. Today arrowheads and other hand-chiseled relics are still being unearthed in residents' backyards.

Around 1606 King James granted a Virginia trading company a charter to colonize this land. When Captain Edward Hardie visited Agawam in 1611, he found the Agawam tribe to be very friendly. English trading companies would often stop to fish along the coast and to trade with the Indians, but by 1616 several European diseases had killed about 80 percent of the native population.

When Captain John Smith came to this territory in 1614 he reported a problem that would affect the economy for the next two hundred years: the land had great potential, but the sandbars at the harbor's entrance would keep Agawam from becoming a port city. The need for farmland in the 1630s led William Wood to observe this area favorably. He wrote, "Agowamme is nine miles to the north from Salem, which is one of the most spacious places for a plantation, being near the sea, it aboundeth with fish, and flesh of fowls and beasts, great Meads and Marshes and plaine plowing grounds, many good rivers, and harbours and no rattle snakes." In March 1633 John Winthrop, Jr., son of Governor Winthrop, started a permanent settlement in Agawam with twelve men. A year later, on August 4, 1634, the name was changed to Ipswich, in honor of a famous English port. Ipswich was settled just three years after Boston, making it one of the oldest towns in Massachusetts. Winthrop paid Chief Masconomet 20 pounds for the land, which included the current towns of Hamilton, Essex, Topsfield, Boxford, Middleton, Georgetown, Groveland, and Haverhill.

Many remarkable colonists lived in Ipswich at this time. Winthrop's neighbors included two governors, Thomas Dudley and Simon Bradstreet, one deputy-governor, Samuel Symonds, and one magistrate, Richard Saltonstall. Anne Bradstreet, Simon's wife, was America's first poet. Daniel Denison, whose wife Patience was Anne's sister, became the commander-in-chief of the colonies during King Philip's War. Nathaniel Ward, the first of America's scholarly ministers, lived in Ipswich. He was a preacher, poet, and the lawmaker who wrote the colony's first code of fundamental laws, called the Body of Liberties.

The town was a place of political importance during these early years. One of the Massachusetts Bay Colony's four courts was held in Ipswich, and a school was voted into being as early as 1642.

By 1646 the town population had grown to 800 and included 146 families. Every year ships brought more immigrants to this area, and the pressure to find good farmland steadily increased. The rocky soil made plowing difficult. As large stones were arduously dug up, they were used to set property boundaries, thus producing a complex network of rock walls, many of which still stand throughout Cape Ann. As the town grew, more wealthy colonists ventured to buy land out of Boston and built homes in towns such as Ipswich.

Ipswich could not escape the impact of the Salem Witch Trials. In 1689 the ministers of Ipswich spoke out against accusations of witchcraft, but it was not enough. Some of the accused were jailed in Ipswich, near the Meetinghouse Green. Among these was Giles Corey, who was crushed to death by heavy stones which were placed on him for refusing to admit to practicing witchcraft. In 1692 Elizabeth How of the Linebrook Parish was found guilty of witchcraft and was hung on Gallows Hill in Salem. John Proctor, who had lived in Ipswich and then moved to Salem Village, was also found guilty of witchcraft and was hung, despite the petition sent in by 32 of his Ipswich neighbors. Sadly, many of the accused and killed were later pardoned and damages were paid to their families. _The Crucible_, a play by Arthur Miller, was made into a motion picture telling about these events and was filmed in Ipswich in 1995.

The town's influence and prosperity continued until the late 1700s. A town wharf was built and salt hay was exported. Fishing and lumbering took the place of hunting and trapping, and shipbuilding began to grow as an industry. Now the Massachusetts Bay Colony, including Ipswich, became rich through trading with Europe, and the government of the colony, namely England, was very concerned that it was not getting its share of the wealth. So England imposed regulations on commerce and increased taxes. In 1686, the appointed Royal Governor, Sir Edmund Andros, imposed a royal tax to be collected in every town. The colony and notably Ipswich did not passively accept this.

In 1687, the citizens of Ipswich, led by Reverend John Wise, denounced the new levy of taxes and refused to submit to taxation without representation (see **History of Essex** section). Since Ipswich was the first town to publicly stand against English authority, the town seal reads, "Ipswich, the Birthplace of American Independence."

In 1766 the town's representative in the colonial legislature was fired because he failed to vote in a way that expressed the anger of citizens who voted in town meetings. In September of 1774, during the Ipswich Convention, delegates from 67 towns unanimously decided to stand together against England in a war for independence. By April 1775, Ipswich Minutemen were marching toward Lexington and Concord. The American Revolution had begun.

The first Ipswich soldier to lose his life in the war was Jesse Story, Jr., who was killed at the Battle of Bunker Hill in 1775. Ipswich men continued to fight until the end of the war. They were even present at the battles of Ticonderoga and Saratoga in New York. Although the colonies did not win their independence until six years later, Saratoga was an important victory.

Eight years of war proved a hardship on the Ipswich economy. With most of the men away, farms went under and the fishing and shipping markets were lost. The town owed a huge debt, and there were problems created by the changeover to the new American money system. More losses came. A large percentage of Ipswich revenue was lost to the creation of new towns: in 1792, the Hamlet parish separated and became the town of Hamilton, taking away many of the richest farms, and in 1819 the Chebacco Parish divided from Ipswich and became the town of Essex, taking with it most of the town's shipbuilding industry.

This poor post-war economy and the construction of Route 1 are the two main reasons for the survival of so many old houses in Ipswich. The sandbar at the mouth of the Ipswich River kept the town from becoming a major port city like Boston, Salem, and Newburyport, all of which have deep harbors. With the construction in 1803 of the Newburyport Turnpike (Route 1), all overland communication between Boston and important cities to the north (such as Newburyport and Portsmouth, New Hampshire, as well as Portland, Maine) now ceased to flow through Ipswich. Families were faced with economic hardships and could not afford to modernize their houses. Instead they made repairs to existing homes, and this small town became a museum for 17th-century architecture.

After the war, one of the few industries still left in Ipswich was lace making. The first U.S. census in 1790 recorded that Ipswich produced almost 42,000 yards of pillow lace the previous year. This number was so large that the federal government sent a letter back assuming a clerical error had been made, but upon recount the report was verified. About 600 men, women, and children worked at home to manufacture the handmade lace, and it became known as a "cottage industry." From the 1790s to the mid-1830s, Ipswich was the only place in America to commercially manufacture lace, and it remained a steady supplier of lace up to the Industrial Revolution. But by the 1820s, even that industry was failing and the population had dropped to half of what it had been thirty years before. (Visit the Whipple House Museum to view the only collection of handmade American lace in the country.)

The handmade lace industry came to a halt when, in 1822, two men appeared with a frame knitting machine they had smuggled out of England. This machine led to the 1824 incorporation of the Ipswich Lace Factory. By taking advantage of the water power created by damming the Ipswich River, the hosiery mills in Ipswich started to flourish in the mid-1800s. In 1868, Ipswich Mills incorporated and began to produce stockings that developed into Ipswich's single major industry for the next seventy years. The Ipswich Mills became the largest hosiery factory in the nation until it closed in 1928.

During the late 1800s, many immigrants were brought to Ipswich to work in the mills. First came the Canadians from Quebec and Nova Scotia. Then, when they no longer wanted to work in the factories, the mills brought in Greeks, who were followed by the Polish. With new people came a new influence to this largely Protestant town, the Catholic Church.

When the mills finally closed, the newcomers remained. The church was very important to the new immigrants and helped them keep their customs and native languages alive. Each group had its own church: the French Canadians had St. Stanislaus'; the Irish and English-speaking Catholics had St. Joseph's; the Greeks had the Church of the Assumption of the Virgin Mary; and the Polish had Sacred Heart Church. Each was a living memory of the world they had left behind.

Prohibition came to Ipswich in January 1920. The *Ipswich Chronicle* reported that the new law would be enforced by the local authorities. Thus began thirteen years of rum-running and bootlegging that certainly kept plenty of alcohol coursing through local veins. Ships large and small anchored in a strip called Rum Row, which stretched from Thacher's Island off Rockport to Cape Cod. Most of the ships came from the maritime provinces of Canada. During the summer smaller vessels would go out to the ships and pick up the illegal liquor. In winter small cottages on Little Neck, Eagle Hill, and Grape Island were used to store incoming cargo.

Because of its beaches, wharves, and hidden creeks, the coast of Ipswich and Cape Ann was an easy place to unload liquor without attracting undue attention. One of the most favored spots was Gould's Creek Bridge. When the tide was right, rum runners could sail right in and unload directly onto waiting trucks. Many trucks could be heard rumbling down Labor-in-Vain Road at all hours of the night. Others would use the Town Wharf. One night bootleggers set ablaze an ice house on Cavelly's Lane. While the police and fire departments were busy with the fire, smugglers unloaded the ship.

During this time there were many raids on Ipswich properties. Johnny Post's place on Grape Island was raided and the Coast Guard found over 1,000 gallons of contraband. The Bull Brook Farm was raided and the police found a 150-gallon still, 50 gallons of distilled spirits, and 1,700 gallons of sour mash. One time a large vessel with a $175,000 cargo ran aground on Treadwell Island and the crew buried the liquor in the surrounding flats. Clammers and other townspeople spent the next two weeks digging up cases of scotch and champagne. A thriving industry came to an end when prohibition was repealed in 1933.

PLACES OF INTEREST

Ipswich has more 17th-century houses than any other American community, and portions of the two original town greens still remain. Over forty houses built before 1725 are still lived in, making this community an invaluable treasury of early American history. Guided walking tours are available for the historic homes found mostly on High Street and throughout town. The following places of interest are not in alphabetical order but have been listed in the order in which you will find them if you want to take a self-guided tour. Note the small white wooden plaques on the historic homes which indicate the original owners' names and dates. For more information about Ipswich, stop by the Ipswich Visitor Information Center in the Hall-Haskell House or the Ipswich Public Library.

The Whipple House Museum is at 1 South Village Green. Around 1655 John Whipple, a Deputy to the General Court, built a two-and-a-half story, two-room house with a large hall at the corner of Market and Saltonstall Streets. In 1670 his son, Captain John, added the east half, which was even larger—an uncommon practice at this time. (Usually additions were smaller than the original structure.) Around 1700 his children added a lean-to off the back of the house. For over 200 years the Whipple family owned this house, but now it is the headquarters of the Ipswich Historical Society. To preserve the house it was necessary to move it to its present location.

The Whipple House has some features common to late 15th-century English homes, such as casement windows and a steep-pitch roof. It also has 17th-century American architectural characteristics, such as clay-and brick-filled walls, pine paneling with shadow molding, heavy chamfered oak and tamarack beams, gunstock posts, and enormous fireplaces. The house contains many significant domestic objects from Ipswich's colonial period, including textiles, porcelain, and glass. The Whipple House also has the only collection of American handmade lace in the country. New England landscape architect Arthur Shurcliffe designed the typical 17th-century herb garden found in front of the house, and author Ann Leighton planted the many types of flowers and herbs found there. The museum is open May–October 15, Wednesday–Sunday, from 10 to 4; admission is charged. Call 356-2811.

South Village Green is located across from the Whipple House. This green was used as a training ground for town militia in the 17th and 18th centuries. On September 15,

1775, two notorious characters from American history, Benedict Arnold and Aaron Burr, marched past this spot on their way to Quebec to fight the French. Today the green is still surrounded by houses which depict several styles of early American architecture. The old South Cemetery lies adjacent to the green.

The Swasey Tavern is a private residence at 2 Poplar Street. The tavern, which is across from the northeast corner of the South Green, was built in the early 1700s. Increase How was the first to use the house as a tavern, and it stayed a popular inn for many years. In 1789 George Washington visited here and had a drink with Ipswich resident, Major Joseph Swasey, who had served with honor in the Revolutionary War.

The Heard House Museum is at 54 South Main Street. In 1795 a wealthy merchant, John Heard, built this Federal-style house. His family owned the house until 1936, when it was bought by the Ipswich Historical Society. Notable features include the Palladian window over the entrance and the Chippendale-style staircase inside the hall. Many Oriental treasures brought to America during the China Trade era are among its furnishings. These include inlaid and carved teak chests and cabinets, Japanese prints and scrimshaw, and Chinese garden seats. On the third floor is a collection of Native American relics, seafaring memorabilia, and children's toys. A notable collection of paintings by Arthur Wesley Dow is on display. In the carriage shed is an excellent collection of 19th-century horse-drawn carriages. The museum is open May–October 15, Wednesday–Sunday, from 10 to 4; admission is charged. Call 356-2641.

The Hall-Haskell House is at 36 South Main Street. In 1819 Mary Hall acquired the property and present house and lived above the general store she ran on the first floor. In 1825 the Haskells bought the property and later sold it to Abraham Caldwell, a well-known cabinet maker. He changed the roof line of the house from gambrel to its present pitch, but the house still retained its wide floor boards and Indian shutters. In 1864 John Heard purchased the house and it remained in his family for many years until the town bought it. It is also called the "Little Red House." Today it is used as the Ipswich Visitor Information Center and an art gallery for local artists from mid-May to mid-October. It also houses the Essex Trail Visitor Center, which is part of the National Park Service. Call 356-8540.

The Ipswich Town Hall is at 30 South Main Street. Originally a Unitarian church built in 1833, this building became the Town Hall in 1843. During the Civil War, the building was enlarged and the original building was lifted to add a new ground floor. The belfry was removed and the bell given to the Greek Orthodox Church. The pews were taken out and donated to the Linebrook Baptist Church.

Choate Bridge is on South Main Street. Built to span the Ipswich River, this is the oldest continuously used stone-arch bridge in America. In 1764 John Choate, Ipswich resident and county treasurer, was commissioned to supervise its construction. Fearful of his decision to use stone, many were sure it would collapse. As a test, Choate sat on his horse on the bridge as the supports were taken away; the bridge did not collapse. In fact it is still heavily in use almost 250 years later.

Meetinghouse Green is on North Main Street in front of the First Church of Ipswich. Over 300 years ago on this site stood the first meetinghouse. Since then, there have been five different meetinghouses; the last was destroyed by fire in 1965. On this green the early settlers built a watch tower to guard against possible Indian attacks. The county jail with its whipping post and stocks were nearby, and during the Salem Witch Trials some of the accused were imprisoned here. The Meetinghouse Green was also where Ipswich citizens, under the leadership of Rev. John Wise, refused to pay taxes to England. An historic plaque marks the spot.

Rev. George Whitefield, the famous British evangelist, preached on this green in the mid-1700s. He was a central figure in the Great Awakening, a religious revival that challenged secularism and false theology. According to legend, the devil was troubled by the success of the revival and showed up to hear the reverend preach. As Whitefield spoke to over one thousand people, Satan sat in the belfry to listen. He was so infuriated with the sermon that he leaped off his seat and fell to the ground, leaving a cloven hoofprint that can be seen in a rock in front of the site where the present church stands. Another legend has it that Satan was chased up the steeple and then sent running down the hill by this fiery preacher.

The Ipswich Public Library is at 25 North Main Street. In 1868, Augustine Heard, a local resident and a successful China trade merchant, established and endowed a Free Public Library. Daniel Treadwell, another resident and a professor at Harvard University, also donated funds and books. The library has an excellent collection of reference materials relating to local history as well as genealogical records. Call 356-6648.

Winter Schedule: Mon.–Thurs., 10–8; Fri., 10–5:30; Sat., 9–4.

Summer Schedule: Mon. and Weds., 9–8; Tues., Thurs., and Fri., 9–5; closed Sat.

Children's Room: Mon., Tues., Thurs., Fri., 9–5; Weds., 9–8.

Residents may obtain **free passes** for the Museum of Fine Arts, Children's Museum, Isabella Stewart Gardner Museum, Museum of Science, Peabody Essex Museum, and Wolf Hollow.

The First Post Office (a private residence) is at 42 North Main Street. It was built before 1769. It was the first post office in Ipswich and one of the earliest in the country.

The Rev. Nathaniel Rogers House (a private residence) is at 1 High Street. The Rogers family lived here for four generations. Each generation produced a minister for the church. Reverend Nathaniel Rogers bought the land in 1727 and built a two-story house to which a third story was later added.

Pillow Lace Site (a private residence) is at 5 High Street. As early as the 1700s, handmade lace was produced by tracing a design on pillows and then using pins and bobbins to hold the fine linen thread in place. From this method came the name "pillow lace." This was the site of the New England Lace Company founded by Dr. Thomas Manning in 1828. An historic plaque marks the spot.

The Bradstreet House (a private residence) is on High Street near the Waldo-Caldwell House. Anne Bradstreet moved to Ipswich in 1634 and lived here for ten years. Her husband, Simon Bradstreet, served the Massachusetts Bay Colony for 62 years as secretary, commissioner, agent to England, and deputy governor. Anne Bradstreet was the first American poet, and one of the few women published during Puritan times. The *Tenth Muse Lately Sprung up in America* was published in London in 1650. Her private collections of poetry reveal her great talent and skill, expressing the feelings she had for her husband, her children, and her God. Fortunately she lived among the brilliant scholars who first settled in Ipswich and who allowed her to explore her ideas without prejudice. To anyone who felt women should be involved in more domestic activities than the writing of poetry, she wrote:

> *I am obnoxious to each carping tongue,*
> *Who say my hand a needle better fits.*
> *A Poet's pen all scorn I should thus wrong,*
> *For such despite they cast on Female wits;*
> *If what I do prove well, it won't advance,*
> *They'l say it's stol'n, or else it was by chance.*

The Jonathan Lummus House (a private residence) is at 45 High Street. On this site stood the house of Governor Thomas Dudley and his wife (the parents of Anne Bradstreet). The present house was built around 1712 and has many features common to English homes of the late 1500s.

The Old Burial Ground is on High Street, across from Lord's Square. The cemetery runs up a long hill with a series of terraces. Many old gravestones of the early settlers can still be found here. The first people to be buried in the Old Burial Ground were John Winthrop's wife and child in 1634.

The carvings on some of the stones are examples of early American folk art. Nathaniel Hawthorne used to visit here and noted in his journal that his favorite gravestone was the statue of Reverend Nathaniel Rogers (d.1775). Hawthorne liked to count the buttons on the reverend's gown. Another grave to note is the monument of John Denison (d.1747). This stone is

Goodale Orchards   *Courtesy Ann Fessenden*

decorated with columns and the family coat of arms. The epitaph reads, "His genius, learning, and engaging manners, spoke him the future joy and ornament of his native town. But Heaven meant other wise..."

The Merchant Choate House (a private residence) is at 103 High Street. This first-period house may have been built as early as 1639, which would make it the oldest house in Massachusetts, predating the Fairbanks house in Dedham. It is said to be "a house within a house" because within its 18th-century frame is a 17th-century single-room house. The living room contains an H-frame, one of only three in the United States. The house also has its original fireplace and back door.

Goodale Orchards is at 143 Argilla Road. In operation since 1920, the orchard was bought by Max Russell in 1979. Many varieties of apples, pears, peaches, and apricots are grown, and pick-your-own strawberries, raspberries, and blueberries are available in season. Call for picking dates and conditions for these fruits as well as apple picking in September. In the old-fashioned barn store the Russells sell their own honey, local preserves, maple syrup, candy, and many other items. In addition they make from scratch fruit pies in season; apple

"Prelude to a Concert" *Courtesy of The Trustees of Reservations*

pie, apple roll-ups, and fruit scones are baked every day. On weekends in the fall you can watch cider being made or take a tractor-drawn hay ride through the orchard for a small fee. Try the hard ciders and varieties of fruit wines made in the orchard's own winery. There are also farm animals to delight your family. Open weekends in April and daily from May to November. Call 356-5366 for exact dates.

The Great House at Castle Hill (a property of The Trustees of Reservations) is at 290 Argilla Road. Overlooking the drifting white sands of Crane Beach is the imposing Great House, a 59-room English Stuart-style mansion designed by architect David Adler and built in 1927 for millionaire Richard T. Crane, Jr. The house contains woodwork from the Earl of Essex's castle in England and some exquisite examples of woodcarvings by Grinling Gibbons. The terrace overlooks the Grand Allée, designed by landscape architect Arthur A. Shurcliff. During the summer concerts are performed on an outdoor stage. Picnics on the Grand Allée are delightful preludes to these music programs. Portions of the motion pictures *Witches of Eastwick* and *Shakespeare's Sister* were filmed at Castle Hill. For more information about programs and house tours, call 356-4351 or the box office at 356-7774.

Places of Worship

BAPTIST

Immanuel Church, 37 Central Street. Call 356-2010. Sunday service at 9:30 a.m., Sunday school at 10:50 a.m.

Linebrook Parish Church, 291 Linebrook Road. Call 356-3104. Sunday service at 9:30 a.m., Sunday school at 9 a.m.

CHRISTIAN SCIENCE

Christian Science Church, 15 North Main Street. Call the Reading Room, 356-2020. Sunday service and school at 10:00 a.m., Wednesday evenings at 8 p.m.

CATHOLIC

St. Joseph's, 1 Pine Swamp Road. Call 356-3944. Saturday service at 5 p.m., Sunday service at 9 a.m. and 11 a.m.

CONGREGATIONAL

First Church in Ipswich, Meetinghouse Green. Call 356-2211. Sunday service at 10 a.m. (9 a.m. in the summer); Sunday school Sept.–June at 10 a.m.

GREEK ORTHODOX

St. John The Confessor Orthodox Church, 244 High Street. Call 356-5303. Sunday Divine Liturgy at 9 a.m.

Assumption of the Virgin Mary Church, 9 Lafayette Road. Call 356-2039. Sunday Divine Liturgy at 9 a.m.

METHODIST

United Methodist Church of Ipswich, Meetinghouse Green. Call 356-5533. Sunday service at 10 a.m. Food Pantry open Thursdays, 5:30 p.m.–7:30 p.m. Reach Out Thrift Shop open Thursdays, 5 p.m.–8 p.m.

PRESBYTERIAN

First Presbyterian Church, 179 County Road. Call 356-7690. Sunday service at 8:30 a.m. and 11 a.m.

RUSSIAN ORTHODOX

St. John the Russian Orthodox Church, 16 Mt. Pleasant Avenue. Call 356-1207. Sunday service at 9:30 a.m. year-round. Saturday Vespers at 7 p.m. Call for Great Feast Days schedule and Church School information. (Note: the church also produces and distributes jewelry and replicas of Eastern Orthodox Christian traditions. Call the Gallery Byzantium, 356-0259.)

Antiques

In the 1920s Joseph and Jennie Saltzberg ran "Saltzberg's" at 3 South Main Street (next to the Choate Bridge), where they sold beer, wine, and antiques. Joseph Saltzberg also worked as a cabinetmaker for Israel Sack in Boston. As a famous "picker" of Americana (objects of utilitarian, decorative, or any nature relating to early American life), he was often seen traveling with Hymie Grossman (a Boston antiques merchant) and others in search of treasures. After World War II, Joseph's son, Edward, started the Choate Bridge Club, where locals met in the antique shop to drink, play cards, talk politics, "scheme and pontificate." (Edward's story continues in the Essex **Antiques** section.)

Starting in the 1930s Ralph Warren Burnham and his wife ran a shop at 5 South Main Street and later opened the Antique Trading Post on Route 1A. The Burnhams had gentlemen called "runners" or "scouts," who would drive around the countryside finding antiques for their shops. After excursions the scouts would return with their car roofs and com-

Burnham Rug Repair Shop   *Courtesy of* Rug Hooking *Magazine*

partments piled so high with goods that the running boards almost touched the ground.

Mr. Burnham was also interested in saving old barns and houses. He purchased the 1640 Hart House, which he restored and furnished with antiques and art and then continued his business there. Today the 1640 Hart House is a restaurant and many of the furnishings and pictures still there are from Mr. Burnham (see **Restaurants** section for more information).

Of great interest to him was the collecting and repairing of old hooked and braided rugs. In his rug repair room from six to twenty ladies patiently worked on rugs until they were as good as new. Sometimes repairs required dying wool until it was the correct shade; often coffee and tea were used in order to give the background of a floral pattern a nice creamy color. Mr. Burnham also painstakingly copied beautiful hooked rug patterns and successfully sold the copies by mail order all over the United States and Canada. In addition to rug restoration, he employed a cabinetmaker, Joseph Bakula, who restored, repaired and copied 18th-and 19th-century antique furniture. Some of Mr. Bakula's beautiful reproductions still grace the old homes in Ipswich today. After Mr. Burnham's death in 1938, his wife carried on the business until 1958.

ANTIQUE DEALERS

Baker Sutton House, 115 High Street. Call 356-0447. Architectural items, decorative iron, garden ornaments, and primitives.

Calico Collectibles, 4 Lord's Square. Call 356-3965. "A one-owner shop with eclectic merchandise."

Eliza Gray's Goods, 37 South Main Street. Call 356-8757. Folk art, found objects, and antiques.

Edward Hoepfner & Daughter Antiques, 103 High Street. Call 356-1245. 18th-and 19th-century American furniture and accessories.

Art

At the turn of this century a group of artists lived and painted here. They shared similar experiences, styles, interests, and exhibitions. Arthur Wesley Dow, Henry Rodman Kenyon,

John Worthington Mansfield, Francis Henry Richardson, and Theodore Wendel all knew one another. In Europe, Dow, Kenyon, Richardson and Wendel studied at the Académie Julian in Paris, and some of them had exhibited their work in the French salon. Their rigorous formal training is reflected in their work. The effects of light and color intrigued them. The natural beauty of the Ipswich River, creeks, and salt marshes, as well as the rural character of this community with its numerous 17th-century houses drew them here and inspired their work.

Arthur Wesley Dow (1857–1922) was born in Ipswich and is the artist most associated with this community's art history. In 1891 he returned from France to found an internationally famous summer art colony here. He sought to preserve and protect the rustic character of his hometown and helped found the Ipswich Historical Society. An early artistic pursuit included pen and ink sketches of treasured local 17th-and 18th-century houses.

Henry Rodman Kenyon (1861–1926) came from a well-to-do Quaker family in Providence, Rhode Island. After finishing his studies at the Rhode Island School of Design in 1882, he sailed to Europe. He and Arthur Dow met in Paris and became lifelong friends. They treasured the variety of the Norman landscape and shared a studio in Pont-Aven, France. In 1889 Dow persuaded Kenyon to return home with him to share a studio in Ipswich. The Choate Bridge, the marshes, and the forests became favorite subjects of theirs, and Kenyon also sketched and painted all over New England. When he died of pneumonia, his wife, Caroline, tried to liquidate the paintings he had strewn all over the house and signed the unsigned ones herself. As her eyesight was failing, though, she often signed them twice.

John Worthington Mansfield (1849–1933) loved to draw as a child. He went on to study at the National Academy of Design in New York. He was well traveled and found Germany's landscape and legendary castles especially paintable. In 1879 he spent the summer in the Adirondacks and produced a masterful charcoal self-portrait which now hangs in the Essex

Institute in Salem. At Myopia Hunt Club he found customers who were willing to pay huge sums to have him paint their horses and dogs. These are masterpieces of detail and composition. The Ipswich Historical Association has an example of his work, a copy of an 18th-century portrait of John Winthrop, Jr., the first governor of the Massachusetts Bay Colony.

Francis Henry Richardson (1859–1934) was the son of a prosperous Boston merchant family. He studied art while pursuing a career in civil engineering. In 1886 he went to Paris to further his training and connected with Boston artist friends who were also there. Arthur Wesley Dow's summer art colony attracted Richardson to Ipswich when he was forty-one years old. Henry Kenyon and Theodore Wendel, two painters he had met in Europe, were also calling Ipswich their home.

The Ipswich School adopted the themes of the Barbizon School of painters (who focused on shadows, reflected light, and cloudy skies) and applied them (minus classical allusions) to Ipswich scenes of marshes, forests, and beaches. Richardson's canvases were brighter, more colorful, and more detailed than the Barbizon examples and those of his peers. Although most of his paintings are in private collections, the Ipswich Savings Bank and Ipswich Public Library have some examples of his work on display.

Theodore Wendel (1859–1932) was perhaps Boston's most-successful landscape painter at the turn of the century. He came from Midway, Ohio and was the son of a German shop owner. He joined a circus when he was fifteen years old; later in life his friends would applaud his ability to balance a chair on his chin while juggling and playing the harmonica.

Wendel was schooled in Cincinnati and in Munich. Soon he became associated with a talented group of young artists called "Duveneck Boys," who traveled with the group's mentor, Frank Duveneck. Winters in Florence were followed by summers in Vienna. In 1885 Wendel met Dow, Kenyon, and Richardson at the Académie Julian in Paris, and in 1886, Claude Monet attracted Wendel and other avant-garde painting students to Giverney. Wendel's style decidedly changed at that point. He achieved a vibrancy and depth of expression rare in all but the most notable luminists, such as Thomas

Cole or Frederick Church. Wendel used color more lavishly, and he was one of the first in Europe to recognize Monet's originality. Wendel later introduced Monet's work to New York and Boston audiences.

In 1897 Wendel married a woman who was the heiress to a spectacularly beautiful tract of land. The views of Ipswich fields, marshes, and drumlins rivaled similar landscapes in France. He went on to immortalize some of the grandest scenery in the nation and won honors for the entries he sent to competitions throughout the hemisphere. Though most of his paintings are in private collections, the Museum of Fine Arts in Boston owns two of his oils. One is the well-known "Bridge at Green Street."

GALLERIES

Today few people realize that there are talented artists quietly at work in this quaint New England town. Each year in July Olde Ipswich Days celebrates this diverse community of artists: sculptors, watercolorists, painters working in oil and acrylic, printmakers, portrait artists, photographers, potters, engravers, basket weavers, and quilters. For more information about this traditional event or to enter your work call 356-0115. In addition, the Annual Art Show sponsored by the Ipswich Arts Council is held in July at the Winthrop School. To exhibit or for more information, call 356-3602.

Artesanias is at 80 Rear High Street (Route 1A). Located in an antique building previously used by the Railway Express Agency, the shop sells "the best in affordable folk art." Open Tuesday–Saturday from noon to 4 p.m., from late April through Christmas Eve; open Sundays between Thanksgiving and Christmas. Closed Mondays. Call 356-5222.

Hall-Haskell House Art Gallery is open Friday–Sunday from 11 a.m to 4 p.m., from mid-May to mid-October (with additional hours by appointment). For information about exhibiting or viewing the collection, call 356-4809.

The Norris Gallery & Frame Shop is at 40 Essex Road. Watercolors by E. Heywood Norris and original work in oil,

Ocmulgee Pottery Shop   *Courtesy of Barbara King*

watercolor, and acrylics by area artists are on display. Open Monday–Friday from 10 a.m. to 5 p.m. and Saturdays from 10 a.m. to 4 p.m. Call 356-0115.

Ocmulgee Pottery is at 317 High Street. Stoneware and porcelain pottery; "no two pieces are exactly alike." Ongoing clay workshops are available. Call 356-0636.

ARTISTS (BY APPOINTMENT)

Susan K. Burton, acrylics: marsh scenes, still lifes, landscapes. Call 356-0408.

Mary Fosdick, color photographs of Ipswich scenes. Call 356-3082.

Susan Ingram, watercolorist and private art lessons. Call 356-7683.

Dorothy Kerper Monnelly, photographer. Call 356-0679.

James T. McClellan, sculptor. Call 356-5271.

Lois Moore, portraits of children and adults in charcoal and pastels (also does house portraits in pen and ink and watercolor). Call 356-2796.

For information about arts-related grants, contact the Ipswich Arts Council chairperson, Georgia Flood, 356-3602 or 356-3077.

Music, Theater, and Dance

ALONG THE WAY COFFEE HOUSE

The coffee house is in the United Methodist Church on North Main Street. Folk, jazz, blues, and country performances at 8 p.m., one Saturday per month from Sept. to June; donations requested. Desserts available. For information call the Crystal Ice Cream Shop, 356-1636.

THE CANTEMUS CHAMBER CHORUS

Cantemus is a non-profit organization dedicated to performing chamber chorus music. Repertoire ranges from medieval and Elizabethan to Early American, Romantic, and contemporary. Cantemus (Latin for "let us sing") members come from the North Shore. The chorus performs in Beverly, Hamilton, Newburyport, and Ipswich. Major concerts are held in May and December. For more information write to P.O. Box 784, Ipswich, MA 01938, or call 1-888-CHORUS1.

CASTLE HILL EVENTS

Castle Hill is at 290 Argilla Road and sponsors a variety of events and recreational activities throughout the year: an Independence Day Celebration on July 4th at 5 p.m. with family fun and fireworks; Picnic Concerts in July and August, from 7 p.m. to 8:30 p.m. on the Grand Allée; a Concours d'Elégance in September with pre-World War II American and European cars and a jazz band; a Choral Christmas Concert with holiday sing-a-long by the fire; a Children's Winter Musicale and a Children's Christmas Party, both in December. For a current schedule or information write to P.O. Box 563, Ipswich MA 01938, or call 356-4351.

THE IPSWICH COMMUNITY BAND

Members of the band are adults, college, and high school musicians from Ipswich and surrounding communities. Newcomers are welcome and no audition is necessary. Rehearsals are Wednesday evenings at the Ipswich High School during June and July. A number of performances are planned. For further information call Gerry Dolan, director of bands for the high school, at 356-3137 ext.135.

TOWN OF IPSWICH, RECREATION DEPARTMENT

The recreation department is located in Memorial Hall at 23 Central Street. Summer picnic and concert series held from June to Aug. for children and families. There is a teddy bear picnic, a magician, and "Red Wagon Theater," where children act out stories and the audience participates. Call 356-6644.

THE IPSWICH MOVING COMPANY STUDIO

The studio is at 62 East Street. Come see dance theater performed with live music, seating is limited and reservations are suggested. For a current schedule, call 356-0334.

IPSWICH RIVER FESTIVAL

The festival program includes fireworks, music, and a block dance. Extra events are planned during the 10th anniversary of this popular event in June 1997. Call the Ipswich Recreation Dept. for details, 356-6644.

Recreation

ANIMALS

New England Alive is at 163 High Street. Founded by Lyle Jensen in 1978 to provide care and recovery for injured and orphaned wildlife and to preserve and share the treasures of a native New England woodland environment with the public. Visitors will find a petting farm and nature study center featuring Yogi the Black Bear and other wild animals that are native to the region, as well as baby farm animals in the barnyard who love to be petted. Enjoy pony rides, reptiles, an aquarium, and more. "Creature Coach" brings animals to your school; or bring your class on a field trip here. Restrooms and picnic area on premises. Open May–Nov.; Monday–Friday, 10 a.m.–5 p.m.; Saturday and Sunday, 9:30 a.m.–6 p.m. Admission is charged. Call 356-7013.

Wolf Hollow is at 98 Essex Road. Here is a unique place to see the North American Gray Wolf in a natural habitat, learn about its role in our environment, and discover what you can do to help prevent its extinction. Open all year Saturday and Sunday, 1 p.m.–5 p.m. Presentations at 1:30 p.m. and 3:30 p.m. From Dec. 15 through Feb. presentations are at 1:30 p.m. only. Groups by reservation weekdays. Admission is charged. Call 356-0216.

BEACHES

Crane Beach (a property of The Trustees of Reservations) is at end of Argilla Road. Covering 1,400 acres of diverse habitats, the white sandy barrier beach stretches for more than four miles along Ipswich Bay. This narrow beach with high sand dunes is separated from the mainland by Essex Bay and the Essex and Ipswich River estuaries. There is also a drumlin (known as Castle Hill) as well as cranberry bogs, salt marsh, and maritime forests. In keeping with the reservation's goal to protect natural resources by balancing public use with ecosystem preservation, the Trustees maintain programs to protect the beach and dune habitats for rare and endan-

gered birds such as the piping plover and the least tern.

Crane Beach has been called the North Shore's best beach. Its sandbar protects the beach from dangerous surf and provides great family swimming. A refreshment stand and public bath house are available. Lifeguards are on duty only on weekends in May and from May 30 to Labor Day lifeguards are on duty daily from 9 a.m. to sunset. The beach is open year-round from 8 a.m. until sunset. Horseback riding is permitted in the fall and winter. A parking fee is charged. Beach Office: 356-4354.

BOATING

Foote Brothers is at Willowdale Dam, 230 Topfield Road. A family-owned canoe rental business, operated since 1955. Equipped with 15-ft. and 17-ft. top-of-the-line Grumman canoes; they also provide a shuttle bus to several drop-off points upstream and instruction for beginners. Reservations and a minimal non-refundable deposit are required. Open every day in season from 8 a.m. to 6 p.m. For more details, call 356-9771.

Ipswich Bay Yacht Club is on Quay Road. Call 356-2502 or (dockhouse) 356-2029.

Public Boat Launch Facility is located at the Ipswich Town Wharf on East Street.

Tsalta Sail Charters (see Manchester-by-the-Sea **Recreation** section)

BOWLING

Ipswich Lanes (candlepin) is at 6 Saltonstall Street. Call 356-4300.

FITNESS CENTERS

Ipswich Family YMCA, 29 County Road. Call 356-9622.

Town of Ipswich Recreation Department, 23 Central Street (Memorial Building). Call 356-6644.

GOLF

Candlewood Golf Club is a public course located at 75 Essex Road (Route 133). Call 356-5377.

HORSEBACK RIDING

Ascot Riding Center is next to the Argilla Farm on Argilla Road. The Argilla Farm has been in existence for over 300 years. This land is part of the 300 acres John Winthrop, Jr. bought from Chief Masconomet. Governor Samuel Symonds bought the land from Winthrop in 1637 and changed its name to Argilla. Boarding, training, and lessons in H/J seat available; call 356-5932.

Linebrook Farms is at 383 Linebrook Road. Boarding, training, and lessons available; call 356-9739.

OPEN SPACE, PARKS, AND PLAYGROUNDS

Bay Circuit Trail starts at the Rowley-Ipswich line off Route 1A at the foot of Prospect Hill (parking available). The Bay Circuit Alliance wants to establish a 180-mile-long trail on conservation lands for non-motorized recreation from Newbury in the north to Duxbury just south of Boston. Currently eleven miles of this trail exist in Ipswich for hikers, mountain bikers, horseback riders and cross-country skiers. A map with route and parking information is available at the Ipswich Visitors Center, from the Ipswich Conservation Commission at the Town Hall (356-6605), or from the Bay Circuit Alliance, 3 Railroad Street, Andover, MA 01810. Call 508-470-1982.

Bialek Park is located on Linebrook Road. For more information, call the Ipswich Recreation Department at 356-6644.

Bull Brook is at High Street behind the Dow Reservoir. In 1926 a stone spear point was discovered here between the ribs of an extinct species of bison. Since then archaeologists have uncovered evidence that the Palaeo Indian arrived in Ipswich around 8500 BC. This stone tool with its fluted point was the hallmark of the Palaeo Indian and is only found in America. The leg and foot bones of a mastodon have also been found here.

Crane Wildlife Refuge (a property of The Trustees of Reservations) is at the end of Argilla Road. Board the *Osprey* for a trip across the Castle Neck River to tour Hog Island and Long Island by hay wagon. On these 650 beautiful, tranquil acres, you will see the 250-year-old Choate family homestead. Also featured is the "Proctor" house, built by Twentieth Century Fox for the filming of *The Crucible*. A stop at

Crane Island Tour   *Courtesy of Kate Wollensak (TTOR)*

the visitor center and a breathtaking ride to the top of Hog Island are included. The island abounds with plants and flowers and sustains more than 180 species of birds, from herons to hawks and warblers to waterfowl. Open May 25–Oct. 27 (1-hour hay wagon tours daily at 10 a.m. and 2 p.m. except Wednesdays and Thursdays). Admission is charged. Call 356-4351.

Greenwood Farm (a property of The Trustees of Reservations) is reached by taking Route 1A to East Street and proceeding along Jeffrey's Neck Road. This 213-acre property is open every day from 8 a.m to sunset. On the farm is a fine example of a first-period house built by Robert Paine in 1702. In the mid-1800s the property was sold to Thomas Greenwood, who built his farmhouse next to the Paine House. In 1993 the Dodge Family donated the house and land to TTOR. There is a path through the salt marsh with board walks which make it possible to walk out to the river. A great place for picnics and viewing salt marsh, tidal creeks, fields, wooded area, and clapboard farmhouses. Parking is free. Call 356-4351.

Ipswich River can be seen running along Topsfield Road, Market, County, and Water Streets. Its gentle waters flow quietly through beautiful forests, fields, and farmland. It is navigable for almost 30 miles and runs through a Massachusetts Audubon Society sanctuary, two state parks, and much undeveloped land. Accessible only by canoe, it is a paradise for birders, botanists, and fishermen. Maps for the Ipswich River are available from Ipswich River Watershed Association, 51 South Main St. Call 356-8939.

Little Neck Causeway and Pavilion Beach can be reached via Route 1A to East Street to Jeffrey's Neck Road and onto Little Neck. This is a park and sandy beach for fishing and boating with a playground and picnic tables. Parking is free.

Rev. Daniel Boone Memorial Park is on Spring Street. This little park near Baker's Pond can be enjoyed year-round. Bring a picnic in summer or go ice skating in winter.

Sally Weatherall Memorial Reservation (a property of Essex County Greenbelt) can be reached via Route 1A to East Street to Jeffrey's Neck Road. The reservation is located near the intersection of North Ridge Road and Little Neck Road. This is a wooded area and salt marsh with an access point and trails off Neck Road. Limited free parking.

TOWN WHARF, RIVER WALK, AND WATER STREET

Park your car at the Town Wharf and follow the Ipswich River along Water Street until you get to the Green Street Bridge (one of the oldest keystone bridges in Massachusetts). Next to the bridge is River Walk, a wooded walkway along the Ipswich River with benches and a pleasant view of the river and old houses. Follow the river as you walk behind the Whipple Middle School and come out on County Road. Turn left over a bridge and you will reach the corner of South Village Green. Turn right at the green and follow the street to the Quebec Labrador Foundation buildings, where you will find a garden and a place to enjoy the view across the river to the old hosiery mill, which is now the location of Ebsco Publishing. Ebsco has recently reconstructed a fish ladder at the factory falls and there are plans to make a bridge across the dam and build a riverfront walkway behind the stores on Market Street. Retrace your steps until you arrive at the pond behind the Whipple House. Follow the river and you will arrive at a set of stairs leading to an old cemetery. Turn left at the road, pass the green and head down County Road back to the wharf. This trail is a little over a mile.

SPORTING GOODS, SALES AND RENTALS

America In-line, 40 Market Street. In-line skates. Call 356-1988.

Foote Brothers, 203 Topsfield Road. Canoe rentals. Call 356-9771.

Skol Ski Shop, 20 Central Street. Four-season sporting goods (including sales, rentals, and repairs of skis and bikes). Call 356-5872.

TENNIS

Bialek Park, Linebrook Road. Lights are turned on at the Ipswich Recreation office at 23 Central Street. Call 356-6644.

Ipswich High School, 136 High Street. Courts are reserved at the Ipswich Recreation office at 23 Central Street. Call 356-6644.

TOURS

Crane Wildlife Refuge (see **Open Space, Parks, and Playgrounds**). Call 356-4351.

The Great House at Castle Hill (see **Places of Interest**). Call 356-4351.

Olde Ipswich Tours, 8 Herrick Drive. John Moss provides a full-service group tour; escorted, customized, and package tours; host escort services; and local guide services. Tours can be given in French and Spanish. Call 356-9540.

Ipswich Brewing Company, Ltd. 23 Hayward Street. Tour this small-town microbrewery and taste Cape Ann's award-winning English-style ales. Tours Saturdays at 1 p.m. and 3 p.m. Call 356-3329 or 800-477-4253.

Lodging

Town Hill Bed & Breakfast, 16 North Main Street. Ten individually decorated rooms. Built in 1850 and located in the historic district. Room includes a full breakfast. Rates begin at $75. Open year-round. Call 356-8000 or 800-457-7799.

Whittier Motel, 120 County Road (Route 1A). 20 rooms; outdoor pool, effi- ciencies, color TV, and lounge. Children under 18 stay free. June 1 summer rate begins at $65. Nov.–May off-season rates apply. The restaurant on premises serves a full breakfast menu and is open Tuesday–Saturday, 6 a.m.–11 a.m., and Sundays, 7 a.m.–11 a.m. Open year-round. Call 356-5205.

Restaurants

Chipper's River Cafe, 11 South Main Street. Open daily year-round, 7 a.m.–10 p.m. Contemporary American cuisine with a screened summer deck for outside dining on the Ipswich River by the old Choate Bridge. Full liquor license. Call 356-7956.

Chipper's Brick Alley Bakery, next to Chipper's River Cafe. Open daily year-round, 7 a.m.–5 p.m. Fresh-baked bread, muffins, calzones, etc., for take-out only. Call 356-7956.

Choate Bridge Pub and Restaurant, 1 Market Square. A casual pub atmosphere with great burgers, steak tips, sandwiches, and pizza. Call 356-2931.

Clam Box, 206 High Street. Open March–Dec. This sixty-year-old landmark serves great fried clams and other seafood. Eat in or take-out. Call 356-9707.

Crystal Ice Cream & Yogurt Shop, Essex Road at Bruni's Market Place. Open in season at 1 p.m. daily (Jan.–Feb. open Friday and Sunday 1 p.m.–7 p.m. and Saturday 1 p.m.–9 p.m.). Serves Richardson's Ice Cream, homemade pies, and specialty cakes. Call 356-1636.

Five Corners Deli, corner of Market and Central Streets. Offers breakfast, lunch, and dinner; features cappuccino, a 12-ft. salad bar, and over 45 sandwiches and five homemade soups daily. Call 356-7557.

Full House, 146 High Street. Open year-round, Sunday–Thursday, 11 a.m.–11 p.m.; Friday and Saturday, 11 a.m.–midnight. Czechuan and Thai food; eat in or take-out. Call 356-9199.

The 1640 Hart House, 51 Linebrook Road. Originally a one-room first-period

THE · 1640 · HART · HOUSE

Courtesy of the Hart House Restaurant

house and the home of Ipswich's first selectman, Thomas Hart, today the house has five levels, five staircases, and a 350-year-old fireplace. The wall panels inside are original hand-painted tea boxes from the Revolutionary War. The Hart House's original room, the Keeper's Room, was sold to the Metropolitan Museum of Art, and the Hart Room, directly above the Keeper's Room, was also dismantled and now sits in the Winterthur Museum in Delaware. After Prohibition, the Hart House was considered one of the few glamorous places to go outside of New York City, Newport, or Boston. Eleanor Roosevelt, James Cagney, and others used the Hart House as a summer retreat up through the 1940s. You can expect fine dining in a casual atmosphere. Local bands as well as live theater are presented during

the year. For information or reservations call 356-9411.

Henrich House, 24 Hammett Street. Open year-round; luncheon 11:30 a.m.–4 p.m., dinner 4 p.m.–10 p.m. daily. Hot and cold appetizers, American continental menu. Call 356-7006.

Lucky Island Chinese Restaurant, 11 Depot Square. Open year-round, Monday–Wednesday, 11:30 a.m.–10 p.m.; Thursday–Sunday, 11:30 a.m.–1 a.m.. Cantonese and Mandarin food. Call 356-9878.

Millstone Restaurant, 108 County Road. Open year-round for lunch and dinner; Monday–Friday, 11:30 a.m.–9 p.m.; breakfast, lunch, and dinner Saturday and Sunday beginning at 7 a.m.; full bar, function room, and homemade bread. Call 356-2772.

Riverview Restaurant, 20 Estes Street. Open daily 4 p.m.–11:30 p.m. Closed Mondays. The best pizza any way you love it and a full-service bar. Eat in or take-out. Call 356-0500.

Salad Bowl Restaurant, 146 High Street in the Ipswich Shopping Center. Open year-round, Monday–Friday, 6 a.m.–2 p.m.; Saturday breakfast only, 6:30 a.m.–11 p.m. Closed Sundays. Will "shrink-wrap" your lunch to take to the beach. Salads, sandwiches, subs, soup in season. Call 356-2733.

Steep Hill Grill, 40 Essex Road. Open year-round every day at 4 p.m. for dinner. Sophisticated menu of innovative new American cuisine. Call 356-1121.

Stone Soup Cafe, 20 Mitchell Road. Open Tuesday–Friday 7 a.m.–2 p.m., breakfast and lunch. Closed Sunday and Monday. Open on Saturday 7 a.m.–noon, serving breakfast only. Dinner on Thursday, Friday, and Saturday with seatings at 6 p.m. and 8:30 p.m. Make your reservations weeks in advance. This unique restaurant offers meals ranging from breakfast specials and blue collar lunches to exquis-ite white tablecloth fine dining. BYOB; no credit cards accepted. Call 356-4222.

Super Subs, 5B Wildes Court off Hammett Street in Market Square. Open year-round. Serves a quick breakfast express 6 a.m.–10 a.m. daily. Sunday–Wednesday, open until 7 p.m.; Thursday–Saturday, open until 8:30 p.m. "A Meal in Every Sub." Call 356-0900.

White Cap Sea Food, 141 High Street. Taste the tradition that made Ipswich famous: hand-shucked fried native clams. Broiled, baked, and grilled seafood; fresh fish market; casual dining indoors or out. Call 356-5276.

White Farms, 326 High Street. Open 11 a.m. April–Oct. Serves light lunch menu, grilled food, and many flavors of soft-serve ice cream, hard-ice cream, and hard-yogurt. Call 356-2633.

Williams Bakery & Restaurant, 39 Market Street. Open year-round, Monday–Friday, 7 a.m.–2 p.m., breakfast and full lunch menu; Saturday and Sunday, 7 a.m.–12:30, breakfast only. Fresh bread and pastry baked on the premises; specialty is "Roast Turkey Dinner with _real_ mashed potatoes." Call 356-2225.

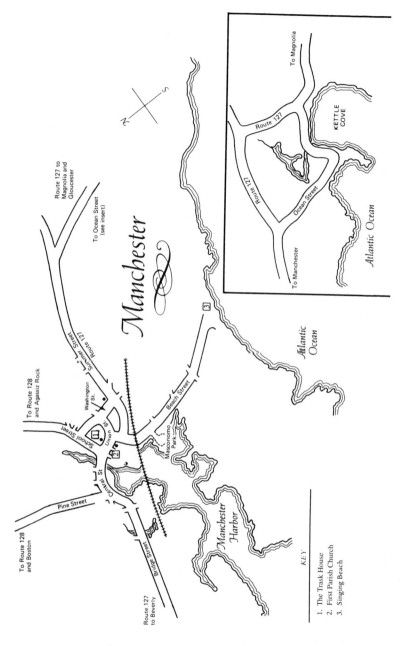

Manchester

To Route 128
and Agassiz Rock

To Route 128
and Boston

Route 127
to Beverly

Route 127 to
Magnolia and
Gloucester

To Ocean Street
(see insert)

Sumner Street

Route 127

Washington
St.

School Street

Central St.

Pine Street

Bridge Street

Union St.

Masconomo
Park

Beach Street

*Manchester
Harbor*

*Atlantic
Ocean*

3

To Magnolia

Route 127

Route 127

Ocean Street

To Manchester

KETTLE
COVE

Atlantic Ocean

N
S

KEY

1. The Trask House
2. First Parish Church
3. Singing Beach

Courtesy of J. W. Murray & Associates

The *Arbella*   *Tom O'Hara*

Manchester-by-the-Sea

HISTORY

The first European settlers came ashore in 1626 at Kettle Cove (see map at left). The *Talbot* arrived in 1629 and dropped anchor in Manchester Harbor but stayed only a few days. In 1630 a fleet of seven ships sailed into the harbor. This was a most memorable occasion, as aboard the *Arbella* was the charter for the Massachusetts Bay Colony—the first charter to come to the New World; all others had been kept in England. The fact that the charter came to New England gave the settlers a sense of independence.

The *Arbella* was the second ship to bring women into the New World and, Anne Bradstreet, the first English poet to arrive on these shores, was one of those on board. Her husband,

Simon Bradstreet, would become the governor of the Massachusetts colony and her father, Thomas Dudley, would serve after him. (See **History** and **Places of Interest**: Ipswich.)

Masconomo, chief of the Agawam Indians, came to greet the colonists when the *Arbella* arrived. Masconomo was fortunate to have survived the great plague that destroyed most of the Agawams. Diseases brought over from Europe proved to be certain death to the Indians. John Smith had sailed along the shore of Manchester in 1614 and had seen a large Indian population, but after the first European settlers arrived, he noted their numbers were greatly reduced.

Manchester was named Jeffreys Creek, after William Jeffreys, one of the few men sent over in 1626 to set up stages for drying fish. (Fish was caught, cleaned, and spread out on platforms called stages to cure and dry. Afterwards the fish was packed into barrels and shipped to England.) The inhabitants of Jeffreys Creek petitioned Salem for a change of name in 1645 and the settlement received the name of Manchester.

For over a century the fishing industry was the primary means of support. The Massachusetts Bay Colony had a monopoly on "fishing and curing" on New England shores by a royal proclamation made in 1622. The General Court also encouraged the fishing industry by not taxing fishing vessels and exempting their men from military duty in 1639.

Manchester men were good mariners. In all kinds of weather, vessels shipped out a variety of fish and returned with freights of bacon, salt, corn, rum, sugar, molasses and coffee. Through rough seas, lost men, and seasons of feast and famine, these men were the breath of life for their community for many years.

Cabinet making began in 1775, when Moses Dodge opened his shop at 21 School Street. Along with Moses Dodge and his family, some of the leading cabinetmakers were Ebenezer Tappan and John Perry Allen. Manchester was known for manufacturing fine furniture, though the business actually began as a way to produce sturdy, everyday furniture with a reasonable price tag. This substantial industry thrived and finally peaked in 1865, with 160 cabinetmakers. Manchester carpenters invented the process of veneering; unfortunately, the process was not patented and is now used everywhere.

Many pieces of Manchester's fine furniture grace the homes of fortunate North Shore residents. Locally you can see several examples when you visit the Trask House on Union Street, owned by the Manchester Historical Society. There you can see pieces crafted by skilled artisans such as Cyrus Dodge, John Perry Allen, Rust & Marshall Cabinetmakers, and Rufus Stanley.

As the woodworking industry declined, the community increased in popularity as a summer resort. Richard H. Dana became the town's first summer resident when he purchased 30 acres of land and built a home in 1845. Many prominent and wealthy inhabitants soon followed. When the railroad came to Manchester in 1847, the community became easily accessible to visitors. Some modest summer places were built along the shore, but most of the "summer cottages" were actually castle-like homes.

Many diplomats escaped the heat and humidity of Washington for the lovely seaside climate of Manchester, and several embassies (Holland, Russia, Italy, and Austria) did their

Furniture Manufactory   *Courtesy of the Manchester Historical Society*

summer business here. Manchester has been visited by Presidents Woodrow Wilson, William Howard Taft, and John F. Kennedy, as well as the children of Theodore Roosevelt. The crown Prince and Princess of Sweden also summered here.

Junius Booth, brother of the infamous John Wilkes Booth who assassinated President Lincoln, built a "summer cottage" here in 1860 and expanded it into an elaborate 106-room hotel. The Masconomo House was located near Singing Beach and had a 77-foot-long dining room that could seat 300 people. Complete with an elevator, five beautiful staircases, a wraparound porch, bowling alleys, tennis courts, and dance halls, it had all the luxuries. Since Junius Booth was an actor, many actors and literary notables were drawn to the Masconomo House with its lively program of plays and concerts. Prior to World War I, a devastating fire destroyed most of the hotel and it was never restored to its former glory. Today a portion of the Masconomo House remains as a private residence.

Manchester still has a number of summer residents, but because of its close proximity to Boston and businesses located along Interstate 95, it is now a suburban community for year-round residents. In 1990 the town's name was officially changed by an act of the legislature to Manchester-by-the-Sea, because townspeople wanted to distinguish their community from the other Manchesters of New England.

When Manchester-by-the-Sea celebrated its 350th Anniversary in 1995, the entire community got involved. The townspeople enjoyed a year-long series of events, including a re-enactment of the arrival of the *Arbella*, parades, crafts, music, dancing, and a bonfire. The grand finale was a beautiful display of fireworks that illuminated the harbor.

PLACES OF INTEREST

Visitors arriving in Manchester-by-the-Sea for the first time will appreciate the attractive downtown area as well as the boat activity in the picturesque, sheltered inner and outer harbors. Shops, restaurants, parks, and beautiful Singing Beach are within easy walking distance. Curbside parking in the downtown area is for one hour only, and visitors who plan to remain longer are asked to park in a municipal lot directly behind the Town Hall, at the North Street lot, or the train station. Singing Beach has a pay-per-car parking lot that fills up quickly, so come early in the day. Manchester is easily reached by scenic Route 127 or by Route 128 (Exits 15 and 16), or by train from either Boston or Rockport.

Manchester (Memorial Hall) Public Library is on Union Street. This building, built in 1887, was designed by Charles Follen McKim, who also designed the Boston Public Library. The funding for this lovely building was made possible by summer resident T. Jefferson Coolidge. The building is constructed of cut Ashlar with natural seam face. The stones used were selected in quarries where the ledges have occasional seams—places where the moisture and air work their way down through and give the stone a reddish brown color. The building is similar in design to ones found in Brittany, France, in the 16th century. The weathervane at the peak of the library is a reproduction of one of Columbus's ships. During the town's 250th anniversary in 1895, two bronze tablets cast by the Paul Revere Brass Foundry in Boston were placed in Memorial Hall in memory of the soldiers and sailors who died in earlier wars. Call 526-7711.

    Winter Schedule: Mon., 10–8; Tues.–Thurs., 1–8; Fri., 10–6; Sat., 10–1.

    Summer Schedule: Closed on Sat., July 1–Labor Day.

    Residents may obtain **free passes** for the Museum of Fine Arts, the Isabella Stewart Gardner Museum, the Children's Museum, the New England Aquarium, the Peabody Essex Museum, and the Museum of Science.

The Trask House is on Union Street. Abigail (Nabby) Hooper was already established as a businesswoman when she married the sea captain Richard Tink (or Tynke), a widower. She had bought the land on Union Street and built the house around 1823, before her marriage. In the oldest part of the house she ran a small store, cared for the sick, and "acted as an attorney by drawing up wills and deeds for other people." When she married the sea captain, Nabby did not want to be known as "the Mistress Stink," so about a year after her marriage she had his name changed to Trask (his mother's maiden name). Mrs. Trask kept the title of the house after she and her husband were married; she was a very liberated woman. The couple resided here with their son Charles during the 1800s. They were a prominent family in the community.

Today the Trask House is the headquarters of the Manchester Historical Society and is open as a museum for residents and visitors. Here you can find out more about Manchester's past, and see some actual pieces of furniture made in Manchester by famous carpenters such as John Perry Allen and Cyrus Dodge. The Trask House is open weekends during the summer or by appointment. For information call 526-7230.

7 Central Street was originally known as the "Lee Place," named for Captain John Lee, who built it in 1754. When Delucena Lathrop Bingham bought it in 1792, it became known as the Bingham House. Mr. Bingham was appointed the first postmaster of Manchester. This old building has served as a private home, tailor shop, tavern, post office, and other establishments and has maintained its charm over the years. Today it still functions as a fine restaurant known as 7 Central.

Rabardy Block (Floyd's Store) at 15 Central Street is a lovely Victorian house originally known as Rabardy Block, built in 1884 by a French cabinetmaker, Julius Rabardy. In 1885 the post office moved to this location from 7 Central Street with Mr. Rabardy as postmaster. At the time postal boxes were scarce, and Mr. Rabardy began the custom of placing letters and other small printed matter in the window, so people who did not have boxes could see they had mail. As the volume of mail increased and people could no longer see their letters in the window, he placed an octagonal drum behind the glass, which anyone could turn and then take their letters. Eventually a law was enacted which disallowed public display of private mail.

Floyd's Store is named after Lyman Floyd, who opened his general store around the turn of this century. The popular general store became a family business that would last through four generations. Children still go up to the counter and select candy while Mrs. Rice (granddaughter of Lyman Floyd) waits patiently for them to make their choices.

Seaside 1   *Courtesy of Merritt Miller*

Seaside "1" is on Central Street. This little building was erected in 1885 as a firehouse to hold the town's first steam engine, *Seaside*. *Seaside* and another old steam engine, *Torrent*, are once again on display (both were previously exhibited at the Peabody Essex Museum in Salem). The recently renovated Seaside "1" is now open to the public as a museum. Summer hours are Saturdays, 10 a.m.–4 p.m., and Sundays, noon–4 p.m. For information, call the Trask House at 526-7230.

The First Parish Church is located at 10 Central Street. Prior to 1656, the first settlers met for worship in private houses. Between 1656 and 1809, three different meetinghouses were built; as the structures deteriorated and the peoples' needs changed, they were razed and rebuilt. Finally, in 1809, the beautiful Congregational Church on the parish green was constructed. It occupies about the same focal point in the center of town as the former meetinghouses. The steeple, which is rather large and includes a bell tower with a beautiful clock, has served as a landmark for many people, including mariners offshore, since the structure was built. In recent years the chimes in the bell tower have been restored

Steeple of the First Parish Church   *Liz Mackie*

and now play well-known hymns each day at noon. A golden cock weathervane sits atop the steeple and picks up breezes off the harbor.

Outwardly the building has changed little, but, in 1845 the interior was remodeled. The old square pews were removed, and other changes were made, including the removal of a large arched window at the rear of the pulpit. During the bitter winter months, parishioners brought foot stoves to church with them. After much opposition, heat (in the form of one absurdly small cast-iron stove) was installed in the church in 1821. The early settlers did not mind listening for hours to sermons and prayers; on the contrary, they believed too much comfort would make young people puny and endanger the health of the congregation as a whole.

The organ in the First Parish Church was built in 1861 by E. and G.G. Hook of Boston for the Congregational Church at Woodstock, Vermont. When the Woodstock church bought a new organ, the Ladies Social Circle of the Manchester church bought the Hook organ for $1,200. The organ has a tracker action mechanism, which means that the connection between the keys and pipes is made by moving wooden parts. The instrument is made of the finest grade of walnut and some of the pipes are of California pine. There are 758 pipes, the smallest of which is the size of a pencil. The largest wooden pipe is about 12 inches wide by 8 feet high; on top of it is a "bung" that amplifies the vibrations, so it becomes the equivalent of a 16-foot pipe. Originally air was supplied to the bellows by a hand pump, then by water power, and finally by an electric motor. The tone is silvery and cohesive, fine for congregational and choir singing.

Organist Bernice V. Baker Lipsett was born in Manchester and grew up on the Baker Farm on upper School Street. She organized the Junior Choir at the First Parish Church and in 1934 took over the senior choir and the organist duties. The church honored her 50th anniversary as church organist in 1986; many former pastors attended. When Bernice Lipsett passed away in 1996, the church was filled to capacity as many paid tribute to this woman who was greatly admired and had been an organist for 67 years.

1661 Burial Ground is at the intersection of Washington and Summer Streets. When the first settlers arrived, they had to build shelters for themselves and their families and then set aside a piece of land as a burial ground for their dead. The first cemetery was located near the site where the town library now stands and a second burial ground was set aside along the road to Magnolia. Unfortunately, no written records remain. In 1661 the town took by eminent domain the land at the intersection of what is today Washington and Summer Streets from Samuell Friend and gave him a grant of land elsewhere in town in exchange. Originally this cemetery property extended across Summer Street, since the road to Magnolia came up Summer Street from town and then bore right down Sea Street, out toward Eagle Head, and back out onto Summer Street, down by what is today Sweeney Park. The town voted in 1760 to erect a handsome entrance gate and a stone wall around the cemetery. Several times between 1661 and 1760 town records mention the problems briers caused. By 1772, townspeople again were forced to try to find a solution to the persistent briers, which encumbered the living and followed the dead to their graves. The oldest legible stones are those of Joseph Woodbury and Wife (1714); George Norton (1717); Elizabeth, wife of Thomas Lee (1720); and Lieutenant William Hilton (1723). Another old stone is a plain piece of granite with the initials E.H., for Edward Hooper. Many stones are older, but the epitaphs can no longer be deciphered. These rough, hand-hewn stones are simple memorials to the humble lives of our forefathers.

Places of Worship

BAPTIST

First Baptist Church, 20 School Street. Call 526-4283. Sunday service at 10:45 a.m.(summer, 9:30 a.m.); Sunday school Sept.–June, 9:30 a.m.

CATHOLIC

Sacred Heart Church, 62 School Street. Call 526-1263. Sunday service at 9 a.m. and 11 a.m. (summer, 8 a.m. and 10 a.m.); services on Mon., Tues., Thurs., and Fri. at 7 a.m.; Sat. at 9 a.m. and 5 p.m.; CCD classes Oct.–June.

CONGREGATIONAL

First Parish Church, Central Street. Call 526-7661. Sunday service at 10 a.m. (summer, 9:30 a.m.); Sunday school Sept.–May, 10 a.m.

EPISCOPAL

Emmanuel Church, Masconomo Street. Call 526-4446. Sunday prayer, sermon, and story for children at 10 a.m. (summer only).

Antiques

Dorfman Antiques & Estate Jewelry, 36 Union Street. Call 526-1973.

The Stock Exchange, 3 Beach Street. The Stock Exchange began in 1975 down the street from its present location. The shop's owner, Elaine Perkins, said her mother tried to dissuade her from opening a consignment shop and selling "used clothing," but Elaine trusted her intuition. "It was pretty sparse at first, but people came and purchased and also brought in their things; slowly the shop filled with merchandise." Customers sense a harmonious environment from the moment they enter and are greeted by pleasant staff, music, and lots of colorful merchandise creatively arranged. The store is open year-round Monday–Saturday, 10 a.m.–5 p.m., and Sundays, 1 p.m.–5 p.m. Consignments are taken anytime except Sundays. The policy is 50%/50% on clothing; on other consignments customers receive 60%, and on items with a sales price over $100, customers get 70%. The Stock Exchange takes decorative pieces, antiques, furniture, old linens, "upscale" clothing, paintings, and much more. Call 526-7569.

Yankee Peddler at 27 Union Street is an antique and collectible consignment shop. Call 526-8400.

 *Art*

Though this lovely town never established its own art colony or art association, it nevertheless has drawn artists and writers who independently found their expression here. Beautiful Singing Beach with Eagle Head (the rocky headland at the northern end of the beach) has been the subject of artists for many years. The beach has been painted at every season as it reflects the moods and colors of the ever-changing New England weather and the interplay of sea, sand, and sky.

From Masconomo Park, you can observe the picturesque harbor with boats at anchor while fishermen unload the day's catch of lobsters or fish, still others prepare to sail, and rowboats, powerboats, and yachts provide endless visual delights. The harbor is a stage for photographers, artists, and casual observers of people. The town is nestled around the harbor, and rooftops and façades of diverse house styles and periods lend interest and variety. Notice Memorial Hall Library, Town Hall, private homes, the drawbridge, marinas, and the steeple of the First Parish Church. Cast your eye in another direction and there is Captain Dusty's lobster shack, which has been captured countless times with camera, artists' brush, and pen. It's not uncommon to see an easel and chair set up directly on the sidewalk with an artist busily at work.

Masconomo Park is the setting for the annual Art in the Park exhibit by North Shore artists, held each year in July. For information about exhibiting your artwork or for additional information call 526-2040. During the first weekend in November the Arts Gala is held at the First Parish Church, but only Manchester artists may exhibit (up to three works by one artist may be entered). This Gala is sponsored by the Cultural Arts Council. Call 526-2040 for more details. In addition to these exhibitions, the lobby of Fleet Bank at 17 Union Street displays local artists' works, which are rotated monthly. If you are interested in any of the works displayed or have questions, call Ginny Hughes at 526-7880.

Grant applications for art-related programs are available at the town hall or library and must be submitted by October 15. For more information, contact the Manchester Cultural Council at 526-2040.

Music, Theater, & Dance

THE HELMSMEN

In 1957 The Helmsmen, a barbershop quartet, was founded by Jack Meigs, Fred Chellis, Everett Adams, and director Dick Coons. They had sung together in college and wanted to keep singing as a group. The Memorial School auditorium provided the perfect place for their concerts, which were well attended. With time, new members joined the group. By 1972, they had semi-disbanded until Dick Coons passed away in 1976. Many of the members gathered at the

The *Helmsmen* at Hammond Castle   *Courtesy of Richard Emery*

First Parish Church in Manchester for his memorial service and this gathering spurred a revival. By 1977 Dick Emery became director and the men's singing group expanded and thrived anew. The Helmsmen were twenty-four strong by 1982. They performed in the Great Hall as part of the Hammond Castle Series. On one special occasion, the Helmsmen sang Scots melodies at the Robert Burns Society in Boston. Dick Emery directed and arranged most of the wide variety of music the men sang (folk, classical, jazz, swing, and contemporary). Since 1985 they have only performed twice, both times with the Harmonettes (now the Manchester Women's Chorus). At the memorial service for Jack Meigs at the First Parish Church in 1996, twenty-three Helmsmen came from across the United States to sing. The men were moved by the occasion and the sound of their own voices combined once more. Will there be another revival?

MASCONOTES

This group was formed in the late 1950s, when the Helmsmen and Harmonettes combined men's and women's voices into a mixed vocal group directed by Katrina Schlaikjer and Brad Day. They sang until the late 1960s. In 1966 there was a special Spring Festival at which the Masconotes sang and the Helmsmen and Harmonettes also performed separately. Dick Emery wrote "The Tides," a half-hour piece performed by all the singers, for the occasion. When Manchester celebrated its 350th Anniversary in 1996, Dick Emery wrote the music and Herbert Kenny wrote the lyrics for a special hymn, "Mindful of Thee." A performance was held at the First Parish Church, where the hymn was sung by a choir made up of choirs from different churches in town as well as members of the Manchester Women's Chorus.

THE MANCHESTER WOMEN'S CHORUS

This singing group was formed as an extension of the Harmony Guild of the First Parish Church in September 1958. Patricia Perry, who began her soloist career at the age of sixteen, was the first director. She stayed with the group until the early 1980s. In 1983 Fred Broer became director. He is an experienced conductor, composer, and performer, as well as director of the North Shore Conservatory of Music at Endicott College in Beverly.

The chorus has performed for private organizations throughout the North Shore. In October 1996, the Manchester Women's Chorus performed at Simmons College in Boston as part of the "Massachusetts Conference on Women," which was a response at the local level to the "International Conference on Women" held in 1995 in Beijing, China.

Approximately forty North Shore women rehearse on Monday evenings at the Manchester Congregational Chapel. Each year the group performs an annual Christmas concert, and for the spring concert in Manchester and Gloucester they are joined by The Apollo Club of Boston. (Founded in 1871, the Apollo Club is the oldest continuously active men's singing club in the United States.) The choir members also present a "Manchester Women's Chorus Scholarship" each year to a Manchester High School senior who aspires to enter the field of fine arts (preferably music). If you would like to join the Chorus or want more information about their concerts or the scholarship, call Fred Broer at 283-9021.

The Manchester Community Center is located at Harbor's Point and sponsors music programs throughout the year, such as concerts in the park, ballroom dancing, swing band night, and Sunday night sing-alongs. For more information, call 526-7626.

Pat Perry was the original director of the Harmonettes in Manchester. For over fifteen years she has done live theater productions. Pat has performed on Queen Elizabeth II cruises, at WGBH-TV Channel 2 benefits, and currently performs with *An Illusion...* (contact the 1640 Hart House in Ipswich for performance schedule). During Manchester's 350th Anniversary in 1995, Pat took on the character of Mary Todd Lincoln. She does other one-woman, "in character" performances for public or private occasions and would be happy to discuss her repertoire; for more information, call 526-1511.

Recreation

BEACHES

Black Beach is on Ocean Street (off Route 127). Rocky shore, pebbly beach, and scenic drive-by. No parking available.

Singing Beach is at the end of Beach Street. From the center of town or the train station it is a pleasant walk to this lovely sandy beach surrounded by a rocky shore. Restrooms and food concession. Parking fee.

Tuck's Point is a short drive from the center of town. From Route 127 take Harbor Street. After crossing the railroad bridge, bear left and go to the end of the road. This is a small park along a rocky shore with a tiny sandy beach on the scenic harbor. Grassy areas with picnic tables, restrooms; parking for residents only.

White Beach is reached by taking Ocean Street (off Route 127) between Manches-ter and Magnolia. It is a lovely drive to this sandy beach surrounded by a rocky shore. Parking is for residents only.

BOATING, CRUISES, AND MARINAS

Crocker's Boat Yard, 15 Ashland Avenue. Call 526-1971.

Manchester Harbor Boat Club, P.O. Box 1405. Call 526-4290.

Manchester Marine, 17 Ashland Avenue. Full-service yacht yard and marine supplies. Call 526-7911.

Tsalta Sail Charters is based in Ipswich but sails out of Manchester-by-the-Sea. Captains Diane and Charles Cooper will take up to six people on the 35-foot *Tsalta* for a 2-hour sail. There is also a 5-hour sail that includes lunch. For details and reservations, write to Tsalta Sail Charters,

Singing Beach   *Peter H. Gertsch*

6 Poplar Street, Ipswich, MA 01938 or call 356-4122.

COMMUNITY CENTER

The Manchester Community Center is located at Harbor's Point; office hours are Monday, Wednesday, and Friday from 9 a.m. to 12:30 p.m. The center is a nonprofit, privately funded organization with the sole purpose of promoting community spirit through sponsorship of community events and activities for all ages (social, educational, fraternal, or recreational). Throughout the year many town organizations hold their functions here: for example, scout troops, senior citizens, the North Shore Horticultural Society, and the Seaside Garden Club all meet here. Each month there is sure to be something going on that will interest you. In January there is a Speakers Series called "Winter Wednesdays," in February there is a children's activity such as a concert or puppet theater, and in March there is a Members' Party with evening entertainment for everyone in town. Each year the calendar holds traditional as well as new activities. The Community Center building is available to rent for your next meeting, party, wedding, or reunion; there is a full kitchen and the hall seats up to 140 people. Call 526-7626.

FITNESS CLUBS

Manchester Athletic Club is on Atwater Avenue (Exit 15 off Route 128). A "leader in fitness since 1973," this full-service athletic club offers outdoor activities (including summer camp programs), in the summer and tennis, swimming, aerobics, exercise machines, indoor track, massage, nursery, and a cafe year-round. Open Mon.–Fri., 5:30 a.m.–10 p.m.; Sat. and Sun., 7:30 a.m.–8 p.m. Membership fee. Call 526-1681 or 800-649-4644.

OPEN SPACE, PARKS, AND PLAYGROUNDS

Agassiz Rock (a property of The Trustees of Reservations) is a half-mile west of Route 128 on School Street (Exit 15). Park and Rock (measuring 6,000 square feet) are named for Louis Agassiz, Harvard University professor of Natural History (in the 1870s), who identified the area's Rock and Swamp as two huge glacial erratics deposited by the glacier that covered New England thousands of years ago. From the summit of Agassiz Rock is a panoramic view of land and sea. Street parking only. For information call 921-1944.

Cedar Swamp, Blue Heron Pond, and Millstone Hill are on old School Street (diagonally across from the Agassiz Park entrance). Park your car outside the gate and walk in. Watch for signs—the trails are marked. Wear sturdy shoes and insect repellent.

Coach Field is at the corner of Brook Street and Norwood Avenue. The baseball diamond, soccer field, and tennis courts are open to residents. Parking is available.

The *Ocean Lawn* at Coolidge Point Reservation   *Courtesy of The Trustees of Reservations*

Coolidge Reservation (a property of The Trustees of Reservations) is located directly off Summer Street (Route 127). When Thomas Jefferson Coolidge, the great-grandson of President Thomas Jefferson, bought the old Goldsmith Farm in 1871, he described this bluff of Crescent Beach as a "wild promontory surrounded by the ocean." In 1873, he built a large country house of white clapboard on the neck of the point looking westward toward Crow Island. This house was soon followed by other houses. Over the years Coolidge Point became a small community of congenial families where privacy was respected.

Mr. Coolidge was president and director of many corporations and was appointed to various important commissions by the Governor of Massachusetts and the

President of the United States. He was an early member of the Metropolitan Park Commission and a friend of Samuel Sawyer of Gloucester (the benefactor of Ravenswood Park). One of his greatest pleasures was reading. In 1887 he gave the Town of Manchester its library. He was a revered citizen of Manchester and the last of our ministers to France. In fact, he is often referred to as "The Ambassador" among the Coolidges. He died in 1920 at the age of ninety.

In 1902, Thomas Jefferson Coolidge, Jr. engaged McKim, Mead, and White to build his new house on the Ocean Lawn. The house was built on the site of the old Coolidge mansion, which was moved back to a higher site. Nothing interrupted the widespread view of the ocean and shore for miles each way. The house was 230 feet long, with two wings of brick and white marble and Roman columns reflecting the Classic Revival style of Jefferson. This Georgian style house, known as the "Marble Palace," embodied ideas which came down from Inigo Jones (English architect, 1572–1652).

Thomas Jefferson Coolidge III followed in his father's and grandfather's footsteps. He was president or director of several corporations and president of the Museum of Fine Arts. He was appointed Undersecretary of the Treasury by President Franklin D. Roosevelt during his first term. Before Mr. Coolidge's death in 1958, the McKim house was torn down and another house was built on the Ocean Lawn; this house remained until 1984. In mid-1970 Frederick Winthrop, Director of The Trustees of Reservations, was walking on the Ocean Lawn with his first cousin, Bill Coolidge of Topsfield (the only surviving brother of T.J. Coolidge III) when the conversation turned to the possibility of preserving the views and land on Coolidge Point. In 1992 the Coolidge Reservation was established. Today 57.8 acres of for-est, wetlands, and rocky headlands, including a portion of Magnolia Beach, and the expansive Ocean Lawn, with its magnificent trees and inspiring ocean views, are there for all to enjoy. Ample parking is available. (Note: The Ocean Lawn is open to visitors on **Saturdays only**.)

Masconomo Park is located downtown next to the harbor. There is a pier, boat landing area, playground, sports field, picnic tables, and a bandstand (concerts are held on Sunday evenings in August). Parking is available for residents at the park; public parking is nearby.

Memorial (Elementary) School is on Lincoln Street. There is a large new playground. It is best to park at the lot on the corner of Brook Street and Norwood Avenue.

SPORTING GOODS: SALES AND RENTALS

Seaside Cycle is at 23 Elm Street. Sales, repairs, and rentals of bicycles and skis. Call 526-1200.

Lodging

Old Corner Inn, 2 Harbor Street. This former Danish summer embassy was built in 1865. It is a gracious manor where you can enjoy a vacation or a weekend get-away. The inn has 9 cozy guest rooms with working fireplaces and four-poster beds. A continental break-fast is served. From Route 128 take Exit 16 (Pine Street), turn left at the bottom of the exit ramp, and drive 1.4 miles to a stop at Route 127. Turn right and drive 0.7 miles. The inn is on your left. Open year-round. For reservations, call 526-4996.

Restaurants

Beach Street Cafe, 35 Beach Street. Breakfast, full meals, subs, sandwiches, salads, and soups. Call 526-8049.

Captain Dusty's Ice Cream, 60 Beach Street. Homemade ice cream and frozen yogurt. Open in the summer only. Call 526-1663.

Captain Tom's, 11 Summer Street. Baked and fried seafood, roast beef, salads, and sandwiches. Call 526-9511.

Coffee Cup Restaurant, 25 Union Street. Breakfast, lunch, and dinner. Open daily at 6 a.m. Call in your pizza order for pick-up, 526-4558.

Edgewater Cafe & Catering, 69 Raymond Street. Authentic Mexican cuisine. For twelve consecutive years voted "Number One People's Choice" (*North Shore Magazine*). Eat in or take-out. BYOB. From the end of May throughout the summer open at 8 a.m. daily; for off-season hours, information, or to order, call 526-4668.

Harbor Point Ice Cream, 40 Beach Street. Call 526-7462.

The Harborside Hofbrau, 37 Beach Street. Genuine German and American cuisine; pub downstairs and fine dining upstairs. Full liquor license; directly on the harbor. Open 11:30 a.m. daily for lunch and dinner. Call 526-7774.

Jane's Place, 7 Beach Street. Full breakfast, soups, salads, subs, pizza, and sandwiches. Eat in or take-out. Open Sunday–Wednesday, 6 a.m.–7 p.m.; Thursday–Saturday, 6 a.m.–8 p.m. Call 526-1202.

Kitchen Witch Eatery, 10 Summer Street. Gourmet coffees, sandwiches, soups and homemade pastries. Open 6 a.m. Monday–Friday; Saturday and Sunday, open at 7 a.m. Call 526-9995.

Seven Central Publick House, 7 Central Street. (For the history of this seaside tavern see the **History** section.) Casual dining and patio. Fireside dining in cold weather. Open daily at 11:30 a.m. Wheelchair accessible. Call 526-4533.

Captain Dusty's   *Liz Mackie*

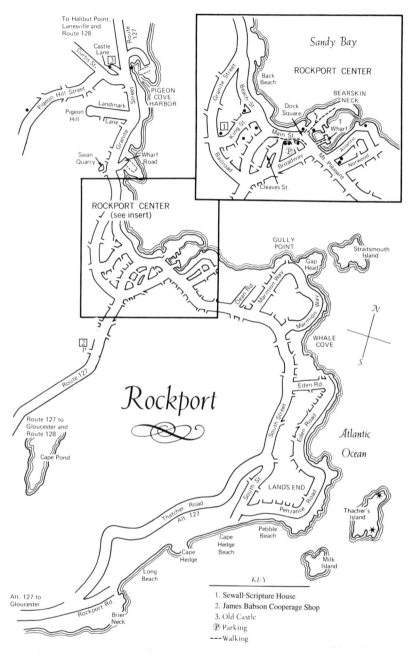

Courtesy of J. W. Murray & Associates

Thacher Island and Twin Lights   *Tom O'Hara*

Rockport

HISTORY OF ROCKPORT

The Indians summering here welcomed Samuel de Champlain ashore in 1605. Had they been as friendly when he returned a year later, Rockport might have become a French colony. Instead, Captain John Smith of England promoted "New England" in a book. He wrote that timber, fish, and stone would provide initial revenues for a town on this "Sandy Bay." It was Smith's successive publications that influenced the ancestors of many a Rockporter to migrate here.

The first extensive land grants were not made until 1688, when qualified voters decided to distribute their common lands "at ye Cape." Every householder and every man over twenty-one years of age who had been born in the town and was still living and paying taxes received six acres, chosen in a lot drawing. Eighty-two units were laid out from Lane's Cove around "holybut point" and past "piggion cove" to Millbrook.

A rash of land transfers broke out following these grants. In the early 1690s the Richard Tarrs came from Maine and built their first shelter on the slope behind what is now 113 Main Street. Then John Pool, his wife, and children moved here from Beverly. Thomas Witham and John Pool erected a grist mill on the brook that runs down into the sea and they dammed-up the brook to provide power. In 1702, the Samuel Gott family purchased land near Halibut Point and built what is said to be the oldest gambrel-roofed house remaining on Cape Ann. Others settled along the shore at locations that became known as Folly Cove, Pigeon Cove, and Front Beach. Further expansion occurred at the bay when roads were laid out to connect these families with central Gloucester.

As the Sandy Bay area developed, the families petitioned for land to build a schoolhouse. Next, the settlers decided that the ten-mile round trip to church on winter Sundays caused excessive hardship. Starting in 1738 they persistently appealed to the first parish in Gloucester to allow them to hire a minister for the winter months. They also wanted a portion of their compulsory church taxes returned to them so they could pay the winter preacher. Finally their appeal went to the General Court in Boston and in 1754 the lower house of the legislature and the governor of Massachusetts concurred; the Sandy Bay parish, Gloucester's fifth and last, was granted. The first church, at the head of Long Cove, was thirty-six feet square, two stories high, and without a belfry or a steeple. John Cleaveland had been installed as minister of the Essex Church and this drew his younger brother, Ebenezer Cleaveland, to Sandy Bay. The parish concurred with the church vote "in chusing Mr. Ebenezer Cleaveland for their Pasture" and he stayed until 1780, when the congregation could no longer pay him a living.

The first residents had come for the virgin timber, but before long fishing and coastal trade supplied the main revenue. Soon a wharf was needed. Benjamin Tarr and John and Ebenezer Pool secured a grant and built the first Sandy Bay pier of timber and stone at what is today the old harbor. As the fleet expanded more docking areas were needed, so a second wharf was approved by the parish, to be built on "Bear Scin Neck flatts." Nearby communities outclassed Sandy Bay in the building and manning of schooners; however, after the Revolutionary War, the partial-decked, small local vessels of Sandy Bay were able to resume fishing sooner than the bulkier ships of the larger seaports. The smaller "Chebacco" boats (named for Essex, where they originated) were ideally suited for catching cod, haddock, and pollock; as the market grew, so did the fleet. From Essex and Annisquam boat-builders, sailors, and others moved to Sandy Bay. By 1800 dozens of sailing vessels, each weighing five, ten, or more tons, anchored in what is today Rockport Harbor.

Like Gloucester, Sandy Bay (Rockport) saw its share of loss of life and vessels. The *Industry* went down with all hands off Salt Island. A Dutch ship with 303 people aboard sank off the cape. A local vessel capsized on the north side of the peninsula and seven were drowned; strangely, one man survived, and he was the only one who could not swim.

When the Sandy Bay meetinghouse was beyond repair, the cornerstone of "Old Sloop" (the Congregational Church) was laid. Ebenezer Cleaveland returned for this event on July 4, 1803, and joined his successor-to-be, David Jewett. Pastor Jewett was ordained in Sandy Bay and remained devoted to this community for more than thirty years.

As the community continued to grow, more wharves, piers, and breakwaters were needed and the Sandy Bay Pier Company was founded. Old wharves came down and stone foundations were laid for a longer, wider wharf. Then the state legislature chartered the Pigeon Cove Pier Company "for the purpose of erecting and maintaining a stone pier." This was followed by the creation of the Pigeon Cove Harbor Company in 1831, to protect the exposed cove by constructing a breakwater on the "North East side of said cove...." Thacher Island had the twin lights, but the Salvages (Savage Rocks) and Straitsmouth Island remained a constant menace. It was not until 1896 that the federal government took over Straitsmouth for the sole purpose of erecting and maintaining a lighthouse there. In 1836 construction of the breakwater running out from the tip of Bearskin Neck towards the Headlands commenced; this turned Long Cove into a genuine harbor. The old fort on Bearskin Neck was taken down in 1837 and wharves were built out on the north side of the harbor and from the south side of Long Cove Brook.

Fishing and commerce boomed on shore and at sea. Cod, mackerel, and fish oil brought high prices. With the completion of the Erie Canal, "western" markets were now accessible. Isinglass (a semitransparent, pure form of gelatin used to settle beer) was a new commercial venture that provided a livelihood along with the granite industry for one hundred years. The isinglass industry thrived until prohibition came to Rockport.

The granite industry provided work for hundreds of local men. The industry began when Nehemiah Knowlton placed an advertisement in a Boston newspaper offering cellar and foundation granite stone for sale. Major Bates from Quincy saw the newspaper and came to Rockport. Major Bates set up operations in two rented locations and was accompanied by William Torrey, who remained to continue the business. Torrey and his sons concentrated their excavations at the Torrey Pit, next to the Rockport Granite Company bridge. Almost all the granite used at government installations in Boston Harbor and the Charlestown and Portsmouth Navy Yards came from this pit, as well as granite for the Chain Bridge over the Merrimack River at Newburyport.

Cape Ann's high-quality granite was easily accessible and the cost of transportation (via the Atlantic Ocean) was low. Tons of stone were shipped across the United States to be used in the building of financial institutions, wharves, jetties, dry docks, railways, and roadways. Before the cutting could begin, the flat surface was marked with a chalkline; this required a keen eye for imperfections. Then holes were drilled a few inches apart and about three inches deep and dynamite or black powder was placed in the holes to blast the stone from the ledge. The work was dangerous and many injuries occurred from premature explosions, flying debris, and falling rock. As soon as the block was freed, it was lifted to the rim of the quarry by hooks fastened to heavy chains and loaded onto flat cars that were moved by gravity. Then hauling animals such as oxen or a locomotive pulled the stone to the waterfront, where it was cut as needed and loaded onto ships.

The hard igneous rock was extracted from the pits for decades by hundreds of Finns, Swedes, Irish, Scots, Italians, and English, as well as the Yankees who were descendants of the first settlers. The industry flourished until the coming of automobile transportation. At first drivers were content with the bumpy surface of a granite-block road, but as they drove farther and faster, they demanded smooth roads of concrete

42-pair of oxen pulling an 18-foot granite threshold   *Courtesy of Gaspar Lafata*

and asphalt. When the need for granite ebbed the small granite companies merged into the Rockport Granite Company. They could not compete for long with the lighter construction materials available: demand declined as costs continued to rise, and the granite industry eventually skidded into history.

During the 1800's, as might be expected, the Sandy Bay parish grew and thrived, and the people became increasingly restless and wanted their independence from Gloucester. Voters were aroused, opposition swelled, and no agreement could be reached at town meetings. Finally, the Massachusetts legislature got involved. Sandy Bay dropped the matter when it was determined that its taxes would be higher after a separation. By April, 1839, Sandy Bay favored a separation by a vote of 319 to 54. New geographical boundaries had to be drawn, property values established, and many more details worked out; sharp clashes ensued. Finding a name for their new town was another matter that caused friction. After repeated voting, since there was so much land with quarrying value, the name Rockport was deemed most appropriate. In February, 1840, Governor Marcus Morton signed a bill setting off Sandy Bay and parts of Pigeon Cove and Annisquam as the independent town of Rockport.

By this time regular steamers were running excursions from Boston to Rockport, carrying hundreds of passengers at a time. Boston to Portsmouth steamers anchored off Straits-mouth Island and smaller boats ferried passengers back and forth to Rockport. A combination of rail (which extended to Gloucester at this time), stagecoach lines, and ships opened Rockport to ever-increasing numbers of summer visitors. These visitors returned home telling others that Cape Ann was an attractive summer place. Richard Henry Dana, Jr. (author of *Two Years Before the Mast*) honeymooned here with his bride. At another time, the Danas brought Mr. and Mrs. William Cullen Bryant to Pigeon Cove. Locals began to take in more boarders. Tourists were attracted by Dogtown, Folly Cove, Pigeon Hill, and the picturesque lighthouses. Visitors yearned to come back to the peaceful surroundings and agreeable inhabitants. Thoreau and Emerson were two such visitors who took kindly to Rockport. Thoreau wrote of his walking tour of Cape Ann, and Emerson was so pleased that he returned the following summer, bringing his entire family.

During the 1800's Rockport's several industries kept the local people employed: shipbuilding (with its related businesses), an organ factory, a cotton mill, numerous shops with a variety of goods, and summer visitors. Lectures, dances, theater, concerts, and even a natural history society provided for lots of social activity. People went walking, rowing, and sailing, and regattas were also catching on. Baseball, picnics, and fishing parties were all the rage. Artists were drawn to Rockport and needed materials such as easels, paints, and brushes. The first provider of artists' materials and frames was G. Tucker Margeson, who also served as the local telegraph agent in the 1870s. Artists were attracted to Rockport by the odd-shaped buildings, the sheer walls and smooth angles of the quarries, the rocky cliffs, and many other paintable subjects. Visitors who were not artistically inclined enjoyed riding bicycles around Cape Ann; others found collecting algae fun and joined the Sea Moss Club. Some were happy to pass lazy days on verandahs, enjoying pleasant views and good books. One local resident was irritated when she counted 202 "idle pleasure carriages and buggies with occupants bent on mere recreation" passing by her house.

The history of Rockport would not be complete unless the Harbor of Refuge is included. The *Rockport Review* convinced townspeople they needed a breakwater to create an enormous protected harbor. The newspaper admonished citizens to petition Congress to construct it. Finally, by the end of 1883, the U.S. Engineers recommended construction of a V-shaped, 9,000-foot breakwater from Avery's Ledge toward Andrews' Point, leaving two broad entrances to a harbor some 60 feet deep and over 1,660 acres in scope. This impossible dream caused one million tons of stone to be quarried, transported, and placed in position to create the breakwater. For more than fifteen years one appropriation led to another as Congress kept the project funded and congressmen came from time to time to inspect this "most-important undertaking." At one point about six hundred feet of the breakwater were complete. Although another newspaper, the *Advertiser*, wrote that at this rate it would take another twenty-five years to finish it, no one seemed able to stop working on the dream. Finally, in 1910 Congress stopped funding Rockport's breakwater and work ceased. The unfinished breakwater is visible from Front Beach and Bearskin Neck and other places along the shore.

One day in 1886, not far off Rockport's shores, a strange creature was spotted. Through binoculars the town clerk and a friend watched a sea serpent's undulations for about ten minutes. They described the creature as being about eighty feet long, with a whitish head the size of a nail cask and a brownish body having a girth larger than a man's. A week later several other people spotted the creature in Pigeon Cove. Many articles appeared in newspapers in the weeks following the sightings, and there was a substantial agreement of descriptive detail. In fact, there was even a $20,000 reward offered to anyone who could catch the creature. But as freely as the creature appeared, it vanished. (For more information about other sightings of the sea serpent, see **Places of Interest**: Gloucester.)

The passage of time has not diminished the appeal of Rockport's coast, quaint old houses, fishing shacks, and picturesque harbor. Visitors can picnic at the shore, bicycle around the cape, attend a world-class concert, or see award-winning canvases at the Rockport Art Association. Rockport's charm and the hospitality of its people draw visitors from around the world.

PLACES OF INTEREST

A s you enter Rockport via Route 127 from Gloucester, you'll see the Visitors Information Booth on your right, on upper Main Street. Should you come into Rockport via Route 127A and need information, stop at the Rockport Chamber of Commerce and Board of Trade at 3 Main Street or call 546-6575.

In the historic central district of Rockport, 19th- and 20th-century buildings of brick or frame construction run along both sides of Main Street, one of the town's earliest roads. The following places of interest are in geographic order with the most central attractions listed first, followed by those increasingly farther away.

Bearskin Neck got its name in 1710, when John Babson killed a bear there, skinned it, and laid the skin on a rock to dry. Some Essex fishermen saw the sight and called out to Babson that he should call the spot "Bearskin Neck." The Neck was the shipbuilding center of Rockport for 150 years; today it is still a commercial center with many quaint art galleries, gift shops, restaurants, and a motel. Many of the businesses here are closed during the winter, but you can walk to the end of the Neck anytime and enjoy the picturesque setting.

Motif #1 is the most painted building on the Eastern seaboard. Located on Bradley Wharf on Bearskin Neck, this fishing shack became famous when artist Lester Hornby brought his students here during art classes. The blizzard of 1978 swept the shack into Rockport harbor; later it was reconstructed and painted the original color.

Old Stone Fort was located at the end of Bearskin Neck to protect against British warships during the War of 1812. Muskets, powder horns, and decorative swords are on display at the Sandy Bay Historical Society at 40 King Street.

Old Fort Gallery is located at 71 Bearskin Neck Road (at the site of the Old Stone Fort). Take the flight of stairs up to the observation platform for a panoramic view of Rockport. At the top are several signs pointing out events of historic significance. A token admission is charged.

Rockport Art Association is at 12 Main Street. In 1929 the Association purchased the Old Tavern of 1787, originally a one-story house with a gambrel roof, which the owner, Captain Josiah Haskell, converted into a tavern. Later Caleb Norwood bought it and the building was used as an inn, a store, a restaurant, and a dance hall on the second floor. For years the Old Tavern was the last stop of the Salem–Rockport stagecoach. After the Art Association bought it, the rooms were remodeled and an exhibition hall was added at the rear. Today the Association occupies three large buildings on Main Street. Open year-round: Monday–Saturday, 9:30–4:30; Sunday, 1–5. Call 546-6604.

First Congregational Church on Main Street incorporates both Federal and Greek Revival elements. This is the second church building; its cornerstone was laid in 1803. The architect was Jacob Smith of Gloucester. In 1814 the tower was shattered by a British bombardment.

Rockport Public Library is located at 17 School Street, in the 1847 steam Cotton Mill. The original building was 200 feet long, had a four-story entrance tower with a belfry, and a five-story detached smokestack. At one time over two hundred looms operated, using 1,000,000 pounds of cotton per year to produce award-winning cotton duck, yarn, and "India Rubber cloth." The four almost identical large frame houses still standing today, across Broadway from the mill, were once dormitories for mill workers. Fire destroyed the mill in 1883 and 235 workers were without jobs.

In 1987 local sculptor, poet, and philanthropist Franz Denghausen left a bequest in his will of $1,000,000 for the provision of suitable new library space in memory of his wife Luisita. Mr. Denghausen had read encyclopedias and dictionaries cover to cover and received his education from libraries when he was growing up. The new Rockport Public Library opened its doors in 1993 and offers many services: the film series, local repertory theater performances, exhibitions in the upstairs mezzanine hall, and an outstanding doll collection in the

Children's Room. Library patrons come from all over the North Shore to attend the Millbrook Meadow summer reading program. The Friends of the Library promote the library's goals and new members are always welcome. Call the library at 546-6934. **Winter and Summer Schedule:** Sun., 1–6; Mon. and Wed., 1–8; Tues., 10–5; Thurs., 1–8; Closed on Fri.; Sat., 10–5.

Residents may obtain **free passes** for the Museum of Fine Arts.

James Babson Cooperage Shop is on Route 127 (upper Main Street) between Rockport and Gloucester. When James Babson turned twenty-one, he was granted 22 acres of land at Beaver Dam by the colonial settlement. Here, in 1658, he began making barrels with lumber he got from the mill at Cape Pond Brook. The hoops were soaked in the brook before they could be bent, and then Babson used fire to heat and shape them. After the barrels were filled with dried fish they were shipped to England. Years later Colonel James Foster built his farmhouse in front of the present shop and the cooperage became the kitchen portion of his house. When the house was torn down in 1924, Roger W. Babson had the granite exterior of the shop refurbished before the building was made into a museum. The cooperage contains early Americana (ancient kitchen tools and iron wares used to make barrels). Open during July and August, Tuesday–Sunday, from 2 to 5.

Sandy Bay Historical Society is located in one of Rockport's finest old homes, the Sewall-Scripture House, at 40 King Street. The house was built in 1832 by Levi Sewall with granite from his own quarry. It stands out as a fine example of the Federal style, delicately handled in stone. Sewall's descendants lived in the house until it was purchased by the Society in 1957; the house was placed on the National Register of Historic Places in 1982. Visitors will see oil paintings by Alfred L. Wiggin (1823–1883), a prize-winning reed organ designed and made by William Manning at his factory on King Street, a large granite industry collection, a marine exhibit, samples of local isinglass, and objects and photos from the steam Cotton Mill (1847–1883). In the Children's Room are beautifully dressed old dolls, toys, and furniture. In the Hannah Jumper Room, visitors learn how on, July 8, 1856, Hannah led sixty normally prudent housewives on a five-hour rampage to stamp out "demon rum" in their fishing village. The men had left bills unpaid and wasted their hard-earned wages on drink, leaving no money for food and provisions for their families. The women declared Rockport to be a dry town and it still is, 140 years later. Open July 1–Labor Day, daily from 2 to 5, or by appointment. Admission fee includes the Sewall-Scripture House and the Old Castle in Pigeon Cove. Call 546-9533.

The Sewall-Scripture House
Courtesy of Sandy Bay Historical Society

Granite Keystone Bridge was built in 1872 and is listed on the National Register of Historic Places. Directly next to the bridge on the ocean side of Route 127 is a roadway leading down to the Granite Pier. From a short roadway that connected the adjacent Flat Ledge Quarry to the Granite Pier, you can view the single arch, which spans 65 feet and is 32 feet wide, as well as the granite blocks used in the bridge's construction.

Pigeon Hill is reached by taking Landmark Lane off Route 127, near Pigeon Cove (north of Rockport center). This lovely picnic spot above Sandy Bay has always been a landmark for mariners. At one time there was a 2,000-ton granite boulder on the top of this hill left behind by the last ice age; the boulder produced thousands of feet of stone comparable to quarry granite. The town of Rockport purchased the five-acre summit of Pigeon Hill as a perpetual piece of common ground for all people to enjoy.

The Old Castle on Granite Street in Pigeon Cove center, directly behind the former Story Library, also is owned by the Sandy Bay Historical Society. It is believed that the Old Castle may have been standing on the original 100 acres purchased by Jethro Wheeler in 1712. It is one of the oldest remaining houses on Cape Ann. Six successive generations of Wheelers lived here. The 1853 assessment record refers to the house as the "Old Castle." This first-period house's only notable architectural feature is the overhanging second story on the front and east end, reminiscent of the Gothic architecture the early settlers had known in England. The purpose of this overhang is to gain floor space in the upper stories. This house has an overhang of two to four inches obtained by hewing the outside of the posts to a smaller dimension on the first floor than on the second. Since use of an overhang died out early in eastern Massachusetts, its occurrence here points strongly to an early date for this house. Over time the lean-to was added and many changes were made. The Old Castle contains exhibits on Dogtown, quarry tools, local history, and five early fireplaces. Open daily from 2 to 5 from July 1 to Labor Day, or by appointment. Admission fee includes the Sewall-Scripture House and the Old Castle. Call 546-9533.

The Paper House at 52 Pigeon Hill Street, off Curtis Street, is reached via Route 127 from Rockport on the way to Halibut Point. Built during the 1920s by Elis Stenman, this two-room house has walls made of 215 thicknesses of newsprint and contains furniture made of rolled-up newspapers. Over 100,000 newspapers were used in making the house and furniture, and through the shellac you can still read the print! Open daily from 10 to 5 during July and August, or by appointment in the spring and fall. A small fee is charged.

Halibut Point is on Gott Avenue, off Route 127 north of Pigeon Cove. Halibut Point Reservation (a property of The Trustees of Reservations) includes twelve acres and Halibut Point State Park includes fifty-four acres. This point is where sailing vessels had to tack, or "haul-about," as they rounded Cape Ann's northernmost tip. At Halibut Point, Joseph Babson and Benjamin Hale operated quarries and shipped stone from their own wharf. As you walk the well-maintained trails you will see the abandoned quarry, which has naturally filled with fresh water. At the shore are huge piles of cut granite left over from the quarrying operation. This is a great place to picnic, sketch, go fishing, and explore the rocky shoreline and tidal pools. If you are a bird watcher, you may see eight types of gulls and over 100 other species of birds. (For more infor-

Halibut Point   *Courtesy of Dorothy Kerper Monnelly*

mation, see **The Sea, the Land, and the People** in the Cape Ann section.) Open daily, with guided tours offered throughout the year. Handicap accessible restrooms. Parking fee in the summer (Trustees members park free). Visitor center open 8–6 in the summer (closes at 4 p.m. in the winter). Call 281-0041 or 546-2997.

Straitsmouth Island has an 1896 lighthouse (which is a copy of the 1890 Eastern Point Lighthouse) that was placed there for inshore navigation of Rockport's harbor. (For lighthouse cruises, see **Recreation** section for Rockport and Gloucester.)

Thacher Island (Twin Lights) is the only double set of lighthouses remaining in America. They were constructed to warn ships of the savage rocks of Big Salvages and Little Salvages, located between the two islands of Thacher and Straitsmouth, where many a vessel has been destroyed. Congress appropriated funds to replace the original pair of wooden lights in 1859 and the contract went to a New Hampshire granite quarry. No local stone was used in the 150-foot high lighthouses!

The island is named after Anthony Thacher, whose vessel was wrecked in a violent tempest in 1635. Anthony Thacher wrote a letter which was later printed in Increase Mather's *Remarkable Providences* telling of the remarkable gale that turned buildings over, tore thousands of trees up by the roots, and left destruction visible for years afterwards. The now legendary tale of "Thacher's Woe" follows.

A vessel set sail from Ipswich bound for Marblehead (they had to go around the cape because the cut had not yet been made to create a passageway via the Annisquam River) with a reluctant Parson Avery aboard. He was supposed to start the first church in Marblehead but had not wanted to go there because the fishermen were "loose and remiss in their behavior." So he had gone instead to Newberry (Newbury), and now, after solicitations by men and magistrates, he finally consented. Avery and his family plus his cousin and his family were among the twenty-three "souls" on board when, on August 14, 1635, at 10 o'clock at night, the gale split the sails. They did not hoist new ones because of the storm and the darkness but instead threw over the anchor, which would not hold. The wind and waves drove them with its fury "upon a rock between two high rocks, yet all was one rock." The ship was broken and filled with water and people were swept away, drowned, and dashed upon the rocks. The children wailed, the men prayed, and all prepared to die. Parson Avery, one daughter, and his eldest son, along with Anthony Thacher, washed upon the rocks, bruised and beaten but alive. Thacher saw his children crying and clutching each other on a rocky ledge and watched as they were swept away to their death. The survivors remained for a week on the island before they could be rescued and continue on to Marblehead. John Greenleaf Whittier wrote a poem, "The Swan Song of Parson Avery," based on "Thacher's Woe."

At the present time, there is no transportation to Thacher's island, since the last of many landing ramps was destroyed by the sea. The Thacher Island Association is currently raising funds to build a new landing ramp so visitors will once again be able to explore the island. Call George and Dorothy Carroll in Rockport (former Thacher lighthouse keepers) at 546-7697 for more information or to make a contribution to the landing ramp fund.

Places of Worship

BAPTIST

The First Baptist Church in Rockport, 2 High Street. Call 546-6121. Sunday service at 10:30 a.m. and Sunday school at 9 a.m., Sept.–June. Church school for the developmentally delayed and a nursery are provided.

CATHOLIC

St. Joachim's, Broadway. Call 546-6756. Sunday Mass at 8:30 a.m. and 10:30 a.m.

CHRISTIAN SCIENCE

Christian Science Church, Main Street. Reading Room is at School Street. Call 546-2392. Sunday service and Sunday school at 10 a.m.; Wednesday service at 8 p.m.

CONGREGATIONAL

First Congregational Church, 12 School Street. Call 546-6638. Sunday service at 10 a.m.; Sunday school at 10 a.m., Sept.–June; nursery for infants–age 2.

METHODIST

Rockport United Methodist Church, 36 Broadway. Call 546-2093. Sunday service at 10:30 a.m. and Sunday school at 9 a.m.

NON-DENOMINATIONAL/ EVANGELICAL

Pigeon Cove Chapel, 155 Granite Street. Call 546-2523. Sunday service at 10 a.m. (summer) and at 10:30 a.m. (winter); Sunday school at 9 a.m., Sept.–June.

UNITARIAN-UNIVERSALIST

First Unitarian-Universalist Church, 8 Cleaves Street. Call 546-2989. Sunday service and Sunday school at 10:30 a.m.

Antiques

Matt Jackson owns **Ye Olde Lantern Antiques** at 28 Railroad Avenue. He started collecting old coins, bottles, and rocks when he was twelve years old. His first job was doing maintenance on the grounds of Beauport, where the curators, Mr. and Mrs. Blanford, asked him to come inside one day and help clean an old Irish Waterford chandelier. Beauport with its many rooms and variety of old things—especially the beautiful designs in the hooked rugs, the Jacobean furnishings, and the old English Staffordshire—made a lasting impression on him. In 1972 he started his first shop in Hamilton, and hung up an old lantern framed by a wooden sign where the shop "Ye Olde Lantern" stood. Then in 1979 he bought the Rockport property at 28 Railroad Avenue, renovated the shop over a period of three years, and at the same time ran his Hamilton store. Matt Jackson's favorite antiques include "Historical Blue" Staffordshire pottery made during the early 1800s. This pottery bears historical scenes or buildings commemorating special places and was made by transfer patterns. He does appraisals and house clean-outs, and will also buy and sell one piece or an entire estate. The shop is open by appointment; call 546-6757.

MORE ANTIQUE DEALERS

Aud Froystein Antiques, North Road (Bearskin Neck). Call 546-3387.

Buried Treasures, 17 South Road (Bearskin Neck). Antique jewelry. Call 546-3432.

Geraci Galleries & Art Center Ltd., 6 South Street. Paintings by masters, sculpture, and antiques. Parking on premises. Call 546-7854.

Hanna Wingate of Rockport, 11 Main Street. Call 546-1008.

Intique, 6 Dock Square. Call 546-2970.

Joan's Rainbow Legend, 7 Bearskin Neck. Antique jewelry. Call 546-7823.

Marian Titus Antiques, 34 Granite Street. Call 546-6804.

Rockport Quilt Shoppe, 2 Ocean Avenue (Pigeon Cove). Specializes in antique quilts. Call 546-1001.

Rockport Trading Company, 67 Broadway Avenue. Call 546-8066.

Scott's Barn, 151 Upper Main Street. Call 546-6365.

Woodbine Collection, 35 Main Street. Call 546-9324.

Art

Artists began coming to Rockport in the mid-1800s, but by the early 1900s their numbers had increased. When Rockport celebrated its centennial in 1940, G. Tucker Margeson's art studio was already sixty-seven years old. "Sunday painters" and summer dabblers moved in. Some stayed only for the summers; others, like Harrison Cady, who illustrated *Peter Rabbit*, bought property and became perennial residents. W. Lester Stevens was Rockport's first native painter to achieve prominence for his painting, "Quarry at Rockport." Eric Hudson Jonas Lie was born in Norway and came to Rockport before World War I; his specialty was marine paintings. He became president of the National Academy in 1933 and held this position for several years. Other artist pioneers in Rockport were Galen Perrett and Harry A. Vincent. Both Perrett and Vincent painted marine and waterfront scenes, though only Vincent was self-taught.

When Aldro T. Hibbard came to Rockport in the summer of 1920, he moved into a deserted livery stable on the waterfront and started the Rockport Summer School of Drawing and Painting. Eight World War I veterans were his first students. The school evolved into a club, and the *Gloucester Times* wrote about the fifty Rockport artists who gathered and planned "the first exhibit of the work of professional artists ever given in Rockport." In August 1921, the vestry walls of the first Congregational Church displayed about one hundred pictures. Some of the artists sensed that changes were coming to Cape Ann. They recorded in oils, watercolors, and lithographs the scenes they loved: the quarries at work, sloops docked at Pigeon Cove wharves waiting to haul the stone away, lobstermen and fishermen with their traps and nets, streets with shingled houses and picket fences. In time the growing art community appealed to the town to preserve these treasures and maintain the town's character. Fishing shacks and old barns became studios and homes.

Exhibits continued at the church and other locations in Rockport, until finally the **Rockport Art Association** was incorporated in 1928 by Hibbard, John M. Buckley, Kitty Parsons Recchia, Richard A. Holberg, Charles R. Knapp, Antonio Cirino, and W. Lester Stevens. A year later the Association purchased the Old Tavern at 12 Main Street and remodeled the building to suit their needs.

The Association began the Christmas Nativity Pageant in 1947. The idea originated with Dr. William F. Strangman, who proposed the production of a Christmas tableau at the Association's home. Mrs. Aldro Hibbard suggested a live pageant

Live Nativity   *Sherman Photo, Courtesy Rockport Art Association*

and said that the cast should be made up of people from the community. The committee agreed and the artists created the props and backdrops for the stable and crèche for Nativity Night. Over the years, this event has become a major tourist attraction and now draws December shoppers to downtown Rockport and the many boutiques on Bearskin Neck.

All year the Rockport Art Association presents major exhibitions. The Association offers workshops and adult and children's art classes in addition to the painting, drawing, sculpture, and photography exhibits by artist members. In the Hibbard Gallery, concerts, painting demonstrations, lectures, and other events are held; the internationally known Rockport Chamber Music Festival is held there in June. The Association's exhibits are open to the public free of charge. Artist members must live in Rockport, or spend their summers here, or have lived and worked in Rockport. For information about joining the Rockport Art Association or about its year-round programs, call 546-6604.

GALLERIES

Ahearn Martin Gallery, 102 Marmion Way. Call 546-2648.

Artful Image Pastel Portraits, 6 Dock Square. Call 546-1144.

Bosari Gallery, 12 Tuna Wharf. Call 546-9683.

William Bradley Gallery, Tuna Wharf. Call 546-3404.

John Caggiano Gallery, 76 South Road. Call 546-2414.

Sven Ohrvel Carlson Gallery, 43 Broadway. Call 546-2770.

Carson Studio & Gallery, 31 Broadway. Call 546-5850.

Coty Gallery, Tuna Wharf. Call 546-3979.

Currier Gallery, Bearskin Neck. Call 546-9720.

Demeri Domenic Gallery, Bearskin Neck. Call 546-6082.

Fine Arts of Rockport, 49 Main Street. Call 546-7431.

The Freyda Gallery, 28 Main Street. Call 546-9828.

Gaietto Remo Ray Gallery, 1 Main Street. Call 546-1123.

Geraci Galleries and Art Center, Ltd., 6 South Street. Call 546-7854.

Granite Shore Gallery, 20 Main Street. Call 546-7620.

Kaihlanen Gallery, 47 South Road. Call 546-9818.

Kamalic Ivan N. Gallery, 8 Main Street. Call 546-2654.

Kismet Gallery, 3–5 Main Street. Call 546-9750.

Howard Kline Gallery, 150 Upper Main Street. Call 546-7706.

Lerch R. Gallery, Bearskin Neck. Call 546-7797.

Marston Gallery, 4 Atlantic Avenue. Call 546-3353.

Louis Mastro Gallery, 30 Main Street. Call 546-7469.

Menna Andrew A Barn & Gallery, 1 Wharf. Call 546-7003.

Morrell Wayne Home & Gallery, 25 Main Street. Call 546-2946.

Mosher Art Gallery, 5 Atlantic Avenue. Call 546-2002.

Nicholas Gallery, 71 Main Street. Call 546-9647.

Ocean View Gallery, 38 South Road. Call 546-6363.

Old Fort Gallery, 71 Bearskin Neck. Call 546-8089.

Rockport Public Library, 17 School Street (art display in Brenner Friend's Room). Call 546-6934.

Rockport Quilt Shoppe, by appointment only. Call 546-1001.

Dorothy Russell Gallery, 35 Mt. Pleasant Street (Hannah Jumper House). Call 546-2610.

Small Small World, 47 South Road. Call 546-6426.

Square Circle, 11 Dock Square. Call 546-7100.

Stilson Gallery, 5 Dock Square. Call 546-3400.

Stoffa Michael Gallery, 49 Main Street. Call 546-7108.

Strisik Paul Gallery, by appointment only. Call 546-2871.

Too Fortunate Pottery, 9 Dock Square. Call 546-7590.

The Tracy Tom Gallery, 56 South Road. Call 546-7608.

Tutwiler-Vickery Gallery, 57 Main Street. Call 546-7649.

Wenniger Gallery, 19 Mt. Pleasant Street. Call 546-8116.

Wind, Leslie, 338 Granite Street (Folly Cove). Custom-made jewelry. Call 546-6539.

For grant applications or information about art-related programs, call Suzanne Ingalls at the Rockport Cultural Council 546-9081.

Music, Theater, & Dance

CHORUS NORTH SHORE
(FORMERLY ROCKPORT COMMUNITY CHORUS)

A community concert of "Old Christmas Carols" was presented at the First Congregational Church in 1931. Hundreds of people enjoyed the program of international carols performed by four local choral groups. People said they wished the concert could be held every Christmas season. Inspired by this response, the Community Carol Choir reorganized and changed its name to Rockport Community Chorus. Over time the chorus drew members from other communities and expanded its musical offerings.

Sonja Dahlgren Pryor has conducted the chorus for thirty-five years. She is past music director of Park Street Church in Boston and a guest and interim conductor of the New England Women's Symphony and the Cape Ann Symphony orchestra. Chorus North Shore celebrated its 65th anniversary in 1996 and has over 140 members from many communities. No membership fee or audition is required. Concerts are held from September to May and rehearsals are held Monday evenings at the Community House. For more information, write to Chorus North Shore, P.O. Box 281, or call 546-1740.

ROCKPORT CHAMBER MUSIC FESTIVAL

In 1981 pianist-composer David Alpher, soprano Lila Deis, and a local businessman, Paul Sylva, began an exciting chamber music series. The Rockport Art Association has hosted the Festival's concerts since the premiere in 1982 and the Hibbard Gallery has provided relaxed ambiance and a connection with Rockport's artistic legacy.

The Festival welcomed its new artistic director, concert pianist and outstanding educator, David Deveau, in 1995. He has greatly enhanced the Festival's ability to draw some of the nation's finest musicians to Rockport and offer quality educational programs. A special 15th anniversary season featured world-renowned soloists and chamber ensembles inaugurating a new Festival format: a Thursday evening "Virtuoso Piano Recital Series," Friday night "String Quartet Series," Saturday night "Chamber Music Gala Series," and casual-dress Sundays featuring "Come as You Are" concerts. A special holiday concert, "An American in Rockport," was given on July 3. Several lecture series have been held to introduce young people to chamber music and deepen the appreciation of regular concert goers. During June and July, sixteen different concerts are held. For information or reservations, write to the Festival office at P.O. Box 312, or call 546-7391.

THE ROCKPORT LEGION BAND

Sixty-five years ago a group of local musicians met to provide Rockport with a community band. On Memorial Day they made their debut dressed in white duck pants and blue flannel shirts. The Rockport Legion Band is a non-profit organization and all performances continue to be free, in fulfillment of that original purpose. Of the more than thirty original members, only Eugene Parady is still playing with the band. William S. Crowell is the conductor and director of this twenty-five member band. Some musicians are as young as seventeen. Several years ago a scholarship fund was started for band members still in high school; each year they are eligible to apply for funds for higher education.

The band rehearses year-round on Thursdays at 7:30 p.m. at the Legion Hall to prepare for the summer band concerts, parades, and performances for the elderly. New members are always welcome. Outdoor concerts are given at the bandstand on Beach Street on Sundays from 7:30 p.m. to 9 p.m., from July 5th through August. If you're on vacation and have your instrument with you, come make music! Bring your family, something to sit on, and a picnic dinner. For more information, call 546-2790.

THEATER IN THE PINES

Nan Webber and friends met in the spring of 1987 at her hilltop home under tall pines. The script which launched the fledgling theater company was "Alice in Blunderland," written by two graduates from Oberlin College who had performed the play in Washington, D.C., for the U.S. Congress. What appealed to her thematically and artistically then still does today: the script dealt with long-range implications of nuclear power. Theater in the Pines performed this play on several occasions in various communities.

Theater in the Pines began in the upstairs of Spiran Hall Little Art Cinema. They have been on stage in the Center for Performing Arts at Rockport High School. In December 1996, they performed "A Child's Christmas in Wales" by Dylan Thomas in the new Rockport Library's Friends Room. For Nan Webber, the most thrilling part of her work is watching actors develop from being shy until they become confident performers. Today there are fifty members and shows are held in the spring as well as in late summer. The stage manager and the lighting director have been here for over four years and came from the famous Tavistock Theater Company in Islington, London. In 1997, Theater in the Pines plans to perform at the Rockport Art Association. For more information and programs, call 546-9329.

WINDHOVER CENTER FOR THE PERFORMING ARTS

Herbert and Ina Hahn could not find an arts-oriented summer camp for their teenage daughters, so they bought the

Balzarini farm in Pigeon Cove and started their own arts center in 1967. Herb Hahn loved music and literature and Ina was a professional dancer who loved music, dance, and theater. With little experience in construction but a great deal of energy and vision, Herb worked late into the night. When buildings were torn down on the North Shore, he scavenged for materials and salvaged hand-hewn beams, barn siding, stained glass windows, and cupolas. With these architectural treasures he converted the existing buildings into a dance studio, a library and music room, dormitories, and dining and kitchen facilities in less than a year. At the same time he was head of the Manchester High School English department.

Windhover was named after the poem by Gerard Manley Hopkins about a kestrel that hovers in the air against the wind, symbolizing the soaring of human imagination and the spiritual quest that informs great art. Though Herbert Hahn passed away in 1975, Windhover's spirit continues. Today it is a non-profit performing arts center for adults. Ina Hahn has staged productions where small dance companies on Cape Ann have gathered to perform together. She likes to try things that haven't been done before. The season is from mid-June through August; programs include dance workshops and ballet and dance/theater performances. Windhover is located at 257 Granite Street. For more information and tickets, write to P.O. Box 2249, or call 546-3611.

Recreation

BEACHES

Back Beach Landing on Beach Street is a rocky shore with a sandy beach and on-street parking.

Cape Hedge Beach is off Route 127A on Old County Road. This pebbly beach has a boat landing area, on-street parking, and a resident-sticker parking lot.

Front Beach (School House Beach Landing) on Beach Street has a sandy beach, boat landing, and on-street parking.

Long Beach, next to Cape Hedge Beach, is a pebbly beach with some rocky shore for swimming, fishing, and boating. Vehicular access is by private toll road on the south side. Take Route 127A (Thatcher

Road) and approach from the north over a footbridge at end of lane connecting to Thatcher Road opposite Frank Street.

Old Garden Beach and Landing is reached from Route 127A (Mt. Pleasant Street) to Norwood Avenue to Ocean Avenue. There is a path along the rocky shore and a sandy beach with boating and a scenic vista. Free parking during the week and resident-only parking on weekends.

Pebble Beach is reached by taking Route 127A (Thatcher Road) to South Street to Penzance Road. This is a sandy area for swimming, with some rocky shore and salt marsh. Street parking only.

Straitsmouth Cove Landing is reached by taking Route 127A (Thatcher Road) to Straitsmouth Way. This is a sandy beach and rocky shore with a boating area. Resident parking only.

BOATING AND CRUISES

Old Harbor Yacht Club, 8 Wharf Road (off Bearskin Neck). Open weekends in May, daily June–August, and weekends in September. Rent kayaks, sailboats, fishing boats, and inflatables by the hour, half-day, and full day. Call 546-9411.

Rockport Lobstering Trips and Island Cruises, at T-Wharf. See how lobsters are caught, cruise the islands, and learn the history of Rockport. Reservations suggested. Call 546-3642.

Rockport Schooner Co., at T-Wharf. Cruise under full sail on the *Appledore*.

Scenic views of Rockport and the coast of Cape Ann. See the Headlands and Thacher's Island. Call 546-9876.

CINEMA

Little Art Cinema, 18 School Street. Closed in winter. For shows and times, call 546-2548.

GOLF

Rockport Golf Club, 60 South Street. Excellent 9-hole golf course. Carts and lessons available. Function hall available for rent. Open April 1–Oct. Call 546-3340.

OPEN SPACE

Note: The coastal public access points described below are only a partial listing. In 1997 the town of Rockport Rights-of-Way Committee produced a pocket-sized map book giving the exact location of all coastal public access points. The map book is available at Toad Hall Bookstore in Rockport and at The Bookstore on Main Street in Gloucester.

Andrews Point is reached by taking Route 127 (Granite Street) to Phillips Avenue. This is a rocky shore for hiking. Resident parking only.

Cathedral Point is reached by taking Route 127 (Granite Street) to Breakwater Avenue (Pigeon Cove area). This is a rocky shore for hiking and fishing and a boat landing. Free parking.

Halibut Point Sea Rocks (off Route 127, Granite Street) is near the Atlantic Path, an historic pathway along the Rockport shore, accessed via rights-of-way from Cathedral Avenue, Phillips Avenue, and Point de Chene Avenue (marked by signs). Here are rocks for scenic viewing and coastal hiking.

Halibut Point Reservation (a property of The Trustees of Reservations). See **Places of Interest** for a complete description.

Halibut Point State Park is reached by taking Route 127 (Granite Street) to Gott Lane. See **Places of Interest** for a complete description.

Hoop Pole Cove is reached by taking Route 127 (Granite Street) to Phillips Avenue. This is a rocky shore with resident parking only.

Loblolly and Emerson Points are reached via Route 127A (Thatcher Road) to Penzance Road. Park offers a stone beach, salt marsh, and rocky areas. Sticker parking only.

Pigeon Cove Wharf is reached by taking Route 127 (Granite Street) to Breakwater Avenue. This is a working waterfront protected by a large stone breakwater that is leased to Rockport for commercial fishing purposes by the Boat Owners Association. Free parking.

ROCKPORT (SANDY BAY) HARBOR AREA

Bradley Wharf is accessed from Bearskin Neck on Rockport Harbor waterfront with pier and plaza near Motif #1. No parking.

Cove Court Road is accessed from Bearskin Neck on Sandy Bay. This right-of-way to the rocky shore is accessed by foot at the intersection of Doyle's Cove Road and North Road. Swimming, fishing, and strolling on breakwater and rocks.

Granite Pier is located off Granite Street (Route 127): take Wharf Road directly next to the Granite Keystone Bridge. This is a rocky shore and breakwater with a boat landing area and pier. Free parking.

Harbor South Shore is reached from T-Wharf by heading toward Headlands directly on Rockport Harbor (see below). This includes a small grassy area called Star Island Park.

Headlands is reached by taking Route 127A (Pleasant Street) to Atlantic Avenue. Go to the end of road. This park has pathways along a steep bank overlooking the harbor and rocky shore.

Lumber Wharf is downtown near Front Beach with a rocky shore, boating pier, and picnic tables. Street parking only.

T-Wharf is inside Rockport Harbor at town center. Pier, plaza, marina, boat landing area, restrooms, and free parking available.

SWIMMING POOLS

Sandy Bay Motor Inn, 173 Main Street. Indoor heated pool open year-round. Individual saunas and changing rooms also available. Adult memberships only. Call 546-7155.

Lodging

For more information about lodging places, contact them directly or contact the Rockport Chamber of Commerce & Board of Trade, 3 Main Street, Rockport, MA 01966, or call 508-546-5997 or 6575. As you enter Rockport on Route 127 (upper Main Street) the Chamber Visitors Center is on your right. Price ranges below are: ($) = $50–$75, ($$) = $76–$125, ($$$) = $125 and up. All information was verified at time of publication.

BED & BREAKFASTS

Addison Choate Inn, 49 Broadway. 7 non-smoking rooms and a cottage. Continental breakfast plus. Pool, ocean view, walk to beach. Year-round. ($$) Call 546-7543 or 800-245-7543.

Beach Knoll Inn, 30 Beach Street. 10 rooms. Continental breakfast, ocean view. Year-round. ($–$$) Call 546-6939.

The Blueberry, 50 Stockholm Avenue. 2 rooms. Full breakfast; pets welcome. Year-round. ($) Call 546-2838.

The Cable House, 3 Norwood Avenue. 4 rooms. Full breakfast; non-smoking; ocean view, walk to beach. Seasonal. ($$) Call 546-3895.

The Captain's House, 109 Marmion Way. 5 rooms. Continental breakfast; ocean front. Seasonal. ($$) Call 546-3825.

Carlson's B&B, 43 Broadway. 2 rooms. Full breakfast; pets welcome; walk to beach. Year-round. ($$) Call 546-2770.

Eden Pines, Eden Road. 6 rooms. Continental breakfast plus; ocean front, walk to beach. ($$$) Call 546-2505.

The Inn on Cove Hill (historic B&B) at 37 Mt. Pleasant Street. 11 rooms. Continental breakfast; non-smoking; walk to beach. ($–$$) Call 546-2701.

Lantana House, 22 Broadway. 7 rooms. Continental breakfast plus; non-smoking; walk to beach. Year-round. ($$) Call 546-3535.

Linden Tree Inn, 26 King Street. 18 rooms. Continental breakfast plus; walk to beach. Year-round. ($$) Call 546-2494 or 800-865-2122.

Old Farm Inn, 291 Granite Street. 9 rooms. Continental breakfast plus; walk to beach. Seasonal. ($$) Call 546-3237 or 800-233-6828.

Peg Leg Inn and Restaurant, 2 King Street. 33 rooms. Continental breakfast; wheelchair access; ocean view, walk to beach. Seasonal. ($$) Call 546-2352.

Pleasant Street Inn, 17 Pleasant Street. 8 rooms. Continental breakfast plus; walk to beach. Year-round. ($$) Call 546-3915 or 800-541-3915.

Rocky Shores Inn & Cottages, 65 Eden Road. 11 rooms. Continental breakfast plus; ocean view, walk to beach. Seasonal. ($$) Call 546-2823 or 800-348-4003.

Sally Webster Inn, 34 Mt. Pleasant Street. 8 rooms. Full breakfast; walk to beach. Seasonal. ($–$$) Call 546-9251.

Sea Robin Guest House, 1 Tregony Bow. Call 546-7072.

Seacrest Manor, 131 Marmion Way. 8 rooms. Full breakfast; non-smoking; ocean view, walk to beach. Seasonal. ($$) Call 546-2211.

The Seafarer Inn, 86 Marmion Way. 7 rooms. Continental breakfast; non-smoking; ocean view, walk to beach. Seasonal. ($–$$) Call 546-6248.

Seven South Street Inn, 7 South Street. Continental breakfast plus; swimming pool, walk to beach. Seasonal. ($$) Call 546-7973.

The Tuck Inn, 17 High Street. 11 rooms. Continental breakfast plus; non-smoking; pool, walk to beach. Year-round. ($–$$) Call 546-7260 or 800-789-7260.

MOTELS & COTTAGES

Bearskin Neck Motor Lodge & Coffee Shop, 74 South Road (Bearskin Neck). 8 rooms. Ocean front, walk to beach. Seasonal. ($$) Call 546-6677.

Captain's Bounty Motor Inn, 1 Beach Street. 24 rooms. Wheelchair access; ocean front, walk to beach. Seasonal. ($$) Call 546-9557.

Eagle House Motel, 8 Cleaves Street. 15 rooms. Walk to beach. Seasonal. ($$) Call 546-6292.

Five Corners Vacation Apartments, 6 Railroad Avenue. Non-smoking; walk to beach. Seasonal. ($) Call 546-7063.

King Street Cottage, 20 King Street. 2 1/2 rooms. Walk to beach. Year-round. ($$) Call 546-9920.

Peg Leg Motel, 10 Beach Street. 15 rooms. Ocean view, walk to beach. Seasonal. ($$) Call 546-6945.

Sandy Bay Motor Inn, 173 Main Street. Swimming pool; pets welcome; wheelchair access. Year-round. Call 546-7155 or 800-437-7155.

Sea Ledges Apts., 10 Gap Head Road. 4 rooms. Ocean view. Seasonal. ($$) Call 546-2366.

Seven Smith Street Court, 7 Smith Street. Non-smoking; ocean view, walk to beach. Seasonal. ($$$) Call 508-695-1715.

Tregony Bow Guest House, 4 Tregony Bow. 2 rooms. Call Rory Cassidy at 546-7827.

Turk's Head Motor Inn, 283 South Street. 28 rooms. Swimming pool, walk to beach. Seasonal. ($$) Call 546-3436.

INNS

Ralph Waldo Emerson Inn, 1 Cathedral Avenue. Swimming pool, ocean view. Seasonal. ($–$$) Call 546-6321.

Seaward Inn, 62 Marmion Way. 38 rooms. Serves full breakfast and dinner;

non-smoking; swimming pool; wheelchair access; ocean front, walk to beach. Seasonal. ($$$) Call 546-3471 or 800-648-7733.

Yankee Clipper Inn, 127 Granite Street. 26 rooms. Serves full breakfast or continental breakfast plus and dinner; non-smoking; swimming pool; ocean front, walk to beach. Seasonal. ($$$) Call 546-3407 or 800-545-3699.

Restaurants

The price ranges below are as follows: ($) = $3–$10, ($$) = $11–$16, ($$$) = $17 and up.

Arnie's Eatery, 28 Bearskin Neck. Call 546-6900.

Beach Front Restaurant, at rear 16 Beach Street. ($) Call 546-9060.

The Blacksmith Shop, 23 Mt. Pleasant Street. Serves lunch and dinner; children's menu and take-out available. Relaxing atmosphere. Great food with a delicious view of Rockport harbor. ($$) Call 546-6301.

Brackett's Ocean View Restaurant, 27 Main Street. Serves lunch and dinner; sandwiches, salads, seafood, and much more. Beautiful ocean view. Open April–October. ($$) Call 546-2797.

Cutty's Harbor Cafe, 14 Bearskin Neck. Call 546-2180.

Dock Square Coffee & Tea House, 25 Dock Square. Serves breakfast, lunch, and dinner; homemade pastry, breads, soups, salads; children's menu. Offers outside seating and take-out. A specialty coffee and tea house with the finest cappuccinos and lattes on Cape Ann. ($) Call 546-2525.

Donut Dream, 229 Upper Main Street. Serves great pastries, sandwiches, soups, and gourmet coffees. ($) Call 546-2171.

Ellen's Harborside, 1 T-Wharf. Serves breakfast, lunch, and dinner; fresh seafood, daily specials; children's menu and take-out available. Casual dining overlooking Rockport harbor. Wheelchair access. ($–$$) Call 546-2512.

Flav's Red Skiff, 15 Mt. Pleasant Street. Serves breakfast and lunch. Take-out available. ($) Call 546-3849.

Flying Saucer Cafe, 27 Mt. Pleasant Street. Call 546-6874.

Folly Cove Pier Restaurant, 325 Granite Street (Route 127). Serves lunch and dinner; fresh seafood and steak. Casual dining, lovely sunsets, ocean view. Open May–Oct. ($$) Call 546-9603.

Greenery Cafe and Restaurant, 15 Dock Square. Serves lunch and dinner; fresh seafood, grilled fish, pizzas, pastas, superb sauté, sandwiches, salad bar, and espresso. Take-out available. ($$–$$$) Call 546-9593.

The Hannah Jumper, 7 Tuna Wharf. Serves lunch and dinner. Overlooks the harbor. ($$) Call 546-3600.

Helmut's Strudel of Bearskin Neck, 49 South Road (Bearskin Neck). Serves breakfast and lunch; fresh pastries, croissants, and sandwiches. Outside seating, ocean view; take-out available. ($) Call 546-2824.

Ice Cream Gallery, 8 Dock Square. ($) Call 546-9219.

Lobster-in-the-Ruff, 29B South Road (Bearskin Neck). ($) Call 546-7833.

Lobster Pool at Folly Cove, 329 Granite Street. Serves lunch and dinner; self-serve seafood restaurant; children's menu available. Casual dining by water's edge,

indoors or out; spectacular sunsets. Wheelchair access. ($–$$) Call 546-7808.

Lograsso's Deli, 13 Railroad Avenue. Serves lunch and dinner; take-out available. ($) Call 546-7977.

Michael's, 173 Main Street. Serves breakfast. ($) Call 546-9665.

MoJack's, 16 Beach Street. Serves breakfast, lunch, and dinner. Family-style restaurant; enjoy spectacular ocean view. Breakfast served all day or try their daily lunch and dinner specials. Children's menu and take-out available. ($) Call 546-3001.

My Place By-The-Sea, 68 South Road (Bearskin Neck). Serves brunch, lunch, and dinner; children's menu and take-out available. Wheelchair access. Breathtaking outdoor oceanfront dining.($–$$$) Call 546-9667.

Nelson's Candies & Ice Cream, 64D South Road (Bearskin Neck). Call 546-7344.

Ocean Cafe, 8 Old Harbor Road. Call 546-7172.

Peg Leg Restaurant, 18 Beach Street. Serves lunch, and dinner; children's menu available. Famous for over 50 years for its fine dining and friendly and gracious service. Outside seating; ocean view. Wheelchair access. ($$) Call 546-3038.

Poet's Corner at Ralph Waldo Emerson Inn, Phillips Avenue. Serves breakfast and dinner; children's menu.

Wheelchair access. Lovely setting with an ocean view and delicious food. Outside seating available. ($$) Call 546-6321.

Portside Chowderhouse 'n Grille, Doyle's Cove Road (Bearskin Neck). Call 546-7045.

Rockport House of Pizza, 19 Broadway. Call 546-6066.

Roy Moore Lobster Company, 31 South Road (Bearskin Neck). Call 546-6696.

Sea Garden Restaurant in Seaward Inn, 62 Marmion Way. Serves breakfast and dinner; children's menu available. Wheelchair access. Oceanfront dining with traditional American cuisine. ($$–$$$) Call 546-3471.

Seaside Restaurant, 21 Dock Square Mall. Serves lunch and dinner; daily specials, native seafood, lobsters; children's menu. Wheelchair access. Located at the entrance to Bearskin Neck with harbor and ocean view from every seat. ($) Call 546-3905.

Sweet Sara, 6 Bearskin Neck. Call 546-9800.

Turk's Head Motor Inn, 283 South Street. Call 546-3436.

Veranda, at the Yankee Clipper Inn, 127 Granite Street. Serves breakfast and dinner; sumptuous meals featuring regional American cuisine and Tuscan dishes. Beautiful oceanfront dining room. ($$) Call 546-3407.

Bibliography

Andrews, Wayne. *Architecture in New England*. The Stephen Greene Press, 1973.

Babson, Roger W. *Dogtown: Gloucester's Deserted Village*. Rotary Address, September 1927.

Boice, Susan H. "Discover a Safe Harbor." *Ipswich Chronicle.*

Carlozzi, Carl. *Ecosystems and Resources of the Massachusetts Coast.* Coastal Zone Management, 1975.

Castonguay, Wayne. *Shellfishing In Ipswich.* 1991.

Cetacean Research Unit, Bass Avenue, Gloucester, MA. 1996.

Chamberlain, Allen, and Thomas Williams. *The Old Castle.* Village Improvement Society, 1939.

Cooley, John. *The Granite of Cape Ann.* Rockport National Bank, 1974.

Cooley, John L. *Rockport Sketch Book.* Rockport Art Association, 1965.

Copeland, Melvin Thomas. *The Saga of Cape Ann.* Bond Wheelwright Co., 1960.

Cramer, Deborah. "Along the Edge: The Barrier Beaches at Crane Beach and Plum Island." *Essex Life: The Magazine of Essex County.* July–Sept, 1981.

Crowell, Reverend Robert D.D. *History of Town of Essex 1634–1868.* Town of Essex, 1868.

Cummings, Abbott Lowell. *The Framed Houses of Massachusetts Bay, 1625–1725.* Belknap Harvard, 1979.

"Descendant of the Witch Trial Victim Presents Linebrook Map to IHC." *Ipswich Observer*, October 1995.

Dolan, John. "The Beauty of Old Memories Lingers On." *Ipswich Chronicle*, November 14, 1996.

Drake, Samuel Adams. *New England Legends and Folklore.* Roberts Brothers, 1888.

Dresser, Thomas. *Dogtown: A Village Lost in Time.* 1995.

Erkkila, Barbara. "Fitz Hugh Lane, Self-taught Artist, Now Recognized Here and Nationally." *Gloucester Daily Times*, August 12, 1953.

Felt, Joseph B. *History of Ipswich, Essex, and Hamilton.* Charles Folsom, 1834.

Floyd, Frank L. *Manchester-by-the-Sea*. Floyd's News, 1945.

Foley, Rosanne Atwood, and James E. Foley, Jr. *Report on Old Burying Ground, Essex, MA*, 1991.

Garland, Joseph E. *The Gloucester Guide*. Protean Press, 1990.

Gaskins, Stephanie R. *The Ipswich Painters at Home and Abroad*. Cape Ann Historical Society, Gloucester, 1993.

Glickstein, David and Linda. "Cape Ann." *The Discerning Traveler*, July 1990.

Gloucester Historic District Committee. "Rocky Neck." June 18, 1991.

Harris, Leslie. *150 Years a Town*. The Cricket Press, 1969.

Hartt, Hildegarde T. *Magnolia, Once Kettle Cove*. H. Hartt, 1962.

Hodgkins, Mrs. George E. "Rum Running: It Was a Growth Industry during Prohibition." *Ipswich Chronicle*, August 2, 1984.

Hoel, Michael L. *Land's Edge*. The Little Book Publishing Co., 1986.

The Ipswich Bay Circuit Trail Committee. *The Bay Circuit Guide to Walks in and around Ipswich*, 1996.

Ipswich Historical Commission. *Something To Preserve*. The Historical Commission, Boston, 1975.

"The Ipswich Moving Company." Ipswich Spy in *Ipswich Observer*, June, 1996.

Ipswich Salt Marsh Committee. *The Ipswich Marshes*, 1962.

Junior League of Boston. *Along the Coast of Essex County*. J.W. Murray and Associates, 1984.

Kenyon, Paul B. *People & Books*. 150th Anniversary Committee, 1980.

Killen, Wendy. "Ipswich Environmental Center Offers Guidance to International Groups." *The Boston Globe*, November 11, 1990.

Kull, Andrew. *New England Cemeteries, A Collector's Guide*. 1975.

Lamson, D.F. *History of the Town of Manchester 1645–1895*. Pinkham Press, 1895.

Longfellow, Henry Wadsworth. *The Complete Poetical Works of Longfellow*. Houghton Mifflin Co. The Riverside Press, 1922.

Massachusetts Coastal Zone Management. *Massachusetts Coast Guide (Volume I: Access to the Public Open Spaces Along the Shoreline*, 1995.

McAveeney, David C. *Gloucester & Rockport*. The Curious Traveller Press, 1990.

McKeon, Robert. "Prehistoric Bones on Display in Salem." *Salem Evening News*, August 6, 1975.

Naisbith, Helen. *Walking Cape Ann with Ted Tarr*. Ten Pound Island Book Co., 1989.

"National Register to Add Two More Ipswich Historical Districts." *Ipswich Observer*, June 1996.

National Trust for Historic Preservation. *What Style Is It? A Guide to American Architecture*. Preservation Press, Washington, D.C., 1983.

Nichols, Christopher. *Early Meetinghouses of Essex, Massachusetts*, 1984.

Pope, Eleanor. *The Wilds of Cape Ann*, 1981.

Potter, Lucy. "Brief History of the Hall-Haskell House," *Ipswich Chronicle,* July 11, 1996.

Potter, Lucy. "The 1640 Hart House," *Ipswich Chronicle,* July 11, 1996.

Quinn, John. "Ipswich: A Long and Storied Past." *Inside Ipswich*, August 15, 1996.

Richardson, Ralph W. *Historic Districts of America* (New England). Heritage Books, Inc., 1989.

Rifkind, Carole. *Field Guide to American Architecture*. New American Library, 1980.

Robertson, Kitty. "They Came with Tags Labled "Ipswich Mills." *Ipswich Chronicle,* March 16, 1972.

Robbins, Sarah Fraser, and Clarice Yentsch. *The Sea Is All About Us*. Peabody Museum of Salem, 1973.

Rockport Historical Commission. *National Register Survey*. Carnegie Library, 1973–1985.

Schuler, Stanley. *Saltbox and Cape Cod Houses*. Schiffer Publishing, Ltd., 1988.

Scully, Vincent J., Jr. *The Shingle Style and Stick Style*. Yale University Press, 1974.

Schilling, Mark. *The Whale Watcher's Companion*. A Guide to Watching Whales in New England. Cetacean Research Unit, 1974.

Stern, Jane and Michael. "Boston's North Shore, The Fried Clam Belt." *Gourmet*, July 1995.

Stickney, Edward and Evelyn. *The Bells of Paul Revere, His Sons & Grandsons*, 1976.

"Stone Age New England: Clues to the Past." *Ipswich Chronicle*, November 19, 1975.

Story, Dana S. *Frame Up*. Barre Publishers, 1964.

Swan, Marshall W. S. *Town on Sandy Bay*. Phoenix Publishing, 1980.

"The Tenth Muse of Ipswich." *Ipswich Today*, July 28, 1972.

Thayer, Lydia Prescott. *Annisquam*. Cape Ann Ticket and Label, 1994.

Toivainen, Ruth, and Helen Stenberg. *History of the Congregational Church of Essex, 1683–1983*.

Town of Manchester. *Manchester-by-the-Sea, 1645–1970*, 1923.

Tozer, Eliot. "The Whipple House." *Early American Homes*, October 1996.

Ursin, Michael J. *Life in and around the Salt Marshes*. Thomas Y. Crowell Company, 1972.

Van Auken, Sarah. *ABC of Cape Ann*, 1991.

"Vivid Minds." Editorial. *North Shore Magazine*, January 9, 1997.

White, Laurence. *The Natural History of Crane's Neck*.

White, Laurence B., Jr. *Life in the Shifting Dunes*. Museum of Science, 1960.

Wonson, Agnes Choate. *Candles of Memory*, 1925.

Index

Note: Page numbers in italics refer to illustrations.

Adams, Ben (cottage), *107*
Agassiz Rock Reservation, 17, 184
Adventure, 101
Agawam Indians, 23, 139, 170
American beach grass, 21
Andrew, A. Piatt, 96
Andros, Sir Edmund, 51, 141
Animals, *150*, 160, 161
Annisquam, 102
  Artists, *105*
  Toll Bridge, *104*
Antiques
  Essex, 59, 65
  Gloucester, 113
    Annisquam, 104
  Ipswich, 153
  Manchester-by-the-Sea, 178
  Rockport, 203
Arbella, 84, *169*
Architectural styles, 35
  Adamesque, 41
  Bracketed, 43
  Cape Ann cottage, *39*
  Cape Cod cottage, 37, *38*
  Federal Period, 40, *41*
  First Period, 35, *36*
  Georgian Period, 40
  Gothic Revival, 43
  Greek Revival, 42
  Italianate, 43
  Queen Anne, 43
  Saltbox, 37
  Second Period, 35
  Shingle Style, 42, 44
  Stick Style, 43
  Third Period, 35
  Victorian Gothic, 43
  Victorian Period, 42
Area of Critical Environmental
    Concern (ACEC), 25
Art
  Essex, 70
  Gloucester, 114
    Annisquam, 104
  Ipswich, 154, *158*

  Manchester-by-the-Sea, 179
  Rockport, 197, 204
Art in the Barn, *71*
Art in the Park, 179
Art Show, annual, 157
Arts Gala, 179
Avery, Parson, 202

B & B reservations, 13. *See also*
    Bed and Breakfast under
    Lodging.
Babson Cooperage Shop, 198
Babson, Isabel, Memorial
    Library, 93
Babson, James, 85
Babson, Roger W., 89, 93
Bait and tackle shops, 122
Bathrooms, public, 12
Bay Circuit Trail, 162
Beach(es)
  Back, 211
  Barrier, 23
  Centennial Grove, 72, 75,
    78
  Crane, 23, 161
  Cressy, 122
  Front, 211
  Good Harbor, 122
  Half Moon, 122
  Long, 211
  Magnolia, 109
  Niles, 122
  Old Garden, 212
  Pavilion, 122, 163
  Sandy, 21
  Singing, 18, 173, *183*
  Wingaersheek, 21, 122
Bearskin Neck, 190, 196
Beauport, Sleeper-McCann
    House, 96, *97*
Bicycles, 123, 164
Birdseye, Clarence, 86
Blackburn, Howard, 95
Blackburn Tavern, 95
Blackwood, Lucille, 65

Boating and Cruises
  Essex, *76, 77*
  Gloucester, 123
  Annisquam, 104
  Ipswich, 161
  Manchester-by-the-Sea, 183
  Rockport, 212
Booth, Junius, 172
Bowling, 123, 162
Bradstreet, Anne, 140, 149
Bradstreet House, 149, 169
Bridge(s)
  Blynman, 98
  Choate, 147
  Granite Keystone, 199
Bull Brook, 139, 162
Burial ground(s)
  Essex, 54, 59
  Ipswich, 149
  Manchester-by-the-Sea, 1661,
    177
Burnham, Ralph Warren, *153*
Burnham, T.O.H.P., 57

Cabinetmaking, 170, *171*
Calendar of traditional events, 5
Campgrounds, 13, 132
Canoe rentals. *See* Sporting
  Goods.
Canoeing. *See* Boating.
Cantemus Chamber Chorus, 159
Cape Ann Community Band,
  118
Cape Ann Historical Museum, 94
Cape Ann Symphony, 118
Cape Ann Symphony Youth
  Chorus, *119*
Cape Anne, History of, 83
Cape Pond Brook, 85
Captain Dusty's, 179, *187*
Castle Hill events, *151,* 159
Chambers of Commerce, 13
Chebacco, 47
Cheap Champagne, 73
Choate House, *62*
Choate Island. *See* Hog Island.
Chorus North Shore, 208
Christmas Nativity Pageant, 205,
  206
Churches. *See* Places of Worship.
Cinema, 123, 212
City Hall, 94
Civil War monument, *103*

Clam Industry, 28, *30*
Clam, soft-shell, 22, 28, *29*
Cleaveland, Rev. Ebenezer, 190
Cleaveland, Rev. John, 53, 56
Coffee House(s)
  Along the Way, 159
  One World, 75
Cogswell's Grant, 59
Commons Settlement, 85, 89
Conant, Roger, 84
Congregational Church, 50, 61
Coolidge Reservation, 185
Cormorants, *21*
Coolidge, T. Jefferson, 173, 185
Cox, Allyn, 71
Cox Reservation, 71, *78*
Crane Wildlife Refuge, 162, *163*
Craske, Leonard, 98, 115
Crucible, The, 141
Cruises *See* Boating, Whale
  watching.
Cultural Council. *See* Art, by town.

Daisy Nell, 74
Dana, Richard H., 171, 194
Dance. *See* Music.
Dancers Courageous, 120
de Champlain, Samuel, 35, 83,
  189
Deep sea fishing, 123
Deer ticks, 26
Dog Bar Breakwater, 99
Dogtown, 85, 89
Dorchester Company, 84
Dow, Arthur Wesley, 146, 155
Drumlin, 17
Dunfudgin Landing, 98

Eagle Head, 18
Eastern Point Lighthouse, *99*
Ecosystem, 17
Eel grass bed, 20
Ellery, William, 85
Essex Antique Dealers'
  Association, 66
Essex County Greenbelt
  Association, 71
Essex Historical Society, 49
Essex Music Festival, 72
Essex River, 61
Essex Shipbuilding Museum, 49, *63*
Essex Town Hall and Memorial
  Library, 44, *57*

Essex Waterfowl Museum, 64
Estuary, 18, *19*

Fall Foliage, 14
First Congregational Church,
    Rockport, 197, 203
First Parish Church, Manchester,
    175, *176*, 178
First Post Office, Ipswich, 148
Fishbox Derby Race, 124
Fisherman Statue *See* Man at the
    Wheel.
Fishermen's Wives Memorial, 88
Fishing and hunting, 14, 77
Fishing industry (history of), 85,
    170, 190
Fishtown Artspace, 114
Fitness centers, 124, 162, 184
Fox Creek Canal, 34
Future Art-Kids of Cape Ann, 114

Gertrude L. Thebaud, 49
Glaciers, 16, 90
Glasswort, 20
Gloucester Fishermen, *83*
Gloucester Fishermen's Wives
    Association (GFWA), 88
Gloucester Stage Company, 120
Golf and tennis, 78, 162, 164,
    212
Goodale Orchards, *150*
Goose Cove Reservation, 126
Granite industry, 192
Gravestone carvers, 56
Great House at Castle Hill, 151
Greenhead flies, 26
Greenwood Farm, 163
Gundalow, 34

Halibut Point, 23, 200, *201*, 212
Hall-Haskell House, 146, 157
Hammond Castle, 109, 121
Harbor of Refuge, 194
Harvey, George Wainwright, 104
Harvey, Martha Hale Rogers, 104
Helmsmen, *180*
Heard House Museum, 146
Hearse House, *55*
Hibbard, Aldro T., 205
Hiking. *See* Open Space.
Historic shipyard, *47*
Hog Island, 17, 62
Horseback riding, 78, 162

Hospital and Health Services. *See*
    Phone numbers, emergency.
Houses, historic. *See also*
    Architectural styles and
    Places of Interest, by town.
Adams, Ben (cottage), *107*
Beauport (Sleeper-McCann), 96,
    97
Bradstreet, 149
Castle Hill (Great House), 151
Choate, 62
Cogswell Grant, *59*
Hall-Haskell, 146, 157
Hammond (Castle), 109, 121
Heard, 146
Lane, Fitz Hugh, 94, 125
Merchant Choate, 150
Sanders, Thomas, 93
Sargent, 41, 91, *92*
Sewall-Scripture,
    1640 Hart,
Trask, 171, 173
Whipple, 37, 143, 145
Wise, John, 64

Independent Christian Church,
    92, 112
Ipswich Community Band, 160
Ipswich lace, 143
Ipswich mills, 143
Ipswich Moving Company
    Studio, 160
Ipswich Recreation Dept., 160
Ipswich River Festival, 160
Ipswich River Watershed
    Association, 163
Ipswich Town Hall, 147
Isinglass, 192
Island Mid the Marshes (poem), 62

Jeffreys Creek (town of), 170
Joan of Arc Statue, 95
Johnsen, Alfred "Centennial," 87

Kayaking. *See* Boating.
Kenyon, Henry Rodman, 155
Kettle Cove, 107, 169

Lace making, 143
Lane, Fitz Hugh (House), 94, 125
Le Beauport, *35*
Learning Umbrella, 114
Leonard, Rev. Ezra, 102

Libraries
  Annisquam, 106
  Essex, 59
  Gloucester, 93
  Ipswich, 148
  Magnolia, 108
  Manchester-by-the-Sea, 173
  Rockport, 197
Lighthouses, 24, 100
  Annisquam, 103
  Eastern Point, *99*
  Straitsmouth, 191, 201
  Ten Pound Island, 99
  Thacher Island (Twin Lights),
    189, 201
Little, Bertram K. and Nina F., 60
Little Neck Causeway, 163
Lodging
  Essex, *79*
  Gloucester, 129
  Ipswich, 165
  Manchester-by-the-Sea, 186
  Rockport, 214
Lummus, Jonathan, 149
Lyme disease, 26

Magnolia, 106
Magnolia Historical Society and
    Museum, 108
Man at the Wheel (Fisherman
    Statue), 88, *98*, 115
Manchester Community Center,
    174, 182, 184
Manchester Historical Society,
Manchester (Memorial Hall)
    Public Library, 173
Manchester Women's Chorus, 181
Mansfield, John Worthington,
    155
Map(s)
  Cape Ann and vicinity, xii
  Essex, 46
  Gloucester, 82
  Ipswich, 138
  Manchester-by-the-Sea, 168
  Rockport, 188
Margeson, G. Tucker, 194, 204
Marinas, 76, 125
Marsh grasses, *20*, 32
Masconomo (also Masconomet),
    Chief, 24, 140, 170
Masconomo House, 172
Masconotes, 181

Massachusetts Bay Colony, 84,
    140
Meetinghouse Green, 85, 147
Meetinghouses, 52
Merchant Choate House, 150
Mesquita, Capt. Joseph, 96
Mosquitoes, 26
Motif #1, 196
Motif #2, 70, *80*
Murray, Rev. John, 92
Murray, Judith Sargent, 92
Museums. *See* Places of Interest,
    by town.
Music, Theater, and Dance
  Essex, 53, 72
  Gloucester, 118
  Ipswich, 159
  Manchester-by-the-Sea, 180
  Rockport, 208
Music at Eden's Edge, 74

New England Alive, 160
Norman's Woe, 109
North Shore Arts Association,
    114
Norton Memorial Forest, 90

Old Castle, 199
Old Cold Tater, 121
Old Fort Gallery, 196
Old Ipswich Days, 157
"Old Sloop," 191
Old Stone Fort, 196
Old Town Hall (Gloucester), 95
Open Space, Parks, and
    Playgrounds, 14
  Essex, 78
  Gloucester, 125
  Magnolia, 110
  Ipswich, 162
  Manchester-by-the-Sea, 184
  Rockport, 200, 212
Our Lady of Good Voyage
    Church, 96, 111
Owascoag, 32

Palaeo Indians, 139
Paper House, 200
Parks, 14. *See also* Open Space,
    by town.
Patrons' Museum and Educational
    Center, 97
Perry, Pat, 182

Phone numbers
  Area codes, 2
  Emergency, 2, 3, 4
Pickering, Rev. Theophilis, 56
Pigeon Cove Harbor Company, 191
Pigeon Cove Pier Company, 191
Pigeon Hill, 199
Pillow Lace Site, 148
Pinkie, 48
Places of Interest
  Essex, 59
  Gloucester
    Annisquam, 102
    Central, 91
    Dogtown, 89
    Magnolia, 106
  Ipswich, 144
  Manchester-by-the-Sea, 172
  Rockport, 196
Places of Worship
  Essex, 65
  Gloucester, 111
  Ipswich, 152
  Manchester-by-the-Sea, 178
  Rockport, 203
Playgrounds. *See* Open Space
    by town.
Poison ivy, 27
Profile of the Area
  Essex, 2
  Gloucester, 3
  Ipswich, 3
  Manchester-by-the-Sea, 4
  Rockport, 4
Prohibition, 144
Puritans, 84

Rabardy Block (Floyd's Store), 174
Ravenswood Park, 110
Recreation. *See also* by type.
  Essex, 75
  Gloucester, 122
  Ipswich, 160
  Manchester-by-the-Sea, 183
  Rockport, 211
Red tide, 29
Restaurants
  Essex, 80, *81*
  Gloucester, 132, *134*
    Annisquam, 104
  Ipswich, 165
  Manchester-by-the-Sea, 187
  Rockport, 216

Revere, Paul (bell), 53
Richardson, Francis Henry, 156
Rockport Art Association, 195,
    197, 205
Rockport Chamber Music Festival,
    206, 209
Rockport Granite Company, 192,
    193
Rockport Legion Band, 209
Rockport, town of, 189
Rocky headlands, 18
Rocky Neck, *116*
Rocky Neck Art Colony, 115
Rocky shore, 22
Rogers, Rev. Nathaniel, 148

Sailing. *See* Boating.
Salt marshes, 32, *33*
Saltzberg, Edward, 66
Saltzberg, Joseph, 153
Sand dunes, 21
Sanders, Thomas (House), 93
Sandy Bay (town of). *See*
    Rockport.
Sandy Bay Historical Society, 198,
    199
Sandy Bay Pier Company, 191
Sargent House Museum, 41, 91,
    92
Sawyer Free Library, 93
Sawyer, Samuel E., 110
Scuba diving, 127
Sea serpent, *101*, 195
Seaside "1", *175*
Seaweeds, 23
Separatists, 52
7 Central Street, 174, 187
Sewall-Scripture House, 198, *199*
Shipbuilding
  Essex, 47
  Rockport, 191
1640 Hart House, 154, 165, *166*
Shore birds, *22*
Smith, Capt. John, 83, 140, 170,
    189
Snow skiing, 14
Society for the Preservation of
    New England Antiquities,
    39, 60, 96, *97*
Soldiers' Monument, 58
South Village Green, 145
Spartina alterniflora, 20, *32*
Spartina patens, 20, 32

Sporting goods, 164, 186
Stage Fort Park, 84, 100
Starlighters, The, 121
State Fish Pier, 101
Stavros Reservation, 79
Steam Cotton Mill, 197
Stevens, W. Lester, 205
Straitsmouth Island, 191, 201
Swasey Tavern, 146
Swimming pools, 213

Ten Pound Island, 99
Tennis. *See* Golf and tennis.
Terminal moraine, 17, 90
Thacher, Anthony, 202
Thacher Island, *189*, 202
Thacher Island Association, 202
Theater in the Pines, 210
Theater. *See* Music.
Tidal flat, 22, 28
Tidal marsh, 19
Tidal pools, 23
Tides, 17, 27, *28*, *29*
Toivainen, Ruth, 67
Tours, 164
Town Wharf, River Walk, and
    Water Street, 164
Transportation, 1, 14
Trask House, 171, 173
Twin Lights, *189*, 201

U. S. Coast Guard, 25

Varney, Madame, 50
Visitor Information, 14
Visitors Welcoming Center, 100

Walker Creek Band, 75
Ward, Nathaniel, 140
Weatherall, Sally, Memorial
    Reservation, 163
Wendel, Theodore, 156
Whale watching, 129
Whales, *127*
What's Where? 12
Whipple House, 37, *139*, 143,
    145
White Elephant Shop, *67*, 70
Whitefield, Rev. George, 52,
    147
Windhover Center for the
    Performing Arts, 210
Winthrop, John Jr., 140
Wise, John (House), 64
Wise, Rev. John, 51, 54, 56, 141
Witchcraft, 51, 141
Wolf Hollow, 161
Woodman, Chubby, 31
Wreck of the Hesperus, *109*

Zip codes, 2

Order Form

To order copies of *CAPE ANN AND VICINITY* directly
from the publisher, complete the form below and send
it with your check or money order to:

ACORN PRESS
P.O. Box 403
Manchester-by-the-Sea
MA 01944–0403 U.S.A.

Quantity	Price	Total
_____	$14.95	_____
	MA residents add 5% sales tax	_____

Postage & Handling:
   add $2.95 for the first book,
   add $1.00 for each additional book.   _____

                    TOTAL ENCLOSED   _____

Please print:

Your Name   _____
Address   _____
City, State, Zip _____

**Orders from outside the United States must be prepaid
in U.S. funds drawn on a U.S. bank.**

Note: for quantity discount information, please write to the publisher.